CULTURES IN CONFLICT
THE AMERICAN CIVIL WAR

Steven E. Woodworth

The Greenwood Press Cultures in Conflict Series

GREENWOOD PRESS
Westport, Connecticut • London

Library of Congress Cataloging-in-Publication Data

Woodworth, Steven E.
    Cultures in conflict—the American Civil War / Steven E.
Woodworth.
        p. cm.—(The Greenwood Press cultures in conflict
    series, ISSN 1526–0690)
    Includes bibliographical references and index.
    ISBN 0–313–30651–6 (alk. paper)
    1. United States—History—Civil War, 1861–1865 Personal
narratives. 2. United States—History—Civil War, 1861–1865—Social
aspects. 3. Culture conflict—United States—History—19th century
Sources. I. Title. II. Title: American Civil War. III. Series.
E464 .W66 2000
973.7—dc21   99–43165

British Library Cataloguing in Publication Data is available.

Library of Congress Catalog Card Number: 99–43165
ISBN: 0–313–30651–6
ISSN: 1526–0690

First published in 2000

Greenwood Press, 88 Post Road West, Westport, CT 06881
An imprint of Greenwood Publishing Group, Inc.
www.greenwood.com

Printed in the United States of America

∞™

The paper used in this book complies with the
Permanent Paper Standard issued by the National
Information Standards Organization (Z39.48–1984).

10 9 8 7 6 5 4 3 2 1

To Denton and Emily Elliott,
whom I expect to meet someday

To God Alone be the Glory

Contents

Part III   Reflecting

Preface

The term "Culture Wars" came into prominence in the 1990s after presidential candidate Patrick Buchanan aptly used it at the 1992 Republican National Convention. Yet the reality of conflicting cultures and views of culture was not new then nor was it the first occurrence of such conflict in America's history. The profoundly deep divisions that ultimately motivate men and women to drastic action and fundamental change are always at least partly cultural. The swirling maelstrom of political conflict, important though it may be, is often merely the surface manifestation of deep cultural currents.

Such was the case in the conflict of the 1860s. Over the preceding decades North and South, free society and slave society, had grown farther and farther apart in many of the areas of culture that ought to bind a people together and make them one nation. What Abraham Lincoln called in March 1861 "the mystic cords of Union," springing from every "hearth and heart-string" in the nation, had by that time been strained to the breaking point by the two-generation-long conflict over slavery. Though Lincoln was ultimately proven correct in his assessment that the ties that bound the nation would at last prove stronger than the forces tearing it apart, four years of America's bloodiest conflict were required to resolve the "culture war" of that era.

My purpose in this book is to help readers understand that conflict better by showing them some of the cultural currents that caused and shaped it. My method for accomplishing that is to present excerpts from the writings of actual participants and eye-witnesses in those dramatic events. These writings include letters, diaries, and memoirs. Those who produced them include Northerners and Southerners, common soldiers, junior officers, a general's wife, a plantation mistress, a school teacher, a nurse, an army chaplain, as well as ordinary farmers and business men—in short, a cross section of the bulk of the common people of the era. We can never hope to sample every conceivable segment of society between the covers of one book, and I was naturally limited by the availability of written sources. For example, illiterate persons, a class which included most slaves, are, for obvious reasons, not represented in these excerpts. In such cases history is forced to depend to a large degree on the accounts of others. Still, the selections here should give a fair representation of those who experienced the Civil War and wrote down what they lived.

The events and situations that these participants describe range from mundane life on the farm to the scenes of a military hospital to race relations on a plantation to experiences of soldiers and the anxious vigils of those who waited for them back home. I have striven especially to select passages that reflect the intersection of military and civilian life—the process of enlisting and going off to war, the ways in which the war affected those who were left behind, and the ways it affected those to whom it came in the form of invading armies.

A timeline, a chapter on the military course of the war, and another on the cultural conflict beneath the surface set the scene for the documents that follow and help to put them in perspective. The documents themselves have been arranged into four roughly chronological chapters. For each chapter I have provided a general introduction and for each document an individual introduction. These should provide the necessary perspective and knowledge of specific information necessary to understand and appreciate the documents. A final chapter offers suggestions for comparison, analysis, and further exploration of these rich, original sources. Students, particularly, may find that chapter useful as a possible source of ideas for essays and other short papers.

For all readers, students of the Civil War both formal and informal, I hope that these pages will provide an opportunity to get to know a number of Civil War Americans on a personal basis, as it were, to know something of how they thought and felt and why they acted as they did. Above all, I hope it will help them to come to see the

Civil War not merely as vast armies marching or great generals moving them across their headquarters maps but also as a great event—often the great event—in the lives of individual people, people not so different from ourselves.

A Civil War Timeline—Key Events, 1860–1865

1860

November 6—Abraham Lincoln elected president of the United States.

December 20—South Carolina secedes.

1861

January 9–January 26—Mississippi, Florida, Alabama, Georgia, and Louisiana secede.

February 1—Texas secedes.

February 4—Convention of seceded states meets in Montgomery, Alabama, to form the Confederate States of America. On February 9 it elects Jefferson Davis as provisional president of the Confederacy.

February 18—Davis is inaugurated as Confederate president.

March 4—Lincoln is inaugurated as U.S. president.

April 12—Confederates open fire on Fort Sumter, initiating hostilities. U.S. troops surrender the fort the next day.

April 15—Lincoln issues a proclamation declaring that an insurrection exists and calling 75,000 state militia into federal service to suppress it. He will subsequently make numerous and much larger calls for troops.

April 17–May 20—Virginia, Arkansas, Tennessee, and North Carolina secede.

May 29—Confederate president Jefferson Davis arrives in Richmond, Virginia, the newly designated capital of the Confederacy.

July 21—Union and Confederate troops fight the first major battle of the war at Bull Run (or Manassas Junction), Virginia.

1862

February 6—Union forces under Brig. Gen. Ulysses S. Grant and Flag Officer Andrew H. Foote capture Fort Henry, Tennessee, opening the Tennessee River to Union penetration as far south as northern Alabama.

February 16—Grant takes nearby Fort Donelson, Tennessee, opening the Cumberland River and sealing the fate of Nashville.

April 6–April 7—Confederate forces under Gen. Albert Sidney Johnston attack Grant's army at Pittsburg Landing (or Shiloh), Tennessee, in an unsuccessful attempt to destroy Grant and recoup the Confederacy's recent losses west of the Appalachians. The battle is drastically more bloody than any previously fought on American soil, with over 23,000 casualties, including Johnston, who is killed.

April 25—Union naval forces under Flag Officer David Glasgow Farragut take New Orleans.

May 3—Union troops under Maj. Gen. George B. McClellan take Yorktown, Virginia, and begin to advance up the peninsula between the York and James Rivers toward Richmond.

May 30—Union troops under Maj. Gen. Henry W. Halleck take Corinth, Mississippi, a key railroad junction in the northern part of that state.

June 25–July 1—In a series of battles known collectively as the Seven Days' Battles, Confederate Gen. Robert E. Lee forces McClellan to retreat back down the peninsula, away from Richmond.

July 22—Lincoln presents the Emancipation Proclamation to his cabinet but is persuaded to delay issuing it until after a Union victory.

August 28–August 30—Lee soundly defeats Union Maj. Gen. John Pope at the second battle of Bull Run (or Manassas).

September 17—McClellan gains an indecisive victory over Lee at Antietam (or Sharpsburg), Maryland, forcing Lee out of Maryland and back into Virginia.

September 22—Lincoln announces the Preliminary Emancipation Proclamation to the country. It stipulates that all slaves in areas still in rebellion against the United States on January 1, 1863, will then be "forever free."

November 7—Disgusted with McClellan's lack of aggressiveness, Lincoln replaces him with Maj. Gen. Ambrose Burnside.

December 13—Lee trounces the inept Burnside at Fredericksburg, Virginia.

1863

January 1—Lincoln issues the final Emancipation Proclamation. Going further, he states that the U.S. government will begin to enlist former slaves as soldiers.

May 1–May 4—At the battle of Chancellorsville, Virginia, Lee and Thomas J. "Stonewall" Jackson defeat yet another Union drive toward Richmond, this one commanded by Maj. Gen. Joseph Hooker.

May 18—Grant caps a dazzling campaign of maneuver in central Mississippi by besieging the key Confederate Mississippi River bastion of Vicksburg, Mississippi.

June 16—Lee's army crosses the Potomac in another major invasion of the northern states.

July 1–July 3—Union forces under Maj. Gen. George G. Meade (with whom Lincoln had replaced Hooker on June 28) defeat Lee at Gettysburg, Pennsylvania, forcing him back to Virginia.

July 4—The Confederate army at Vicksburg surrenders to Grant, and within days the North controls the entire length of the Mississippi River.

September 19–September 20—A reinforced Confederate army under Gen. Braxton Bragg wins an indecisive victory over Maj. Gen. William S. Rosecrans's Union army at the battle of Chickamauga, in northern Georgia near Chattanooga, Tennessee.

November 23–November 25—Grant, brought to Chattanooga to replace Rosecrans, soundly defeats Bragg at the dramatic battle of Chattanooga, opening the way for Union penetration of Georgia.

December 8—Lincoln issues his Proclamation of Amnesty and Reconstruction, containing his lenient "Ten-Percent Plan" for returning southern states to their proper relationship with the federal government.

1864

March 1—Lincoln nominates Grant for the newly created rank of lieutenant general, making him commanding general of all northern forces.

May 5–May 6—Grant moves south with the main Union army and immediately collides with Lee in the bloody and inconclusive Battle of the Wilderness.

May 7—Maj. Gen. William T. Sherman begins to advance from Dalton, Georgia, near Chattanooga, toward Atlanta, deep in the heart of the state; he is opposed by a Confederate army under Gen. Joseph E. Johnston.

May 8–May 21—Grant and Lee fight another inconclusive encounter at Spotsylvania Court House, Virginia, but Grant keeps advancing.

June 1–June 3—At Cold Harbor, Virginia, Lee administers a bloody check to Grant's attempt to press into Richmond, but Grant has forced the Confederates back to the very outskirts of the city.

June 8—The Republican party, styling itself the Union party and meeting in convention at Baltimore, Maryland, nominates Lincoln for a second term; as his running mate it nominates Unionist Tennesseean Andrew Johnson, a Democrat.

June 14–June 18—Grant evades Lee and nearly gains a stranglehold on Lee's army and Richmond at Petersburg, Virginia; failing this, Grant settles down to a siege of Petersburg and nearby Richmond.

July 4—Lincoln angers the powerful Radical Republicans by vetoing the Wade-Davis Bill, the Radicals' harsh plan for reconstructing the southern states.

July 17—With the Confederate army in Georgia backed up all the way to Atlanta, Davis replaces Johnston with the more aggressive Gen. John B. Hood.

July 20–July 28—Hood and Sherman fight three bloody but inconclusive battles outside Atlanta.

August 5—Union naval forces under Adm. David G. Farragut take Mobile Bay, Alabama.

August 30—The Democratic party, meeting in convention in Chicago, Illinois, nominates George B. McClellan for president on a platform that calls the war a failure and calls for immediate peace; McClellan muddies the issue by accepting the nomination but repudiating the platform.

September 2—Sherman takes Savannah.

October 19—Union forces under Maj. Gen. Philip Sheridan decisively defeat Confederates under Lt. Gen. Jubal Early at Cedar Creek, in the Shenandoah Valley of Virginia.

November 8—Lincoln wins reelection to a second term, soundly defeating McClellan.

November 16—Sherman leaves Atlanta on his march through Georgia, bound for Savannah and the sea.

December 13—Sherman reaches the sea near Savannah after a successful march.

December 15—Union forces under Maj. Gen. George H. Thomas decisively defeat Hood's army at Nashville, ending Hood's foray into Tennessee and nearly destroying his army.

December 22—Sherman takes Savannah and telegraphs Lincoln presenting the city as a "Christmas gift."

1865

January 15—Union naval and land forces under the command of Rear Adm. David D. Porter and Maj. Gen. Alfred H. Terry capture Fort Fisher, near Wilmington, North Carolina, effectively closing the last southern port for blockade-running cargo vessels.

January 20—Sherman sets out with his army to march northward from Savannah, through the Carolinas.

January 31—The U.S. House of Representatives passes and sends to the states a proposed constitutional amendment banning slavery; it will become the thirteenth Amendment. On the same day, Davis appoints Lee commanding general of all Confederate forces.

February 3—Lincoln meets with Confederate peace commissioners on board a steamer anchored in Hampton Roads, Virginia, but despite his offer of generous terms, the conference fails when the Confederates continue to insist on independence.

February 17—Sherman's troops reach Columbia, South Carolina; departing Confederates set fire to the city.

March 4—Lincoln is inaugurated for his second term.

March 19–March 21—Weak Confederate forces under Joseph E. Johnston attack Sherman's army at Bentonville, North Carolina, in an unsuccessful attempt to halt his advance.

April 2—Grant's forces break through Lee's lines around Petersburg and Richmond; the Confederate government flees Richmond as Lee's army retreats westward.

April 9—Grant corners Lee's remaining force at Appomattox Court House, Virginia, forcing his surrender.

April 14—Pro-southern actor John Wilkes Booth shoots Lincoln while the latter attends a play at Ford's Theater in Washington; he dies the next morning, never having regained consciousness. Another member of Booth's conspiracy stabs Secretary of State William H. Seward, who nevertheless recovers. Aided by fellow conspirators, Booth evades capture and flees into Maryland.

April 18—Johnston surrenders the remains of his army to Sherman at Durham Station, North Carolina.

April 26—Booth is cornered by U.S. troops in a tobacco barn in rural Maryland. Refusing to surrender, he dies of a gunshot wound, possibly self-inflicted.

May 4—Confederate Lt. Gen. Richard H. Taylor surrenders all remaining Confederate forces east of the Mississippi.

May 10—Confederate president Jefferson Davis is captured near Washington, Georgia. President Johnson declares the rebellion ended.

PART I

THE FIERY TRIAL—THE CIVIL WAR IN HISTORICAL PERSPECTIVE

Chapter 1

A Brief Historical Overview of the Civil War

The seeds of the Civil War lay in the institution of slavery, which had already existed in America for over a century at the time the United States gained its independence. By the beginning of the nineteenth century, slavery was an exclusively southern institution, with slaves providing the labor for the South's extensive staple-crop economy. During the first half of the century, increasing moral objections to the institution led to increasing defensiveness and hostility on the part of the South. A minority of Northerners espoused abolitionism, the position that slavery should be immediately abolished rather than be allowed to continue or even be phased out slowly. Abolitionists in the North (it was worth a man's life to express abolitionist views in the South) condemned slavery. In response, Southerners, coming more and more to think that such views represented all Northerners, reciprocated with charges of bigotry and extremism.

Since the U.S. constitutional system clearly made the domestic institutions of the individual states their own concern, Northerners could do nothing about the existence of slavery in the already existing Southern states, but many Northerners did hope to prevent slavery from spreading to new areas still under federal control. The political struggle thus came to focus on the status of slavery in the territories. When in 1854 the Republican party was born with the central theme of permitting no further spread of slavery into the territories, offended Southerners loudly declared that their states would secede from the Union should a Republican be elected president.

In 1860 the electorate put Southern threats to the test by choosing Republican Abraham Lincoln in an unusual four-way election contest. Though Lincoln received fewer than half of the popular vote (because he got not a single vote in the Southern states), he nevertheless comfortably won the needed majority electoral vote by carrying every Northern state except New Jersey, where he split the electoral vote with Democratic candidate Stephen A. Douglas. Like many other Northerners, Lincoln believed that Southern talk of secession was empty bluster.

Southerners, however, lost no time in making good their threat. On December 20, 1860, South Carolina declared itself no longer part of the Union, and during the next six weeks six other Southern states followed suit—Mississippi, Florida, Alabama, Georgia, Louisiana, and Texas. In February 1861 their representatives met at Montgomery, Alabama, and set up a government for what they styled the Confederate States of America, selecting Jefferson Davis of Mississippi, former army officer, secretary of war, and U.S. senator, as their president. Many Southerners still believed that the North would tamely accept their secession and that no war would follow. Davis rightly suspected otherwise.

In those days the United States inaugurated its new presidents not in January following the election but on the next March 4. Thus the man in the White House while the Confederacy was being formed was James Buchanan, by all odds one of the lamest of lame-duck presidents. Weakly, Buchanan allowed secession and hardly lifted a finger when militia in the seceding states quickly snapped up all the forts and federal installations within their boundaries—except two. These were Fort Pickens, on an island outside the harbor of Pensacola, Florida, and Fort Sumter, on an island inside the harbor of Charleston, South Carolina. In each fort, a small U.S. Army garrison waited, out of reach, for the moment, of Southern militia but taking no steps against the rebels.

In his inaugural address, Lincoln appealed for calm and reason. Asserting that states could not rightly withdraw from the Union, he nevertheless promised not to take aggressive action against them unless they fired the first shot. Significantly, he asserted that he would continue to hold the remaining federal outposts in the South. The two forts, especially the more high-profile Fort Sumter in the harbor of the most radically proslavery city in the South, became important symbols of the continued legitimacy of the federal Union. As such they were intolerable to Confederates, who cut off supplies to Sumter (Pickens could easily be supplied from the sea whether Confederate authorities liked it or not) in hopes of starving the garrison out. To Lincoln's dismay, his advisors informed him shortly after his inaugural that in fact the Sumter garrison would soon be out of food and that the federal government, with a regular army of only 16,000 men and its navy scattered over the seas patrolling against pirates and slave traders, did not have the firepower necessary to shoot its way into Charleston Harbor and resupply the fort.

Lincoln decided to send a supply expedition to Sumter anyway, and he notified the governor of South Carolina of his intention, promising not to send in arms, ammunition, or men—only food. That was not good enough for South Carolina's Governor Francis Pickens, who promptly sent word to Davis in Montgomery. The Confederate president in turn ordered his commander in Charleston, Confederate Gen. Pierre G. T. Beauregard, to demand the fort's immediate surrender. If the fort's commanding officer, Maj. Robert Anderson refused, Beauregard was to take the fort. On April 12, 1861, that is just what happened, as Confederate guns all around the harbor opened fire a few hours before dawn. After thirty-four hours of bombardment, Anderson surrendered. Ironically in this opening round of what would be the nation's bloodiest war, no one was killed.

The North roared its response to the attack on Fort Sumter with expressions of outrage, patriotic rallies, and a rush to enlist in the military. Declaring that a rebellion existed, Lincoln called for 75,000 three-month volunteers to put it down. The quota was met and exceeded within days. The South was excited too and pleased that their leaders had finally struck a blow against the hated Yankees. Davis called for 100,000 one-year volunteers, and Southern men responded with equal eagerness. The slave states of Virginia, North Carolina, Tennessee, and Arkansas, faced with the choice of fighting either for or against their fellow slave states of the Confederacy, chose to go with the South. Eager for the prestige Virginia offered as the home of Washington, Madison, and Jefferson, the Confederacy transferred its capital to Richmond at the end of May.

Four slave states still remained in the Union. Delaware had few slaves and never seriously considered secession. Maryland possessed many slaves, particularly in the eastern part of the state, and that section was virulently pro-Confederate. When the Sixth Massachusetts Regiment passed through Baltimore on its way to Washington, a proslavery mob attacked it, and several fatalities occurred on both sides. Other Marylanders strove to take the state out of the Union and into the Confederacy, but Lincoln moved firmly to quash the secession movement in Maryland, even when he had to bend or temporarily set aside certain legal provisions. Among those was an order from U.S. Supreme Court Chief Justice Roger B. Taney, himself a Marylander, directing him not to jail a man who was endeavoring to recruit troops for the Confederacy within the state. Contrary to what Confederate propaganda maintained, however, Lincoln's infringements on civil liberties were few and slight, considering the exigency that faced the nation.

Another slave state on the border between North and South was Kentucky, the home state of both Abraham Lincoln and Jefferson Davis. The Bluegrass State's populace was sharply divided between Confederacy and Union, and a large segment was simply determined to go with Kentucky, whichever way it went. The result was that the state declared itself neutral and forbade either side to move troops into or through its territory. This bizarre arrangement was an enormous benefit to the Confederacy while it lasted, shielding the heartland of the South from Union invasion. Yet both sides carefully observed the limitation, since, as Lincoln saw it, the loss of Kentucky would fatally tip the balance in the coming war against the North. Kentucky neutrality continued throughout the summer of 1861 until a Confederate general foolishly invaded the state in early September. Thereafter, Kentucky opted for the Union, though a few of its citizens wound up fighting for the South.

The westernmost border slave state was Missouri. Swift and decisive action by federal authorities there staved off an early attempt by pro-Southern forces to snatch power in the state, but Missouri remained bitterly divided and saw ferocious guerrilla warfare, sometimes degenerating into bloodthirsty banditry that continued beyond the end of the war. For the most part, however, the state remained Union territory, rarely visited by main-force Confederate armies.

While the fate of Maryland, Kentucky, and Missouri during the summer of 1861 was of vital importance to the survival of the Union, most eyes in America were focused on northern Virginia, where scarcely 100 miles separated the rival capitals. The Confederate congress planned to meet July 20, and Northern newspapers, particularly the erratic Horace Greeley's *New York Tribune*, took up the cry of "On to Richmond," demanding that Union forces take the city before the Rebel congress could meet there. Maj. Gen. Irvin McDowell, commanding the Union army around Washington, warned Lincoln that his troops were not adequately prepared, but Lincoln insisted on action. Often during this war, Lincoln's military instincts would be far better than those of many of his generals. This time they were not. Thirty miles from Washington, McDowell met a Confederate force under Beauregard, awaiting him behind a stream known as Bull Run. Last-minute reinforcements raised Beauregard's numbers to equal those of McDowell. Still the federal general almost prevailed with a surprise flank attack. At the key juncture, however, the Confederates managed to put together a rally around the resolute stand of a Virginia brigade under the command of Thomas J. Jackson, who that day earned his nickname as "Stonewall." Retreating Union troops became confused, especially as they became entangled with civilians, including congressmen, who had come out to see the show and were now desperately trying to get away. The Federals lost their cohesion, and large parts of the Union army stampeded back to Washington.

The humiliating defeat at Bull Run stung the North into redoubled efforts—more money and more men, with an initial call for 500,000 three-year volunteers, the first of many such calls. Confederate euphoria in the wake of the victory soon gave way to recriminations about why the seemingly great triumph had not secured Confederate independence and ended the war. Both sides now grimly settled in for a war that would last longer, perhaps many months longer. No one yet imagined just how long.

Winfield Scott, the aged and decrepit overall commander of all U.S. armies, suggested to Lincoln a plan to put down the rebellion. The navy should blockade Southern ports, the army should cordon off its land boundaries, and a joint army-navy force should seize the course of the Mississippi River. Then the Union should let time and economic constriction bring erring Southerners back to their senses. Newspapers derisively dubbed Scott's program the "Anaconda Plan," after the South American snake that kills its prey by squeezing it. Yet Lincoln saw merit in the plan. He shared Scott's hope that Southerners would reconsider as well as the general's desire to conciliate Southerners by avoiding draconian solutions. Still Lincoln differed with Scott in that he knew it would be necessary for Northern armies to penetrate deep into the South and, most of all, to crush its armies.

As it turned out, the war that followed was fought primarily in the

South and the border states. With the exception of a few Confederate forays, most notably the offensive that took Robert E. Lee's Southern army to Gettysburg, Pennsylvania, no fighting took place on Northern soil. The states of Tennessee, Mississippi, Georgia, and Virginia would see the heaviest fighting and most significant campaigns.

Throughout the war one of Lincoln's chief problems was finding the generals who could lead the North's large, superbly equipped armies to accomplish that end. In the wake of the Bull Run debacle, McDowell had to go, at least from top command. To replace him Lincoln turned to thirty-four-year-old Maj. Gen. George B. McClellan, who had been successful in the relatively small campaign by which the Union had gained control of what was soon to become the state of West Virginia. To command in Kentucky, Lincoln chose William T. Sherman, brother of a prominent Republican senator. Still farther west, in the Mississippi Valley and Missouri, he chose John C. Frémont, 1856 Republican presidential candidate and, before that, an army officer.

These did not prove to be happy choices. Impressed with the vast amounts of men and materials that would be needed to win the war, Sherman may have had something like a nervous breakdown. At least the newspapers said he was crazy. That was a gross exaggeration, but in any case Lincoln relieved him. Frémont was a bigger problem. His administrative practices were questionable, he showed little eagerness to bring the enemy to battle, and, worst of all, he risked alienating hundreds of thousands of proslavery Unionists in border states like Missouri and Kentucky by issuing a proclamation declaring martial law, threatening to execute guerrillas, and freeing the slaves of rebellious masters. Alarmed at the possibly disastrous political fallout this could have, Lincoln canceled Frémont's proclamation. When after several more weeks the general still failed to do the fighting for which he had been appointed, Lincoln removed him. The biggest problem was McClellan. Through the fall of 1861 and the winter that followed, the young general delayed advancing while he drilled and drilled his large and magnificent army. McClellan's initial popularity with cabinet and congress gave way to bitter suspicions; some Republicans began to wonder if the Democrat McClellan did not really want to win the war at all. In fact it was not patriotism but nerve that the young general lacked.

While Lincoln and the nation waited impatiently for McClellan to feel ready to move, dramatic action took place west of the Appala-

chians. Frémont's successor, Henry W. Halleck, was no more enter-
prising, but under his command was Brig. Gen. Ulysses S. Grant.
Grant sought and received Halleck's permission to move against two
Confederate bastions, Forts Henry and Donelson, which guarded the
Tennessee and Cumberland rivers. Accompanied by a flotilla of navy
gunboats under Flag Officer Andrew H. Foote, Grant took both forts
in February 1862, opening the full navigable length of both rivers to
Union gunboats and transport vessels. This was a devastating blow
to the South. The western two-thirds of the state of Tennessee, including the vital manufacturing center of Nashville, with its surrounding rich agricultural area, were lost, and Union troops were soon
poised near the northern border of the state of Mississippi, just thirty
miles from the Memphis & Charleston Railroad, the South's most
important east-west link and, as one contemporary put it, "the ver-
tebrae of the Confederacy."

Jefferson Davis reacted vigorously, sending all the reinforcements
he could to his western commander, Gen. Albert Sidney Johnston.
Johnston gathered his scattered forces along with the reinforcements
at the key rail junction town of Corinth, Mississippi, on the Memphis
& Charleston and prepared to strike a counterblow. This he could
do because Halleck, jealous of Grant's success and with little understanding of warfare despite long study of it, had ordered Grant to
halt and wait for Halleck to bring up more troops and take command
himself. As Grant's army sat camped beside the Tennessee River at
Pittsburg Landing, Tennessee, Johnston's force struck a massive surprise blow on the morning of April 6, 1862. The ferocious battle that
followed was a bloodbath out of all proportion to anything Americans
had ever seen before. In two days' fierce fighting, more Americans
died than had perished in the Revolution, the War of 1812, and the
Mexican War combined.

Typically of Civil War battles, the horsemen figured little in the
heavy fighting—their numbers were too few and the terrain too
rough and wooded to allow classic cavalry charges. Opposing lines of
foot soldiers, occasionally lying prone but usually standing upright,
blazed away at each other from ranges of about 100 yards or less,
sometimes much less. Clouds of white, sulfurous powder smoke
drifted up from the firing lines and hung thick in the woods, while
each soldier frantically worked to reload his muzzle-loading rifle or
musket, turning it on end, dropping powder and bullet down the
barrel, then tamping them down with a ramrod. Finally he returned

the ramrod to its holder beneath the barrel, inserted a percussion cap at the breech, cocked it, and brought it to his shoulder to fire again. If he was reasonably well trained and not too flustered, he might be able to do that two or three times per minute. The artillerists set up their muzzle-loading cannon wherever a large clearing in the woods allowed it, rammed in their loads, and blasted the opposing side with a variety of ammunition ranging from a solid, twelve-pound iron ball, to an exploding shell, to their deadliest load, a bucket of lead balls known as canister. The last of these turned the cannon into something like a giant sawed-off shotgun. Still, it was the infantryman who did most of the killing—and most of the dying.

By the afternoon of April 6, the first day at Pittsburg Landing, Johnston himself was one of the dead. By that evening, Grant had come within a whisker of suffering annihilating defeat, but the Confederate attack stalled and Union reinforcements arrived. Most of all Grant remained resolute and on the second day drove the Confederates back. The bloody battle of Shiloh, as it came to be called, gave the nation a foretaste of the deadly warfare to come, but, most significant, it had failed to reverse the deadly results of Grant's victories at Henry and Donelson. Confederate fortunes west of the Appalachians never fully recovered.

Meanwhile, back in the East, McClellan had finally begun to move, although not the way Lincoln desired. The undeniably clever young general saw that the easiest way to approach Richmond was from the east, parallel to the many rivers that flow west to east in that part of Virginia. He would have the navy land him at the tip of the peninsula between the York and James Rivers, where they emptied into Chesapeake Bay, and thence he would proceed up the peninsula to Richmond. The trouble with this was that it would take his army out of a position to protect Washington, and by this time Secretary of War Edwin M. Stanton and some Republican lawmakers were beginning to wonder if McClellan meant to give the Rebels the capital. Lincoln was more calm and reasonable than his fellow party members and approved McClellan's plan as long as the general would leave behind enough troops to protect Washington. McClellan took his army down the Chesapeake, but problems quickly arose. A misunderstanding about the number of troops to be left behind further poisoned relations between McClellan and his government. McClellan himself advanced timidly and slowly, giving the Confederates time to counter his move with their main army in Virginia. Finally, bold action by a small Confederate army under Stonewall Jackson in the Shenandoah Valley of western Virginia created fears for the safety of Washington and prompted Lincoln to withhold about a quarter of the troops slated for McClellan's expedition.

That, and McClellan's own timidity, gave newly appointed Confederate army commander Robert E. Lee the chance he was looking for. A recent replacement for the wounded Joseph E. Johnston, Lee aimed at cutting off and destroying McClellan's army, which had by late June reached the very outskirts of Richmond. In a week of fighting known as the Seven Days' Battles, in late June and early July 1862, he failed in that purpose but did drive McClellan back down the peninsula, well away from Richmond.

This was but the beginning of sorrows for the Union cause in the East. Lincoln pulled McClellan and his army off the peninsula, and while the withdrawal was underway entrusted the Union efforts in northern Virginia to another army—which would soon absorb most of the components of McClellan's force—under the command of Maj. Gen. John Pope. Yet the team of Lee and Jackson victimized Pope with a sound drubbing in a second battle of Bull Run. Then Lee audaciously took his army across the Potomac into Maryland, looking for a dramatic victory that might end the war. Lincoln saw no choice but to remove the thoroughly discredited Pope and restore McClellan. Though he had failed on the peninsula, McClellan remained immensely popular with his troops, and Lincoln hoped he could restore their morale in time for the showdown clash with Lee.

That clash took place September 17, 1862, near Antietam Creek, outside the little Maryland town of Sharpsburg. Lee was trapped, his army's back to the Potomac, with no viable route of speedy retreat. If McClellan prevailed, Lee and his army would be finished. McClellan enjoyed a better than two-to-one numerical superiority over Lee's depleted army, but the Union general actually used less than two-thirds of his available forces. Even those troops he sent forward in piecemeal advances, never striking the concerted blow that would have destroyed Lee's army and, perhaps, ended the war. Union troops fought with stunning valor in their uncoordinated assaults, each of which came close to defeating Lee. Yet the Confederate general was just able to shore up his battered front, and his soldiers, fighting with desperate courage, staved off the Northern assaults. When night fell, the two armies had fought the bloodiest single day of combat in American history—a record that has stood to the present day. The combined killed and wounded of both sides numbered well over 20,000. Lee escaped back into Virginia, his army intact.

Lincoln was disgusted with McClellan's performance and became more so as weeks passed after the battle without any action from "Little Mac," as his still-adoring troops called him. Yet Lincoln took advantage of the victory at Antietam, such as it was, to take a step he had been planning for some time.

By midsummer, after the failure of McClellan's peninsula campaign, Lincoln had become convinced that the time had come to discard his early policy of conciliating Southerners and adopt a vigorous course aimed at subduing them. The cornerstone of the conciliatory policy had been the offer to leave slavery untouched, and the death knell of that policy was Lincoln's decision that it was time to lay his hand on the South's cherished "peculiar institution." Abolitionists and others in the North had for some months already been urging him to strike at slavery, but hitherto Lincoln had resisted the pressure. Now he decided to take a carefully measured step against it, basing his action on presidential war powers. In mid-July he informed his cabinet that he intended to issue immediately a proclamation—the Emancipation Proclamation—declaring "forever free" all slaves in areas that remained in rebellion against the United States as of January 1, 1863. Secretary of State William H. Seward suggested that it might be well to wait until after the North had won a victory, lest Lincoln's new strong policy be misinterpreted by foreign powers as an act of desperation. Lincoln saw the wisdom of Seward's objection and put the proclamation in his desk. There it stayed until a few days after McClellan's equivocal victory over Lee at Antietam, when Lincoln promulgated it to the nation.

The Emancipation Proclamation marked a distinct epoch in the war. Northern soldiers had recognized for months that Southerners were not to be conciliated and that the policy of restraining the Union war effort was self-defeating. Many of these bluecoats had already begun to implement their own hard-war policies, appropriating supplies without ceremony where and when they needed them. Now the North's official policy would back them up, demonstrating a determination to prosecute the war as vigorously and severely as necessary to compel Southern submission. It also changed the North's war aims and thus changed the nature of the war from a limited war to save the Union (which Lincoln and others believed would be the ultimate doom of slavery in any case) to an all-out war to shake the very foundations of Southern society by freeing the slaves. Meanwhile, in the South, news of the proclamation brought renewed determination to fight to the bitter end.

If it was now a different war, Lincoln and other observers could have been forgiven, in the fall of 1862, for thinking that it looked depressingly the same as before. McClellan continued to suffer from what Lincoln called "the slows." An incursion by the Confederacy's western armies into Kentucky failed, as did another attempted Confederate offensive in northern Mississippi, but Federal commanders, with few exceptions, proved unenterprising in following up their advantages.

Finally, Lincoln sacked McClellan and Federal commander in Tennessee, Don Carlos Buell, replacing them with Ambrose Burnside and William S. Rosecrans, respectively, but the results were anything but satisfactory. At Fredericksburg, Virginia, that December, Burnside blundered into the most lopsided defeat the North had yet suffered, while at the turn of the year, Confederates under Braxton Bragg surprised Rosecrans and almost beat him. When Bragg subsequently withdrew, Rosecrans, his army battered but intact, claimed victory. Meanwhile, out in Mississippi, other Confederates cut Union supply lines, forcing Grant to retreat, and yet another Union column under Sherman met severe repulse near the key Mississippi River bastion of Vicksburg. Lincoln, who had seen his Republican party take a pounding in the November congressional elections and then on January 1 had carried through on his Emancipation Proclamation and declared the Confederacy's slaves free, was glad to accept Rosecrans's scant victory as the only bright spot in a season of otherwise unrelieved gloom. He later said that the country could hardly have survived another defeat.

Yet by the spring of 1863 the season of Union setbacks seemed to be coming to an end. After a dismal winter of trying to find a way to take the Confederate bastion at Vicksburg, Grant carried out a brilliant campaign in April and May of that year, skillfully outmaneuvering his Confederate opponent John C. Pemberton and placing his army in position to besiege Vicksburg, with Pemberton's major Confederate army trapped inside. In late June, Rosecrans finally launched his long-delayed next step, skillfully maneuvering Bragg almost entirely out of the state of Tennessee.

In Virginia, of course, the news was less good that spring. Burnside's successor, Joseph Hooker, restored the Army of the Potomac's morale and boasted of what he would do when he marched against Lee. Yet when that time came, in May 1863, Hooker made a promising start and then froze like a deer caught in the headlights. In the tangled woodlands around the little crossroads of Chancellorsville, Lee and Jackson trounced him in what would go down as their greatest victory. Yet the news was not all good for the Confederacy, even in the East. Jackson suffered a severe wound, ironically from friendly fire, at the very height of his great victory and died one week later. Then when Lee sought to seize the initiative by leading his army into Pennsylvania that June, he and his subordinates turned in their worst collective performance in suffering a solid defeat in the massive battle of Gettysburg, July 1–3. Maj. Gen. George G. Meade, whom Lincoln had appointed to replace Hooker as commander of the Army of the Potomac, conducted his side of the battle with solid if uninspiring competence, but bitterly disappointed Lincoln by failing to pursue Lee's battered army and destroy it before it could slink back to relative safety in Virginia. Lincoln decided he could not replace the first eastern general to win a clear-cut victory over Lee. Meade stayed on, and the stalemate in the East continued.

Even as Meade was contemplating his gingerly pursuit of the beaten Lee, Grant was winning a truly decisive Union victory in the West. On July 4, 1863, Pemberton surrendered Vicksburg and his 30,000-man army. Within days the Union controlled the entire course of the Mississippi River, sundering the Confederacy and striking a blow from which it would never recover.

The Confederacy struck back that fall, or tried to. Major reinforcements from Virginia and Mississippi rushed to join Bragg's Army of Tennessee as it endeavored to stop and destroy Rosecrans's advancing army in northern Georgia. Bragg won an indecisive victory at Chickamauga. Rosecrans's army retreated to Chattanooga, Tennessee, and Rosecrans himself retired to obscurity by order of his superiors. Lincoln tapped Grant as overall commander of all Federal forces in the West, his own and those formerly commanded by Rosecrans, and Grant routed Bragg at the Battle of Chattanooga that November.

As 1864 began, the Confederacy's remaining chance hung on its ability to survive through another year and the hope that the Northern electorate would come to its rescue in the presidential election that fall. If the South could prevent dramatic Union successes, particularly the fall of the cities of Richmond, Virginia, and Atlanta, Georgia, Northern war-weariness might grow to the point that a peace candidate would defeat Lincoln and negotiate a settlement that left the Confederacy independent.

In preparation for the 1864 military campaign, Lincoln gave Grant overall command of all Union forces. Grant determined to make his headquarters with the hard-luck Army of the Potomac, where he would oppose Lee in Virginia. He gave Sherman command of all Union forces in the West, with the objective of crushing the western Confederate army under Joseph E. Johnston and capturing the city of Atlanta. For the first time, the major Union armies would move in a coordinated effort, instead of being, in Lincoln's words, "like a balky team, no two pulling at once."

In early May the armies advanced. Sherman maneuvered skillfully against Johnston in North Georgia, and Johnston did not hesitate to retreat. Amid constant skirmishing their two armies moved this way and that, but always closer to Atlanta. By mid-July they were on the outskirts of the city, after a campaign that had produced relatively little heavy fighting. In Virginia, things were much different. Grant too maneuvered skillfully, but Lee was only too willing to fight. In a series of vast and savage battles that raged from the Rappahannock River all the way to the outskirts of Richmond and from early May to mid-June, Lee tried and failed to arrest Grant's advance and destroy his army. By midsummer, Grant settled down to a semisiege of Richmond and its neighboring city—and key supply nexus—Petersburg. Lee hung on doggedly.

Yet in Georgia, it appeared that Johnston would abandon Atlanta without a serious fight. His long retreat had already cost the Confederacy dearly in surrendered manufacturing capacity. President Davis determined to replace Johnston with a general who would fight. The general he picked was John B. Hood, a proven veteran of fierce reputation at lower ranks. Hood did indeed fight—three major battles within the space of eight days in late July. Yet despite fairly good concepts, his plans failed through his own and particularly his subordinates' errors and most of all through the very hard fighting of Sherman's battle-toughened veterans. Hood held on to the city, but Sherman now settled down to a semisiege similar to the one Grant was conducting against Richmond.

The summer's campaigns had been much more costly and somewhat less spectacularly successful than many had hoped. Yet these campaigns were indeed producing results. Grant and Sherman had the Confederacy in a death-grip, and it was only a matter of time before Southern resistance collapsed—unless Northern will failed in the election that fall. For a few weeks in late summer that failure seemed probable. Democrats, who had nominated George McClellan as their presidential candidate, loudly denounced the war as a failure. Even some within Lincoln's own party began to call for him to give up his reelection bid, and Lincoln himself, while entertaining no thought of quitting, nevertheless admitted that his success looked doubtful. All across the country, North and South, people believed that the electoral defeat of Lincoln meant the victory of the Confederacy.

But then a different sort of news began to come in from the battle fronts. In August, Union Adm. David G. Farragut won the battle of Mobile Bay. In the fall, Gen. Philip Sheridan spectacularly defeated Confederate forces in the Shenandoah Valley of Virginia. Most important of all, however, in early September Sherman tried one more turning maneuver and successfully captured Atlanta. The Democratic mantra that the war was a failure was thus decisively shown to be false. Lincoln might perhaps have won without these military victories; with them he swept into a second term with a resounding majority.

The Confederacy was now doomed, but not everyone knew it. One who did not know it, or refused to accept it, was Confederate president Jefferson Davis, who steadfastly resisted any realistic efforts at negotiation and successfully urged his fellow Southerners to fight on to the bitter end. Even when Davis finally conceded far enough to the wishes of some of his Southern critics to send a peace delegation to meet with Lincoln, he stipulated emphatically that any negotiated settlement would have to recognize from the outset the complete independence of the Confederacy. This was nothing short of full Confederate triumph, but Davis continued to insist on it even as Confederate defeat became more and more of a reality.

Fall of 1864 gave way to winter of 1865. Grant maintained his bulldog grip on Lee and Richmond. Sherman marched across Georgia, living off the land and showing the people that a Union army could now pass through their countryside at will. By Christmas he was in Savannah, on the Atlantic coast. Meanwhile, Sherman dispatched a portion of his army, under Maj. Gen. George H. Thomas, to deal with his erstwhile opponent, Hood. This Thomas did handily, with the help of Hood's own miscalculations. Hood marched into Tennessee hoping to regain the state for the Confederacy. Instead he wrecked his army against Thomas's forces at the battle of Franklin, Tennessee, and, in mid-December, Thomas destroyed most of what was left of Hood's force at the battle of Nashville. In January 1865, Wilmington, North Carolina, the South's last remaining port for vessels running the Union blockade, fell to Union attack, while Sherman began to march his incomparable army northward through South Carolina, both punishing that state for starting the war and also moving into a position to help Grant finish off Lee.

As it turned out, Grant needed no help. In late March he launched his final offensive, crushing Lee's western flank and fatally threatening the flow of Confederate supplies into Richmond. Sensing Lee's army beginning to crumble, Grant ordered an all-out assault for April 2, even as Lee struggled to extricate his army and evacuate Richmond and Petersburg. The Confederate government fled into southwestern Virginia, and Lee's army attempted to follow. Grant's pursuit was relentless, however, and he finally ran Lee to ground and forced his surrender at Appomattox Court House, Virginia, April 9, 1865.

Nine days later, at Durham Station, North Carolina, Joseph E. Johnston surrendered to Sherman the small force with which he had been endeavoring to oppose Sherman's advance. Throughout the remainder of the months of April and May, remaining Confederate forces continued to make their formal surrender, but with Durham Station, the war was over.

Davis still did not face it and fled with his cabinet through the Carolinas and into Georgia, his party shrinking by the mile as various cabinet members, aides, and the like departed to make good their own escapes. Davis apparently hoped to reach Louisiana and Texas and raise new Confederate troops to fight on from there. He never got the chance to try, however, being captured by Union cavalry near Washington, Georgia, on May 10. He was briefly imprisoned but never brought to trial and lived out the remaining twenty-four years of his life in Mississippi, a popular figure in the South.

By the time Davis was captured, Lincoln was already dead. April 14, Good Friday, Lincoln attended the play "Our American Cousin" at Ford's Theater in Washington and was assassinated by John Wilkes Booth, an actor, a pro-Confederate Marylander, and a member of a Confederate espionage ring. Simultaneously, Lewis Powell, alias Lewis Paine, slashed and seriously wounded Secretary of State William H. Seward at Seward's home, where the secretary of state lay bedridden from injuries sustained in a carriage accident. Powell was a member of the same Confederate espionage cell as Booth. He was later hanged, along with three other accomplices, but Booth cheated the gallows, being shot, or shooting himself to avoid capture, several days after his crime.

Lincoln's death added difficulty to the already troubling problem of reconstruction. While the war still raged, Lincoln had offered Southerners an easy way of getting their states back into a proper relationship with the Union. Whenever ten percent of prewar voters would take an oath of future allegiance to the United States, a Union-loyal government could be set up. Radical Republicans denounced Lincoln's "Ten Percent Plan" and passed their own much more demanding Wade-Davis Bill instead, requiring a majority of prewar voters and more stringent oath requirements. To the disgust of the Radicals, Lincoln vetoed the Wade-Davis Bill.

Still the Radicals had been hopeful of Lincoln's cooperation in the last weeks of his life, taking heart from his suggestions that former Confederate states ought to give voting rights to at least some blacks. After Lincoln's death, the Radicals were even more hopeful of his successor, Andrew Johnson. A Tennesseean of plebeian background who despised rich planters, Johnson proclaimed, "Treason is a crime and must be made odious." But to the Radicals' dismay, Johnson stuck doggedly to Lincoln's old lenient policy, adding few additional requirements on the now-defeated Southern states. This led to a three-year battle of wills between president and Congress in which Congress ultimately prevailed. Overriding Johnson's vetoes became routine for Congress, and when he fired a cabinet member without the Senate's permission (Congress had recently passed a law denying him the power to do so), the House of Representatives impeached him and the Senate came within one vote of the two-thirds majority required to remove him from office.

In the election of 1868, Republicans successfully elected their candidate Ulysses S. Grant; yet even with a Republican president, the era proved to be one of frustration and disappointment for almost all concerned. Southern intransigence and violent resistance, Northern weariness from years of struggle, and the inherent limits to what any government can do to change society kept many Radical Republican goals unfulfilled. Former slaves never received the "forty acres and a mule" many of them, and some of their white advocates, had hoped for. Some gains were made in civil rights for blacks, but most of these were subsequently lost after congressionally supervised Reconstruction ended in the Southern states in 1877. For their part, white Southerners remained bitterly resentful of their defeat and even more so of the changes that Reconstruction had attempted to produce in their society.

Still, slavery was a thing of the past, and the Union had been saved. As Lincoln and numerous Union soldiers believed, those accomplishments assured the survival of "government of the people, by the people, and for the people," and had been eminently worth fighting for.

Chapter 2

The American Ways of Life, North and South

"This is a most beautiful & romantic country," wrote Michigan soldier Charles B. Haydon as he observed Virginia during the first year of the war. "Still there seems something decayed, neglected, mournful about everything. . . . Everything is so unlike Michigan," he continued. "Everybody lives away off the road & seems to have done all that they ever expect to except going through the mere formula of living. The idea of anything new or business like strikes one as exceedingly out of place, a great innovation on customs immemorially established."

The South was clearly a culture very different from anything Haydon had encountered before. After visiting a Virginian's house he noticed another curious circumstance: "There was not a manufactured article in the house which was not made north of Secessiondom [i.e., the seceding Southern states]." The blue-uniformed descendent of generations of industrious Yankees puzzled at a society that did not make its own manufactured goods.[1]

The perplexity was mutual. Captain Reuben A. Pierson of the Ninth Louisiana Infantry Regiment sat outside his tent near Bunker Hill, Virginia, on July 19, 1863, writing to his father back home in Bienville Parish, Louisiana, about the recently concluded Gettysburg Campaign in Pennsylvania. "The country through which we passed," he wrote, "was one of the best improved, and most systematic farming countries I have ever seen." For this young man from an agricultural district of an agricultural state in the overwhelmingly agricultural South, it was a startling revelation that even the farming in a Yankee state such as Pennsylvania showed a marked difference to what he knew back home. "They sow their grain with a patented machine, covering it at the same time," he continued. "They reap, pile in bundles, thrash [thresh], and fan the grain all with different machines." To this Southerner it was a revelation to see Northerners doing with machines what his society did, whenever possible, with slaves.[2]

When the two cultures discussed their differences, especially the single core issue of slavery, they seemed to come no closer to understanding. Theodore Upson, a young teenager living in northern Indiana, recorded a visit by his uncle, Rev. Cooper Dayton of Nashville, Tennessee, in 1859, two years before the outbreak of war. Upson recorded in his diary that his father and uncle argued heatedly. Dayton, who was a slaveholder, maintained that his slaves were better off than they would be if they were free, since as their master he saw to it that they got adequate food and medical care. Upson's father asked if the Tennessean had ever sold one of his slaves. "Only one," was Dayton's answer, and that was because he was lazy and could not be made to work enough. Did he teach them to read? Mr. Upson continued.

"Oh no it would do them no good," the Southerner replied. "They were not like white folks. If they could read it would only make them discontented and put bad ideas in their heads."

"Now honestly," pursued Upson, "would you like to be a slave yourself?"

"No of course not," said Dayton. "The Negro is not like white people, and unless you know him as we of the South do you cannot understand him or know what is best for him and how he feels about these things."

Young Theodore was not impressed. On another day the Upsons' local minister, Rev. Cory, came to dinner. "They got to talking right away," Upson recorded in his diary, "and both got pretty mad for Preachers. After a while Cooper Dayton said, 'Now Brother Cory, if you had your own way, what would you do with the slaves?' "

Cory leaped to his feet, pounded the floor with his cane, and roared, "Free them, sir! Free them at once! You have no right to hold them a day longer in slavery."

Dayton looked at him disdainfully, then said, "My! How you must

A black family entering Union lines with their earthly possessions. National Archives.

love a Nigger." Just then Mrs. Upson entered the room to announce that dinner was ready. "I think it was well she did," young Theodore wrote in his diary.

Some days later the difficult uncle left to return to Nashville. Before leaving he warned his brother-in-law, "If you Black Republicans ever succeed in electing a President we of the South will have to leave the Union." At that Dayton's mother, who was also present, remonstrated. "For shame my son, and your Grandfather a Revolutionary soldier and your Father in the war of 1812."

"Oh, you folks in the North don't understand the South," her son replied.

Theodore's father remarked quietly, "Perhaps you of the South do not understand us of the North very well either."

"Oh yes we do," said he, "you folks begrudge us our Niggers."

Young Theodore thought his Uncle Cooper was talking very foolishly.[3]

AMERICAN ROOTS, NORTH AND SOUTH

Cultures north and south differed sharply by 1861. Indeed, they had been different from the very beginning, and by the second half of the nineteenth century those differences had come to have explosive significance, bringing the two cultures into bitter conflict.

North and South had different beginnings, far off in the colonial past. The New England colonies—Massachusetts, Connecticut, Rhode Island, and New Hampshire—came into existence by a vast migration of English Puritans during the first half of the seventeenth century. These devout Christians came with a vision for a new society, cleansed of Old World corruption and Papist (i.e., Roman Catholic) error and tyranny, a society based on the principles of the Bible and an example to the rest of the world—"a city set upon a hill" and "a model of Christian charity," as Massachusetts's first governor described it.

As years passed and one generation gave way to another and yet another, the original vision sometimes faded partially or entirely from view, but always there remained in the collective personality of New England and its cultural descendants the memory of at least a shadow of the old Puritan dream in a deep-seated consensus that one should be honest, virtuous, thrifty, and industrious. That was significant for more than just what became the northeastern states, for to one degree or another, most of the North became the cultural descendent of New England. By the first few decades after the United States gained its independence, New England's rocky soil and constricted borders provided inadequate opportunities for its rapidly multiplying population. Its sons migrated westward to mingle with the descendants of Dutch settlers in New York and the English Quakers and various Germans in Pennsylvania, both of whom had brought with them— at the very least—their own versions of the Protestant work ethic. Other New Englanders spread across the northern tiers of what were to become the midwestern states taking much of New England culture with them. Occasionally, religious revivals occurred to refresh and spread something like the original Christian fervor of the early settlers, and this was particularly the case with the Great Awakening, which occurred during the first half of the eighteenth century, and the Second Great Awakening, which likewise dominated the first half of the nineteenth, each of which spread across the country.

A culture that places a high moral value on work and that heeds the memory, somewhere at its beginnings, of a large number of idealists hoping to create a good society, is not a likely candidate for significant use of slavery, and such was the case in the northern United States. No colony or state there ever had significant numbers of slaves, and many never had any at all.

Besides, many areas of the North were not suited by soil or climate for the sort of large-scale, staple-crop agriculture that had become dependent on slavery. Modern scholars believe slavery could have been made to function in industrial or other settings, but pre–Civil War Americans generally believed that it was suitable only for the cultivation of vast amounts of certain basic crops such as rice, tobacco, sugar, and, later, cotton. These crops grew primarily or exclusively in southern climates, and most people of that era believed, mistakenly, that blacks were better suited than whites to the warm southern climate and completely unsuited to the more temperate climate of the northern parts of the United States. On top of that, Spaniards operating in the Caribbean and Central America had been first to pioneer the wholesale use of African slaves in the New World, and by the time American Southerners became involved in the practice, use of black slaves was customary for the cultivation of staple crops in southern climates.

Thus initial northern culture, the northern climate, and agricultural customs of the time worked against the adoption of slavery there. At the same time, climate and agricultural custom had just the opposite effect in the South, making it a more "natural" place for slavery to take root.

Yet there were other differences and other reasons for slavery to become the dominant social institution in the South. While the earliest northern colonies had been founded with the vision of creating a good society, the first southern colonies had been all about getting rich. Virginia, founded in 1607, was founded on that motive, as were the Carolinas later in the century. While Maryland and Georgia initially possessed religious or philanthropic motives, they very quickly became precise social and cultural copies of their neighboring southern colonies. Thus if slaves were good for profits, then the more slavery the better. By the time of the American Revolution, slavery formed a sharp social difference between North and South. The states north of the Mason-Dixon Line, the boundary between Maryland

and Pennsylvania, had never had much slavery and were quickly getting rid of what vestiges they still had. South of the Mason-Dixon Line, slavery was, quite literally, big business.

This fact, along with some other differences of climate and resources, made for increasing difference, in many respects, between cultures north and south during the first "four score and seven" years of the nation's existence. The North developed a mixed economy based on manufacturing, trade, and agriculture. Factories sprang up in northern cities, even enormous factories on a relatively modern scale, such as the textile works in Lowell, Massachusetts, as the North followed Britain and Europe in adopting the industrial revolution. A thriving merchant shipping industry carried U.S. products, including southern-grown cotton, to the rest of the world and brought the world's products to American ports, of which all of the most thriving ones, save only Baltimore and New Orleans, were in the North. As the mid-nineteenth century approached, Yankee clippers—tall, sleek, amazingly fast three-masted sailing ships—plied the seas of the world, carrying passengers across the Atlantic and tea across the vast reaches of the Pacific from China toward its ultimate destination on the breakfast tables of Americans from Boston to New Orleans.

THE GROWTH OF AMERICA

The early nineteenth century was a time of tremendous growth for the United States of America, and the two sections of the country did not always grow in the same ways. Within the United States, the first half of the nineteenth century saw massive expansion of transportation systems. Turnpikes, either private-enterprise or government-financed, canals, steamboats, and finally railroads helped link the nation's markets together, boosting trade and linking more strongly than ever the culture of the Northeast with that of what was then called the Northwest but is now known as the Midwest. Better transportation linked places like Cleveland, Cincinnati, Chicago, Pittsburgh, and dozens of other towns to the markets of the world. And the increasing trade within the country, flowing freely with almost no government regulations, brought massive prosperity on a scale not dreamed of before. With the exception of a couple of brief economic slow-downs, the nineteenth century was a period of scarcely interrupted economic growth in the United States, and the great bulk of the factories, seaports, railroads, and the other elements of modern industrial economy were overwhelmingly concentrated in the North.

Yet the North also had its farms. Pennsylvania was the breadbasket of colonial America, and, along with New York state, it continued to have a large and thriving agricultural sector even as it was surpassed by the midwestern states of Ohio, Indiana, and Illinois. Northern agriculture took the form of the family farm. Father and older sons toiled to care for the livestock, plow, plant, cultivate, and harvest the crops. Mother and older daughters cared for the house. Depending on the amount of cash the farm brought in, and thus the degree to which the family could participate in the market system, they might be able to purchase such items as clothing. Then they would "only" have to work at washing, mending, cleaning house, canning and preserving food, and preparing meals for a large and hard-working family. In some cases, they might also spin, weave, and sew the family's clothing as well. At times when the demands of farming became extraordinarily pressing, such as harvest or the need to save a young crop from a potentially killing frost, the womenfolk would probably be called upon to drop their household duties and work alongside the men in the field, fighting for the family's survival.

Although some northern farmers could be racist in some of their attitudes, they were all but universal in their disdain for slavery. They valued their freedom, respected hard work, and did not wish their own labor to be placed in economic competition or social equivalence to the compelled toil of a slave. In many ways they were the embodiment of Thomas Jefferson's ideal of the "yeoman farmer"—sturdy, independent, self-sufficient, usually producing most of what their families used, all of what they needed, and a surplus for the market besides.

Life on a family farm in nineteenth-century America had one thing, at least, in common with life in the cities of that era: It involved enormous amounts of hard work. The rhythms of life were different, however, and the surroundings could be quite alien for the factory-working city-dweller. The sun, instead of the factory whistle, set the boundaries of the day's work, and if the overall hours probably averaged out about the same, the factory workers enjoyed less variety and more stultifying surroundings than their country cousins. The factory worker might be at the mercy of his employer, but the farmer too was at the mercy of the impersonal forces of the market. As for most people at most times and places in human history, life for most Americans in the nineteenth century was hard but on the whole quite a bit better than most other people then or before had enjoyed.

Conditions of life for the city-dwelling factory worker could vary considerably. There were good and bad factory owners: those who paid their workers relatively well and those who took every advantage of them they could. At its worst, such a life could involve long hours of factory labor for most members of the family, including children, and habitation in a foul and crowded tenement.

Yet contrary to popular mythology, the industrial revolution was, on the whole, a good thing for the physical well-being of the common people. True, the rich might grow very rich, if they acted shrewdly, but the poor working man often profited too. The rising tide of prosperity lifted all boats, both large and small. The improved productivity offered by more efficient means of production often translated to at least somewhat higher real wages, and the average family had available to it a much larger array of consumer goods, at lower prices, than had ever been the case before.

The industrial revolution did present new challenges. There were shifts in labor demand and a need for readjustments that the previous economic system had not created. The result was the beginnings of urban poverty. Whether the case was one of a poor working family in a tenement or a completely destitute victim of cyclical unemployment, the appearance of such suffering disturbed many Americans who visited or inhabited the large cities of the North during the decades prior to and after the Civil War. Among the forefront of those who took concrete steps to alleviate such problems were evangelical Christians, who established missions in inner cities. Government dole for the poor was scant to nonexistent, but the Christian organizations provided, or helped provide, food, shelter, and clothing for many. Such help was conditional, however, on the recipient's willingness to do such work as he could—even if it was only token duty chopping wood for the mission—and to give up intemperate habits, such as alcohol consumption or gambling, that could perpetuate his poverty. Along with the material help, Christians naturally also presented the message of Jesus Christ, in hopes that needy hearers might change their eternal destiny as well as undergo such change of heart as would infuse them with the kind of work ethic and temperate habits that might bring earthly prosperity as well.

Another effort to ameliorate the conditions for the urban poor, specifically for poor children, was the Sunday School movement. Observing that many children were receiving no education because they worked in factories Monday through Saturday, some Christians established the first Sunday Schools as means of teaching such poor "street urchins" not only reading and writing, but also the Gospel. Over time, as Sunday Schools became more widespread, they became the arm of many local churches aimed at teaching the Bible to children. As more middle class children came to fill their classes, Sunday Schools, except in inner-city areas, generally gave up their role as teachers of reading and writing. Because of the institution's broad distribution in both the North and South, many a Civil War soldier would write letters from the fighting fronts back to his former Sunday School in his home town.

Education for the vast majority of children in the North took place during the regular work week. Educational institutions varied widely, including private schools, charity schools, Christian schools, and the forerunners of today's public schools. Yet even among the "common schools," as the latter were called, local parents, rather than far-off educational bureaucrats, usually determined who would teach and what, and such institutions were not as all-pervasive as they became in the twentieth century. Despite, or more likely because of, its immense diversity in educational institutions, the North, especially in areas that had been settled up for any length of time, boasted a remarkably high literacy rate. Even on the frontier, children attended small one-room school houses, and when those were not available, they might well receive at least some their first years of instruction at home, literally "at their mother's knee," receiving perhaps the best education of all, as witnessed by the case of famous writer Laura Ingalls Wilder, just a few years after the Civil War.

The North's amazingly widespread literacy was another legacy of its Puritan forebears, who had stressed the importance of reading skills so that every person might read the Bible for himself, thereby finding the way to salvation and escaping the wiles of what an early Massachusetts education law called the "Old Deluder, Satan." The New England Primer, with didactic sentences such as "In Adam's fall, we sinned all," was a common reading textbook throughout the North for decades. Especially widespread in the decades immediately prior to the Civil War was William McGuffey's set of readers, with their strong content of moral teaching. Needless to say, the concept of "separation of church and state," at least as reinvented in the

1960s, was entirely undreamt of in the nineteenth century as in the eighteenth or most of the twentieth century.

LIFE IN THE SOUTH

Certain aspects of this picture may seem at least somewhat familiar to the modern reader—cities, towns, factories, seaports, paved roads, railways, and family farms are all part of life in modern America. That is what makes the Old South such a very different culture than the North of that time or twentieth-century America. It was not that the South had none of such things—though it had a great deal less of most of them—but that its culture was dominated, colored, overshadowed by a different system.

The presence of slavery was the largest single factor separating North from South, and slavery exerted an influence throughout all of Southern society. Economically, the South too had prospered during the first sixty years of the nineteenth century, but its prosperity rested not primarily on mercantile pursuits nor on manufacturing but instead almost solely on staple-crop agriculture. In Virginia and Maryland it was tobacco and wheat; in Louisiana and Texas, cotton and sugar; in the Carolinas, cotton and rice; and in the belt of Deep South states from Georgia to Alabama to Mississippi it was cotton, cotton, cotton. A major proportion of the labor that grew these crops was performed by slaves. Slaves outnumbered whites in South Carolina by about 1715, and the Palmetto State continued to have the largest percentage of slaves of any southern state right down to the Civil War. During the early nineteenth century, the state of Mississippi also came to have a slave majority. By the time of the Civil War, 3.5 million slaves resided in the South, to 5.5 million whites.

The system as a whole, carried mainly by the high price of cotton on the world market, was a profitable one for the South. Cotton was the nation's leading export, and the profitability of the crop helped drive up the price of slaves. By 1860 a prime field hand could bring a price of $1,000 or more, at a time when a laboring man, north or south, would be glad to make $300 in a year. The market for cotton remained strong even during downturns in the economic cycle, such at the Panic of 1857. Southerners looked smugly on the economic slowdown in the North while continuing to enjoy steadily high profits. They were quick to claim this as proof of the economic superiority of the slave system.

Yet while cotton was grown by slaves and the markets of the world were willing to pay a high price for it, the fact remained that the slave system was not, in fact, always profitable to those who ran it. Most of the 3.5 million slaves in the South lived on plantations—defined as farms with more than twenty-five slaves—though plantation owners themselves made up only a tiny percentage of the South's white population. A plantation was a large and complex establishment, and running it required both sharp business skills and the ability to manage slaves well. Too lax a hand and the bondsmen would not work hard enough; too hard, and they might become especially surly, laggard, and uncooperative. Many plantation owners used either white overseers or black drivers to run their gangs of slaves, but then the problem was selecting and acquiring the right man for the task. Like all agriculturists, plantation owners were at the mercy of weather and crop yields, even if the market for cotton did remain steady and strong.

On top of all this, plantation owners considered themselves part of the moneyed and leisured class and expected to live a fairly lavish style of life. To be sure, they were by far the richest citizens of the South, but the dirty and not-so-little secret behind many of the most impressive plantations of the South was that their owners were slipping each year deeper and deeper into debt, often to northern merchants and bankers.

While the majority of the South's slaves lived on large plantations, the majority of its white slaveholders were small operators who owned only a few bondsmen. They were still among the wealthiest of southerners, but they might well live in fairly rough farmhouses and work in the fields alongside their slaves. Together with the owners of large plantations, slaveholding farmers comprised about 25 percent of all southern families.

Below them on the South's economic ladder stood the region's largest economic group, substantial middling farmers who owned no slaves. In many ways they resembled very much their counterparts in the North and Midwest. Theirs were family farms, and the family provided most if not all of the labor. Menfolk "plowed the mules" (i.e., drove a team of mules pulling a plow), planted, hoed, and thinned the cotton; the womenfolk were back at the cabin, washing, mending, cooking, or attending to all the other myriad chores of running a household without a single modern convenience. While a farmer's wife in upstate New York might be called out some frosty

Members of a Virginia family pose in front of their house. Library of Congress.

night to help save a young corn crop from a late cold snap, the wife of a yeoman farmer in the South could expect to be called upon to drag a picksack through the cotton fields during the perennial labor crunch at harvest time.

Yet there was one important difference between the middling farm-ers of the South and those of the North. Whereas northern farmers despised slavery, their southern counterparts considered it a beneficial and indispensable feature of the great order of the universe. They fully approved of the South's "peculiar institution" and hoped to make it into the ranks of the slaveholders themselves someday. They might well have relatives who were slaveholders and felt themselves connected to the slaveholding strata of society by many ties, not the least of which was simply their common whiteness.

This was probably the most important factor in securing the loyalty of slaveless whites to the system of bondage. Southern politicians—almost always slaveholders themselves—encouraged the view that the presence of slavery ensured the equality of whites. No white would belong to the lowest class of society nor do the most menial work—that sort of thing would be reserved for the slaves. The bondsmen would form what one Southern apologist called the "mudsill" of Southern society. The mudsill was the bottom log of the cabin, the part that held the rest of the structure up out of the mud.

The fact was, of course, that the middling white farmer out in his field chopping cotton was doing precisely the same work that tens of thousands of slaves were doing at the same moment all across the South. The farmer differed in that he could at least keep the fruits of his labor, but the necessity of competing directly against slave labor demeaned his work and worsened his lot economically, a fact that Northerners seemed to grasp instinctively, but Southerners, immersed in their culture, did not. When one of them, Hinton Rowan Helper of North Carolina, did grasp the point and expounded it in his 1857 book *The Impending Crisis in the South*, the Southern establishment suppressed the book's distribution in the South. That the middling and poorer whites remained unmoved by such rhetoric of Helper's as may have reached them is borne out by the fact that they shortly thereafter dutifully soldiered through four years of bloody civil war aimed at guaranteeing the perpetuity of slavery. For them, whatever else slavery might do, it at least assured that blacks would be kept from reaching a level of social equality with them.

The different driving force in the southern economy led to a different development of the South's infrastructure. While the growth of commerce in the North drove the construction of major trunk-line railroads linking the Northeast to the Midwest, the South's almost colonial emphasis on staple-crop production led to construction of numerous small, local railroads, designed simply to draw produce from the hinterland and funnel it down to port cities or navigable rivers. Such railroads often failed to interconnect with each other and, even if they had interconnected, could hardly have functioned together since they were of differing track gauges.

As Michigan soldier Charles B. Haydon noted when the Civil War brought him to Virginia, the South retained far more of a rustic and backward appearance and flavor than did the North. Even parts of the South that were far removed from the frontier still displayed an earthy lack of refinement that surprised many Northerners. Partially, this was a result of slavery, which minimized the importance of material improvements by funneling all available capital into human chattels. Slavery also meant that much routine maintenance would be done by those who had no stake of ownership in their surroundings. Partially, it was also the result of enervating heat in summer and of the original cultural heritage of the southern colonies. While early Puritans in Massachusetts had labored diligently to create a good and just society, Virginia settlers lived in tumble-down shacks, the chief design feature of which was that they required the absolute minimum of labor to be taken away from the all-consuming business of making tobacco and thus making money.

Education was also different in the South. While it was by no means a society of illiterates, there could be no denying that the dissemination of learning in the southern states did not approach that in the North. A good education could be a very practical thing for a plantation owner or cotton factor (merchant), and some planters utilized their leisure to seek a broad classical education. Yet on the other hand, a dirt farmer might see little purpose in education for himself or his children.

Education of slaves posed a special problem. In most southern states it was illegal. The reason for this bizarre prohibition was fear of slave revolt. That fear was the foremost waking nightmare of white Southerners—submerged deep or shallow in their thoughts, it arose again and again to haunt their minds. This fact might seem odd in a society that insisted vehemently that its slaves were happy and contented and did not desire freedom, much less revenge. Southerners solved this conundrum by maintaining that their peaceful, happy slaves might be turned into bloodthirsty animals by exposure to foreign ideas—particularly condemnations of slavery by the growing northern antislavery movement known as abolitionism, because of its demand for the immediate abolition of slavery. The surest way to see to it that no slave ever read an abolitionist tract or a newspaper report of some antislavery orator in Congress was to make sure that no slave could read. Southern legislatures were not slow to apply that prescription.

In practice it was no sovereign remedy. Even slaves who could not read could overhear conversations not meant for their ears, and most of the time someone, often another slave, could be found who could and would read to them. The reason for the latter fact was that the slave-illiteracy laws were difficult to enforce and frequently disobeyed, sometimes by other slaves or free blacks (of which the South had a few) and sometimes by benevolent whites.

Some of the whites who might be most likely to flout the laws against teaching reading to slaves were the South's evangelical Christians, and their problem on this point dramatizes the dilemma they faced in trying to reconcile their faith with life and acceptance in a slave society. Although Protestant Christianity had played a much smaller role in the founding of the southern than of the northern colonies, by the mid-nineteenth century it had come to be almost equally predominant in both sections of the country. All of the southern colonies had had at least a nominally Anglican (or, in the case of Maryland, Catholic) establishment. The Great Awakening, during the eighteenth century, had been felt less strongly in the South but had still made a significant impact there. During the latter part of the century courageous Baptists in Virginia braved the persecution of the Anglican establishment to introduce a more real and vital form of Christian faith to that state. Then, during the first half of the nineteenth century, the Second Great Awakening, also known in the South as the Great Revival, swept both North and South, revitalizing churches in the North as well as planting the faith in many areas, particularly recent frontier districts, where it had scarcely existed before.

The problem for Bible-believing Christians in the Old South was that while the Bible does not, in so many words, denounce slavery, it does set forth stipulations about right and wrong behavior that, if followed faithfully, would make American chattel slavery impossible. Abraham Lincoln later summed it up best when he took a famous teaching of Christ and applied it to the specifics of the case of slavery: "As I would not be a slave," Lincoln stated, "so I would not be a master." Very early in the nineteenth century, southern Christians faithfully taught such truths, but as cotton agriculture spread and slavery, as the chief means of making all that cotton, became more and more profitable, the pressure grew for Christians to remain silent. When they did not, the consequences could be severe. When in 1802 Methodist minister George Dougherty was merely rumored—falsely, as it turned out—to have planned on circulating an antislavery petition in Charleston, South Carolina, he was seized by a proslavery mob and held under a water pump until he almost drowned. Indeed, the reluctance of Methodists as a group to abandon their convictions on this subject temporarily retarded the growth of their denomination in the South. In time, however, they succumbed to the pressure. Some who would not compromise, like fiery Kentucky Methodist

Peter Cartwright, moved north to the free states. Others grew old, were ignored, and finally passed on. Many gave in. The other predominant denominations in the South—Baptist, Presbyterian, Episcopal (Anglican)—had already done so. The national denominations tolerated this until the issue finally became too prominent, the rift too broad for further fellowship. Then, during the 1840s and 1850s, every major national denomination, Methodists, Baptists, and Presbyterians, split along North-South lines.[4]

Condemned, quietly or vehemently, by their northern brethren, yet unwilling to make a clear witness against the prevailing culture around them, southern Christians tried two alternatives. One was to advocate a "spiritual" church, a Christianity concerned only with the life to come and not at all with man's life on earth except in his acts of personal piety toward God. Thus the church should have nothing at all to say about slavery or any other real or imagined social issues. The other alternative was to address slavery as a proper institution that needed only certain reforms. Such Christians urged planters to treat their slaves better, with at least modest success. Chief among the measures called for by these reformers was the legal recognition of slave marriages (for such unions had no standing in law) and the right to teach slaves to read. The reason for the latter was, of course, the standard Protestant insistence that each believer be able to read God's Word for himself. In the face of widespread fears that slaves might read more than the Bible, Christian reformers met with little success in changing the statutes banning slave literacy, but some believers did persist in teaching their slaves to read the Scriptures in defiance of the laws. The heart of the problem for those southern Christians who sought to reform slavery was that if all the principles of the Bible were applied rigorously to the "peculiar institution," southern slavery would be no more.

The need to refrain from condemnation of slavery also muted reforming zeal for other issues in the South. While evangelical Christians in the North were at the heart of such reforms as the temperance movement, leading to the banning or limiting of the sale of beverage alcohol in some jurisdictions, the South remained relatively hostile to almost all efforts at reform, since an admission that the principles of the Bible ought to be applied to earthly society might have led to an admission that slavery ought to be abolished. Indeed, it had led to precisely that in the North, where Christians, including the early nineteenth century's foremost preacher, Charles G. Finney, were among the most fervent of abolitionists.

THE SUM OF THE DIFFERENCES

The sum of all this was a nation containing two cultures that were increasingly distinct and bound to come into conflict with each other. The politicians could hedge, trim, and waffle as they might, but as long as the culture wars of the nineteenth century remained unresolved, the clash could at most be postponed. It could not be avoided. One politician, New York Senator William H. Seward recognized as much when he referred to the antagonism between the slave states and the free as an "irrepressible conflict."

The politicians, true to form, did their dead-level best to compromise, temporize, and split the difference. The chief flash point of political conflict was the intersection of slavery and national authority—the one narrow point where conscience-bound northern antislavery voters had both power and responsibility to touch the institution of slavery. The issue of contention was whether to admit new slave states to the Union. Congress compromised the issue in 1820 and again in 1850. In each of these compromises, Congress managed to find the votes for an agreement that settled the issue of slavery in the territories the nation possessed at that time, but such compromises were only good until the nation acquired more territory or until someone upset the arrangement by trying to take for his own side what a previous compromise had given to the other. The Compromise of 1850 seemed to bring sectional peace on the political scene until 1854, but then Illinois Senator Stephen A. Douglas made common cause with southern interests in order to claim for slavery lands that the 1820 Missouri Compromise had reserved for free states. With that, the political battle was on again. Yet even during the four years of quiet in Washington, the cultural pot still seethed beneath it all. The nation was deeply divided over slavery, and those divisions were bound to bubble up to the surface one way or another.

In the North, Harriet Beecher Stowe wrote the most socially powerful novel of the era, *Uncle Tom's Cabin* (1852). Stowe's book, a runaway best-seller, was based on thorough research and strove to present the case that while there were indeed benevolent slaveholders as well as vicious ones, the *system* of slavery itself was evil and ought to be abolished. The argument was effective with many northerners, where outright abolitionism still had no majority, but it aroused outrage in the South.

The South too had its pen-wielding advocates during the 1850s, notably George Fitzhugh. In books such as *Sociology for the South* and *Cannibals All*, he proclaimed slavery the best of all possible systems for organizing labor. He compared it favorably to the free market's system of wage labor, boasting that slavery provided cradle-to-grave employment and security for southern black workers. Northern workers, on the other hand, he depicted as the miserable victims of the caprice of market shifts or the cruelty of callous employers—badly in need of the blessings of southern slavery. While it was true that in purely material terms the most well-off slaves probably fared better than the most ill-used factory workers, nevertheless, despite Fitzhugh's recommendation, no free-born northern worker appeared eager to exchange his birthright of liberty for the pottage of slavery's security.

In 1860, the politicians ran out of ways to compromise the clash of cultures, or perhaps a number of politicians arose to prominence who shared the convictions of their people. Foremost of these was Abraham Lincoln, who believed that slavery was a moral wrong that ought at least to be contained until such time as it could be done away completely, even if that day were still far in the future. When he was elected president on the Republican party ticket in 1860—and when he refused to accept a southern compromise demand that he abandon the very moral principle of containment on which the campaign had been waged—southern leaders set in motion the process of secession in their states. The war that followed finally brought the active clash of cultures that had been growing within the country for more than a generation.

AND YET . . .

It was the third springtime of the Civil War, and dozens of battles had passed into history, several of them bloodier than the sum total of all the wars fought by the United States before the guns had opened on Fort Sumter in April 1861. Now, in April 1864, a couple of Northern officers, veterans of some of the most hideous of those clashes, thought about the new and almost certainly even bloodier campaign upon which they would be embarking in only a few days.

To improve their knowledge of the terrain—and probably to divert their minds from what they must soon face—they decided to take a hike up to the Union signal station high atop Cedar Mountain in Virginia. A long walk brought them to the place, and they gazed about at the beauties of nature in its springtime garb. Then they turned their eyes southward, across the Rapidan River, toward the camps of their enemies, the Rebels. The army signalmen had a powerful binocular mounted on the railing of their observation tower on the side toward the Confederate camps, and through it a man could easily make out individual Southern soldiers. Lt. Abner R. Small, adjutant of the Sixteenth Maine Regiment, peered through the glass and then turned it over to Captain Conley, of the same regiment. The captain gazed intently at the enemies he had been fighting for three long years. They were "lounging in their shirt sleeves and smoking their pipes, and talking," while others were avidly playing the new favorite game of both armies, baseball. Conley watched them for several minutes. Then he slowly turned toward Small and in a solemn voice said, "My God, Adjutant, they're human beings just like us!"[5]

Near Corinth, Mississippi, in the spring of 1862, Union Capt. Luther H. Cowan, of the Forty-fifth Illinois, had his soldiers protect local residents against potential plunderers. That fact along with the behavior of his men amazed several local women, and they told Cowan. To his wife the captain wrote that the Southern women had expected much different. "All that I have talked with say they were much mistaken in the way we have behaved and look," he explained. "They thought a yankee was something hardly in the shape of a human being, some awful wicked, ugly beast or a creature that would commit every outrage on all classes that could be imagined, but when they see us civil, quiet, genteel, orderly, accommodating, they are . . . happily disappointed."[6]

If the conflict of cultures between the Northern and Southern sections of the United States had been complete, if the two had indeed possessed two completely different cultures, the American Civil War would not have been nearly as complicated as it was. Indeed, had the two cultures been completely different, rather than simply rival variants of the same basic culture, the war would almost certainly have been, as many Southerners confidently predicted at the outset, entirely unwinnable for the North. In fact, however, both North and South were indeed one nation and shared more fundamental elements of culture than they disputed between them. The conflicting elements

The U.S. Capitol under construction, 1860. National Archives.

had become the ones that counted—and had indeed become impossible to pass over—but the common elements continued to draw the two together. When Northern military victory brought an end to the armed conflict, they had already begun the process that would ultimately restore a greater degree of unity to American culture.

Some of the ways in which the two cultures were alike were in fact the same ways in which they were different. That is, the differences between them were sometimes matters only of degree. For example, the North differed markedly from the South in that it had far more railroad mileage and was laying down track at a much faster rate during the 1850s. Yet the South, when compared to any other society in the world save only the North, was in fact laying track at a fantastic rate. Indeed, had the Confederacy won its independence, it would have possessed the second highest total railroad mileage of any nation in the world—right behind that portion of the United States that would have remained after the South's withdrawal. It was much the same with many other economic factors. The United States was experiencing a century of unrivaled and astounding economic growth, and the South had a part in that. Yet because of slavery and its effects—the reliance on slave labor rather than machines and the tendency for all available capital to be invested in slaves rather than factories and the like—the South lagged far behind the North in this surge of development.

Ironically, many of the aspects in which Northern and Southern culture were similar are features in which they both differ with modern American culture. Thus, applied to the Civil War, the concept of cultures in conflict becomes a two-edged sword. There were many important ways in which the North and South of the 1860s were cultures in conflict with each other, but there are many other and perhaps equally important ways in which they formed together a culture in conflict with that which prevails in the America of the twenty-first century.

For example, Northern and Southern cultures were alike in their view of women. American women as well as men in the 1860s saw the role of a woman as being primarily to help and support her husband. Americans considered the home to be the appropriate sphere for most female activity, where a wife and mother was to make a wholesome and morally uplifting environment for her family. Women were considered to be weaker than men, but they were also accorded correspondingly high honor—some would say they were put on a pedestal. Interestingly, the Civil War was notable in that it featured enormous armies occupying regions with large civilian populations, and yet, in sharp contrast to most wars in history, it saw very few rapes. Part of the reason for this was the high level of respect that nineteenth-century American culture accorded to women.

Very few women showed any dissatisfaction with this arrangement, though there were a few who challenged it vocally. Their voices were heard mostly in the more populous and more heterogeneous North, though some, such as the famous Grimke sisters, hailed originally from the South. The South was, in any case, less tolerant of the expression of divergent views. Southerners, seeking to discredit Northern abolitionism, charged that the North was the seat of numerous pernicious reform movements, of which such protofeminism was one. In fact, aside from a few loud and sometimes rather shrill voices, the feminist point of view was about as foreign to the North as it was to the South.

Finally, and perhaps most important, another aspect of the 1860s in which the culture of North and South agreed in contrast to that of modern America was religion. The Christian faith predominated, despite differences on the issue of slavery. Both presidents frequently

Members of the Christian Commission at their field headquarters near Germantown, Maryland, September 1863. National Archives.

proclaimed national days of thanksgiving to God or of fasting, humiliation, and prayer, as circumstances might seem to indicate. Neither North nor South would have recognized or liked the modern secular state and culture.

IN THE CONFLICT

Fighting an enormous war placed terrible strains on the cultures of North and South. Taxes rose to unprecedented heights; prices rose too; and vast numbers of men were mobilized for military service. Those who remained at home had to cope with circumstances as best they could.

During the war women in both North and South faced new challenges. "I presume you girls will have to do the work this summer while we do the fighting," wrote David Blair from a Union army camp near Atlanta to his sister Libbie back home in Ohio. "If so," he continued, "you will have hard times, but you must be heroines while we are heroes."[7] In similar vein, a popular song of the early war years had a heroic wife urging her husband to enlist:

Take your gun and go, John; take your gun and go,
For Ruth can drive the oxen, John, and I can use the hoe.

Of course, farm women both North and South had always been wont
to take to the fields in seasons of special need, even in peacetime.
Now the war presented a special crisis that called women to take on
an even larger share of field work and for a longer than usual period.

How much this picture of women doing heavy farm work became
a reality during the war is open to question. Despite the eventual
mobilization of a grand total of about 2 million men over the course
of the war, the North continued to have large numbers of young,
healthy, able-bodied men at home, and they may well have taken up
a good deal of slack. In the little town of Warren, Illinois, not far
from the Wisconsin line, another element of the population stepped
in to take over at least one part of the work that had previously been
done by the menfolk of the town and surrounding farms. A group
of older boys, still too young for war, organized themselves into a
volunteer company, patterned after the units in which their elders
had marched away, and styled themselves the "Sawbuck Rangers."
After electing a captain, a lieutenant, a sergeant, and a corporal from
among their number, they proclaimed their readiness to cut firewood
for the families of soldiers, an important job in a part of the country
where winter temperatures routinely plunge into the double-digits
below zero.

Whether women or boys, or other men, took over the work, no
one expected to have to carry on that way for so long. As the conflict
wore on through year after year, the duration of the sacrifices de-
manded by the war actually seemed to wear down many persons on
the home front faster than it did the soldiers. Certainly, the soldiers
themselves thought so, complaining frequently, and often unfairly, of
the inadequate fortitude of the society they had left behind. In such
complaints, however, they almost always excepted their own relatives,
and this is a clue that, during most of the war at least, the noisiest
discontent was coming from a relatively few people.

The problem for soldiers' wives was exacerbated by the fact that a
soldier's pay ($13 per month for a Union private, $11 for a Confederate) was not really adequate to sustain a family, even at the beginning of the war. The soldier usually needed at least some of that
money to provide for his own needs in the army. Add to that the fact
that paydays were often delayed by months—in the Confederacy,

many, many months—and the presence of inflation that, especially in the Confederacy, badly sapped the buying power of the soldier's already small wages, and the problem for soldiers' families could become dire. A number of localities, both North and South, undertook to pay a specified monthly stipend to the families of soldiers. Other families had to eke out their existence as best they could. Accounts of outright starvation are practically nonexistent, but stories of hunger are not.

Ironically, food shortages became most severe in the overwhelmingly agricultural Confederacy. Partially this was because planters stubbornly refused to shift larger portions of their acreage to the production of corn rather than cotton. Also in part it came from the insufficiency of the South's transportation network to move goods where they were needed, especially after Union military incursions began to damage railroads. Finally, it was also a factor of unwise policies of the Confederate government, policies—such as seizure of produce by the government at ridiculously low fixed prices—that tended to drive foodstuffs out of the market rather than encourage greater production.

So acute did the problem become in the South that in April 1863 a large mob, composed mostly of women, rioted in Richmond, protesting scarce food and high prices. They broke into shops and plundered the contents until confronted by Confederate President Jefferson Davis himself, backed by a battalion of militia. Davis appealed to the crowd to desist, and promised to have the troops open fire on all who had not dispersed within five minutes. Apparently no one doubted his word on this, and the rioters went home. Other riots occurred at various times during the war in other Southern cities, but this was the only one in Richmond. Interestingly, the female rioters were mostly the wives not of soldiers but of workers at Richmond's large Tredegar Iron Works, as well as female employees in the city's textile factories.

The hardship was far worse in the South than in the North and only grew worse with time. Northerners grew tired of the war, and the Northern electorate for a time even appeared to flirt with "Peace" candidates such as Ohio's Clement Vallandigham, who would have ended the war at once, granting Southern independence. Yet ultimately Northern determination proved sufficient for the burdens it had to bear. In the South, however, many gave way to despair under the greater burdens faced by that section of the country. With the war appearing hopeless and destitution facing them at home, many—though far from all—of the wives of Confederate soldiers began to write letters to their husbands begging them to desert, come home, and care for the families. Many Southern soldiers did just that, as desertion became epidemic and seriously sapped the strength of Southern armies during the last winter of the war. Still a large and potentially powerful Confederate force remained in the field to the end. Like their commander-in-chief Jefferson Davis, many Confederate soldiers in the field—like their suffering families back home—remained unwilling to accept anything less than complete victory until the complete and final Confederate military collapse in April 1865 decided the matter for them.

NOTES

1. Charles B. Haydon, *For Country, Cause & Leader: The Civil War Journal of Charles B. Haydon*, Stephen W. Sears, ed. (New York: Ticknor & Fields, 1993), 109, 163.

2. Thomas W. Cutrer and T. Michael Parrish, eds., *Brothers in Gray: The Civil War Letters of the Pierson Family* (Baton Rouge: Louisiana State University Press, 1997), 204.

3. Theodore F. Upson, *With Sherman to the Sea: The Civil War Letters, Diaries, & Reminiscences of Theodore F. Upson*, Oscar Osburn Winther, ed. (Bloomington: Indiana University Press, 1977), 4–12.

4. The story of Dougherty is from Christopher H. Owen, *The Sacred Flame of Love: Methodism and Society in Nineteenth-Century Georgia* (Athens: University of Georgia Press, 1998), 23.

5. Abner R. Small, *The Road to Richmond: The Civil War Memoirs of Maj. Abner R. Small of the 16th Maine Vols. with His Diary as a Prisoner of War*, Harold Adams Small, ed. (Berkeley: University of California Press, 1959), 129–30.

6. Luther H. Cowan to "Dear Wife," May 27, 1862, Luther H. Cowan Papers, Wisconsin State Historical Society, Madison.

7. David Humphrey Blair to "Dear Sister Lib," June 5, 1864, David Humphrey Blair Papers, U.S. Army Military History Institute, Carlisle Barracks, Pennsylvania.

PART II

DOCUMENTS

Chapter 3

The North and South Prepare for Conflict

The country plunged energetically, exuberantly, and very naïvely into the Civil War. The nation had never seen a conflict like this one, and, as a woman of the Civil War generation remarked many years later, "those who know nothing, fear nothing." The greatest fear of many a young man during the months of enlistment and army-building in 1861 was that the war might end before he had a chance to go into battle and prove his manhood. Northern and Southern society each did its best to support and encourage the young men it sent off to war, but individual parents often felt differently when the question involved their own youthful sons. The determined boys usually managed to get into uniform anyway. As the months passed, the nation would gradually begin to realize the first beginnings of what the war would mean to them.

The pieces in this chapter reflect that first eagerness to get into the fight, a feeling that continued to motivate young men coming of age and joining the army in 1862, 1863, and 1864, as some of the accounts here reflect. They also display the impact of the war's outbreak on the people who stayed home, and the dramatic change from peace to war for those who marched off.

JOHN REED HELPS RAISE THE STEPHENS LIGHT GUARD

John C. Reed was a young lawyer, the son of a planter, from Greene County in central Georgia. After Georgia seceded in January 1861, hundreds of other young men all across the lower tier of states—from South Carolina to Texas—joined preexisting "volunteer companies" or organized new ones, eager to show their readiness to defend "Southern rights." Such outfits could be long-established high-class drill teams, virtual uniformed country clubs such as the Oglethorpe Light Infantry of Savannah, Georgia, or they could be spur-of-the-moment groups rallied to go and fight Yankees, as was the case with the "Raccoon Roughs" from the opposite (i.e., northwestern) corner of Georgia. The young men of Greene County, including John Reed, waited until news of the firing on Fort Sumter before getting really serious about military preparation. By that time the great fear of every Southern young man was that the war might end before he had a chance to strike a blow. The company known as the Stephens Light Guard was Greene County's answer to that feeling. It was named after Alexander H. Stephens, vice-president of the Confederacy, also from Georgia. The company later became Company I, Eighth Georgia Infantry Regiment.

Reed wrote these reminiscences in 1888. The action of Lincoln to which Reed refers is the calling into Federal service of 75,000 state militia in order to put down the rebellion.

After the secession of Georgia, there was much sign of preparation for war on all sides. Young men suddenly began to study Gilham and Hardee [authors of military handbooks]. On every public occasion, in a village or town, you would see the parade of a volunteer company. But somehow I belonged to the listless. We said, if war does come we shall go at the very first, but we hardly think it is coming. Fort Sumter fell and the consequent action of Mr. Lincoln occurred. The blindest saw that at least a short war was at hand. By a spontaneous movement, a new company of volunteers rapidly formed in Greene county, where I was then settled as a lawyer. At its organization, we named ourselves the Stephens Light Guard, in compliment of Hon. A. H. Stephens, and elected our officers. Among these, Oscar Dawson, a son of William C. Dawson, formerly a U.S. senator from Georgia, became captain and I first lieutenant.

So many companies had already been organized in the State that Gov. [Joseph E.] Brown had but a small supply of arms left, and this was dimin-

A Confederate soldier from Virginia. Library of Congress.

ishing every day. We had delayed organizing until fighting was certain—so we said proudly to ourselves—and now we must have arms. At a late hour in the afternoon I was deputed to secure them. I hastened to the livery stable in Greensboro, and, hiring the only horse to be had, I was soon driving across the country to catch the first train from Eatonton, as that was the quickest route to Milledgeville, then the State capital. Night overtook me long before I reached the town. I had never gone the road. And so soon as it was completely dark I discovered that my horse was blind. But I used my eyes only the better, and I kept up a staving gait. I caught the train, and got to Milledgeville without detention. There by the exercise of some address and great importunity I obtained the desired number of smooth bore muskets. I had them shipped to Greensboro, and returning to Eatonton drove my blind horse back to the stable.

The company regarded this success of mine as a great military exploit, and I was pronounced worthy to be second in command. But nobody knew

A Confederate soldier from Georgia. Library of
Congress.

anything of tactics. Dawson fell in with Blackwell, a young man of Cobb
county who had taken part of a course in the Georgia military school, and
he accepted my offer to resign in his favor. He was elected in my place, and
I at once elected second lieutenant, a vacancy of that office having been
provided for me by general consent. We stayed at old Liberty campground,
in Greene county, for some days, and Blackwell soon had us familiar with
the manual of arms and the company drill. I myself became able to carry
the company through the common evolutions [i.e., maneuvers], and was
beginning to feel much less regret that I had not received a West Point
education. We believed that there was nothing more to be learned at drill.

We longed and prayed for marching orders. They came. We were to go
by rail to Richmond. Our joy made us wild, for now it seemed probable
that we should participate in a battle before the close of the war. I went to
Woodstock, in Oglethorpe county, in those days the most beautiful of country villages, hidden completely by forest trees until one was really in it—to

tell my parents goodbye. My only brother, two years my junior, was already at the front, in the 6th Georgia, as the first lieutenant of a company from Hancock county. My father and mother—especially the latter—were very serious and sad. Buoyant with the eagerness of beginning manhood, and aflame with the zeal which had made the south a great camp, I felt chilled by their evident lack of sympathy. I can understand now what I could not then. It was a bitter cut to them to send at once their only boys to a war which they both believed would be long and bloody. But they blessed me and gave me up. It pains me now to recall how hopeless and stricken my mother looked as she could not speak her goodbye.[1]

MICHAEL CUNNINGHAM GOES TO WAR

Michael Cunningham was typical of Northern young men who enlisted in the first year of the war, and his account reveals much of what it was like to go to war. In his case, the decision to enlist was made difficult by the fact that, as a nineteen-year-old, he was already the chief financial support of his mother and siblings. The "Mick Shanties" to which he refers were the shacks in which poor Irish immigrant laborers lived. "Mick" was a common derogatory nickname for the Irish, who were looked down upon by Anglo-American society.

I enlisted in the Eagle light infantry, afterward Co. B, 18th Reg. Wisconsin Volunteer Infantry, on the 17th day of Dec. 1861. Was 19 years old that spring. [I] resided on a rented farm near Blanchardville, worked in the lead mines most of the time was so engaged at the time of my enlistment. My Father died the 28th of April 1861 and left a Family of 9 children and in poor circumstances. I was the eldest so that the support of the family rested on my sholders as in fact it had to a great extent for the last three as my Father was not able to do much work for three years before he died. [He] had cancer of the stomach. [Several friends] and myself all enlisted the same day I being the first one to sign the roll. . . . A few days afterward we went to Monroe, Green Co., where we was regularly mustered into the state service. . . . We had our Headquarters in the McKeys Hall on the west side of the publick square I and a number of the boys boarded with Old Mr. Boyington, Father of our 2nd Lieut. Sam Boyington. Some time toward the last of Jan. we was ordered to Millwaukee. when we arived in Millwaukee our Co was quartered on west water St. opisit the 2nd Ward Bank in the American House run by one Veerhine. We had a very soft snap while we

A Union soldier from Ohio. Library of Congress.

was in those quarters plenty to eat and nothing to do onley get into mischief which we very often did. After the 9th Regt. which was quartered north of the City was ordered to the front which was some time in Feb we went into the Barricks that they had ocupyed and was called Camp Seigle I think that we was mustered into the U.S. service the last of Feb or first of March by Capt Trowbridge of the Regular Army and the name of our Camp was changed to Camp Trowbridge About this time we drew our uniforms & arms. our guns was the Belgian Rifles. We passed the time in learning the manual of arms in our quarters, also company drill such as we could in our quarters. I don't remember of ever having Battalion drill but twice as the snow was so deep on our parade ground that we could not get through it. . . . Almost every night there was a detail sent out to hunt up Boys that was out on french leave [French leave: absent without leave]. our camp was about one and one half miles north of the Post Office Square, and at that time the post office was pretty well on the north side of the city. between our

A Union soldier from Michigan. National Archives.

camp and the city proper there was a great many mick shanteys, small frame houses and mostly ocupied by Irish, and nearly all of them sold whiskey. the price was one cent a glass or 5c a pint so a boy could get hilarious for a small sum and I'm hear to tell you they improved the opertunity. The Guard House did not lack for tenants. . . .

so things moved along till the 30th of March 1862 when we was ordered to pack our knapsacks and get ready to march. soon the order came to fall in on the parade ground and then by the right into column of fours forward march. when we halted it was at the Depot on the south side of the city and found a train awaiting us. we was soon all aboard and the train pulled out amid waving of flags and the shouts of the boys. we passed through Chicago and on south. there was considerable of speculation as to the place that we would stop. I don't think that there was a place in the Southern Confedracy but what we had been ordered to if all the rumors was to be believed that was flying around.[2]

DAVID FLEMING AND THE PULASKI VOLUNTEERS PREPARE FOR WAR

David Fleming's account of how the people of Pulaski County, Georgia, raised and sent off their very own company for service in the war gives another glimpse of the homey, sometimes disorganized, sometimes very formal way the armies were formed. The ceremony of flag presentation was a standard feature of nearly every company's send-off. The company flags, lovingly sewn by the ladies of the community and formally bestowed along with a speech by a representative seamstress, were almost never carried into battle. Battle flags were a regimental concern, and the company flags were packed up and stored somewhere or sent home for safekeeping.

Fleming wrote these reminiscences for an article in the local *Hawkinsville Dispatch* in 1879.

Previous to the secession of the State of Georgia from the Union, very little interest was taken in military affairs by the people of Pulaski county. There was no military organization in the county at that time. Early in 1861, when the political skies began to show a warlike appearance, the citizens of Pulaski, in common with all other sections of the State, began to see the importance of organizing and training military companies for our defence, as well as a civil war seemed inevitable. Prominent among the leaders in this interest, and we might say the leader, was Dr. Thos. D. L. Ryan, who, aided by many other notable citizens, such as N. W. Collier, Joseph J. Lowry and others, soon effected the organization of the Pulaski Volunteers, which elected Dr. Ryan as captain. So eager were the patriotic citizens to unite with this first company that the ranks were soon filled and many had to be denied admission, and a second company was organized—the Georgia Rangers.

The services of the company were immediately tendered to the Confederate States Government at Montgomery, Ala., and training of soldiers began. There being no officer or member of the Volunteers acquainted with military tactics to much extent, General O. C. Horne, a well-drilled veteran of the Mexican war, kindly volunteered his services as drill master, and under his careful training our company soon learned the manual of arms and order of parading as well as to place the left foot on the ground at the word "hep." For a company of men utterly unacquainted with the art at the beginning, the company was pronounced by many good judges to be well drilled for so short a time of practice.

We went into camps soon after organization at the old Methodist church. . . . There was a beautiful grove there at the time. We were well supplied with tents, cooking utensils and other camp equipage, and soon realized to a small extent the life of a soldier. The change from soft beds and close rooms to a blanket on boards and in an open tent, did not agree very well with some of us, but nothing serious resulted from the exposure, and we realized the benefit of having a little camp experience at home. . . .

After a few days of first camp life and delay in receiving marching orders, we were all permitted to go home and look after our domestic affairs, to return as soon as orders were received to prepare for departure for the seat of war. The signal to apprise us of the receipt of these orders, we were informed, would be the report of a cannon, which, by some means, had come into possession by our town. Imagine a set of men, scattered in all portions of the county, each eager to hear the welcome news that our services were needed at the front as we toiled, each at his respective avocation—how the heart leaped at the distinct sound even for many miles of the report of that cannon on a calm morning in the early part of May. Reader, you may imagine that we are going too far when we say that we were delighted when our marching orders were received, which may have been in the cases of those whose family ties bound them in strong cords at home. But the great majority of our company being ambitious to immortalize themselves on the battle field, and being men without families dependent upon them, we can truthfully say that they received the news with gladness. A little incident connected with the firing of that cannon will not, we presume, be out of place here. Mr. Sam B. Stevens, the "mischief man" of the company (though a whole-souled man and brave soldier) applied to the captain and received permission to manage the giving of the signal, promising to give a report that would be heard by the members in the remotest corners of the county, even those who were asleep. His promise was fulfilled to the letter. He loaded the cannon, but no one except himself knows how much powder he used in the charge. He placed the cannon on one side of a large tree (on our camping ground) and himself on the other, and managed some way to apply the match, when the citizens thought for a moment that they were in the midst of an earthquake. It is said that only one small portion of the cannon could be found, and that was in the rear of Manning's store (John Henry & Son's present stand) a distance of three or four hundred yards, where it had fallen and killed a hog. Sam was unhurt, but the large tree did not live long afterwards.

From previous understanding, as before stated, we all knew what the report of the cannon meant, and in a few hours every member of the Volunteers was at his post, and we were again in camps. The order being only to prepare to receive marching orders at any moment, our officers went to work more diligently in training the soldiers for service.

We neglected to mention a pleasant little episode in the history of the company which took place previous to the incidents above narrated—the presentation of a beautiful flag to the company by the ladies of Hawkinsville. This took place on the 26th of April. It was presented in a beautiful little speech by Mrs. O. C. Horne, and received in behalf of the company by private (afterwards Captain) W. W. Williamson. The writer has been requested by members of the company to give both these speeches in this sketch, but this would take up too much space, and we give the closing remarks of Mrs. Horne, which, as it speaks the heartfelt sentiments of the ladies of Hawkinsville and Pulaski county at the time, shows that the patriotic hearts of these dear creatures were with us:

> Take it, soldiers! And return with it to your homes with honor, or die beneath its folds in defence of Southern Rights and the independence of the Confederate States, and amidst all the dangers and trials of a soldier's life, let it remind you that you have the earnest prayers of the donors for your safety and success.

We also give an extract showing the gist of Mr. Williamson's speech, which every soldier, looking upon that banner as a symbol of the cause in which he had enlisted, felt was from the hearts of the company.

> But the soldier should speak in acts rather than in words, and here in the presence of all this people, we pledge to defend that proud banner in all its pristine purity and loveliness, unsullied and untarnished, with our lives, our fortunes and our sacred honors.[3]

WESLEY W. BIERLY WORKS AND WATCHES

Wesley Bierly was a plain farmer. His diary for the spring months of 1861 tells us something about the daily life of a Pennsylvania farmer in Civil War times and also about the popular reaction to the outbreak of hostilities. Mentions of great excitement about the rebellion sandwiched between rather mundane comments on farm chores make an interesting contrast. Bierly's diary also reminds us that death was much more present and close at hand to nineteenth-century Americans, and it need not come on the battlefield or in the army's camps. Yet the mortality due to sickness in the army camps, especially for new recruits, was dreadful. The first deaths made strong impressions back home. Abe Lukenback, like many underage boys, tried to enlist anyway. His manner of leaving the army was also not uncommon. The business of "burning lime," to which Bierly refers, is in order to make a preparation to spread on his fields and reduce the acid content of the soil. The "Bellefonte Fencibles" were one of the local volunteer companies—hometown drill-teams really—that enlisted from towns and cities all over the country. *Frank Leslie's Illustrated Newspaper* was a popular periodical of the time.

Wednesday [April] 17th Went to E. Harters in P.M. to exchange oats for sowing. There is great excitement about the war—Companies are enlisting and organizing for Washington City. President Lincoln has made a call for 75,000 men in defence of the country. Thousands are preparing in the north as well as in the south. Was all night E. Harters. Weather cold.

Thursday [April] 18th Came home from E. Harters this A.M. Weather cold and snowy. was told that George Wolfe died yesterday at 4 o'clock. Hammered stones in P.M. for burning lime. Was at the wake at wolfs this night Dear George is now sleeping his long sleep. Having suffered much at Bronchitus & Consumption for over a year has now been relieved from his distress and suffering. More news about war—The Bellefonte Fencibles enlisted to a man and started off for Washington City to day. Friday 19th George Wolfe was buried in A.M. Hauled stones. Parents and girls were at the Funeral. Snowed fast in A.M. for a short time.

April—Saturday 20th 1861. Weather fine and clear. Broke stones for burning lime in A.M. Scrubbed the schoolhouse in P.M. was at Fulmers in the eve and fetched Isaiaks chest. There was a meeting in Town about War— to enlist soldiers for defending ourselves against Southern Rebels. Gen. Wolfe, Geo. Kurty, Rev. Edmunds, Mr. Stover & Jeremiah Haines addressed the meeting. E. J. Buskert and several other enlisted.

Sunday [April] 21st Had Sunday school for this the first time this spring in A.M.—had good attendance. Was in town with E. J. B[uskert]. all P.M. and night. Bro. E. J. B. made his will this eve in case he should not return from War. Monday 22nd Got up at Fousts & Buskerts at 3 o'clock this morning at which time marshal music was herd at the Hotel. E. J. Buskert, Gen. J. Wolfe, Charlie H. Winter, Henry Beck Simon Spangler & Abe Lukenback went off to War this A.M. Old Rev. Lukenback went after his son Abraham in P.M. was in town in the even and helped to raise a pole for a Union Flag. Began to set up our lime-stack. Plowed corn stuble.

Tuesday [April] 23rd Worked at the Limestack and plowed corn-stuble. Weather warm and fair. Was at Meyers in the eve.

Wednesday [April] 24th Sowed Oats to day. Set the Lime Stack on fire.

Old Mr. Lukenback fetched his son Abe home from the Army, at Harrisburg. Was in town in the eve. Had a little shower of rain to day at about noon.

Thursday [April] 25 Hauled stones and plowed corn land. Weather clear, cool and windy.

Friday [April] 26. Harrowed cornland. Father grafted apple trees to day. Old Rev. Lukenback was here in the eve.

Saturday [April] 27th Hauled stones in meadow. Father hauled Oats to Lukenbacks in A.M. It is reported that the southern rebels intend to take Washington City to day. Word came to town that Rev. Henry Hockman's wife died. They have seven children in the family.

Monday [April] 29th Went to Hillheim in A.M. and had three teeth pulled. Picked Stones in P.M. Was in town in the eve. Received a letter from Camp Curtin near Harrisburg of Levi Fulmer.

Tuesday [April] 30 Weather rainy to day. Sheared our sheep to day. . . .

Wednesday May 1st 1861. Weather cold—had snow storm and showers of rain frequently during the day—and at night it was very cold. Made fence.

Thursday [May] 2nd. Had a very hard frost this morning Ice was frozen ½ inch thick made fence in A.M.—Made and hauled posts in P.M. Gen. Wolfe came back from Washington City to enlist some more soldiers. Was in town in the eve. subscribed for Frank Leslies Newspaper.

Friday 3 May, A.D. 1861. Weather cold—snowed in A.M. Picked stones for mowing in New ground. Snow at Chambersburg is five inches deep.

Saturday 4th . . . Received letter from Camp Curtin of E. J. Buskert.

Sunday 5th Was in Sunday school in A.M. . . .

Tuesday [May] 7th Was in Mill in A.M. Father was at Henry Moyers for grape plants. Hauled Lime in P.M.—about 100 bu.

Wednesday [May] 8th Hauled 250 bu lime to day Levi Fulmer came here to day—on returning from Camp Curtin. Was in town in the eve.

Thursday 9th May A.D. 1861. Spread lime and harrowed cornland. Weather fair. Was in town in the eve.

Saturday [May] 11th Weather fair—Father went to Pennsvalley to see Rev. Light. Fetched fish oil at Forsters' store to grease gears. Greased Wagon gears in A.M. Spread & harrowed in lime in P.M. Was in town in singing in the eve.

Sunday [May] 12th Weather fair. Lukenbacks & we went together in the Spring-wagon to meeting in Penns valley, about ½ mile above John Moyers, with whom sister Mary lives at present. The meeting was laying of the corner stone of the building to be erected by the Evengelical Association. Rev's Core & May delivered sermons on the occation. Were in preaching of Rev. Edmunds in the New German Reformed Church near John Moyers in P.M.

Monday [May] 13—Had several showers of rain to day. Finished planting Corn in P.M. & planted also potatoes.

Wednesday [May] 15 Made fence and hauled rail pieces. Weather fair.

Thursday [May] 16.—Worked on the road. Weather cold and fair. Was all night at John Wolfs. their children have the hooping-cough very bad.

Friday [May] 17—Hauled stones in new ground. Weather fair.

Saturday [May] 18. Put the cattle to the mountain. Began to plow fallowed land. Jacob Smith brought Sister Mary home from John Meyers to day. . . .

Sunday [May] 19—Was in Sunday School in A.M.—in preaching in P.M. . . .

Tuesday [May] 21st Weather fair. Began to plow in field No. 8 Father came home from Nippanoe's Mountain.

Thursday [May] 23. Finished plowing in field No. 8. E. J. Buskert & Simon Spangler fetched Charlie H. Winter home from Chambersburg, dead. Charlie was sick only a short time. He was buried at 4 o'clock P.M.—A military procession was held under command of Gen. Buchanan. The Rebersburg Sunday School also followed him to the grave. Just when the preacher—Rev. DeMoyer had given out the text—an alarm was heard about fire—when all the people rushed out of church—found Widow Young's Building on fire. The greater part of the furniture was saved, but the house—and the Old school house were burned to the ground. . . .

Friday May 24— . . . Began to plow in the Mountain Orchard. Weather fair. Was in Literary meeting in the eve.

Sunday [May] 26—Was in Sabbath school in A.M. there seems to be new energy in our school at present. May God bless our Officers and Teachers—that they may do their duty in pointing the Youths to an Eternal Sabbath.

Friday June 7th. Have not written in my Diary for some time, but since my last notes a very solemn event took place in Rebersburg—Geo. H. Buskert was brought home dead, from York—York Co., Pa—Whilst in camp he took sick and growing very weak, he wrote home to his father, who immediately left for camp and found his son yet alive, but being with him only during one night he (Geo.) died at 6½ o'clock A.M. and his father arrived with him at Rebersburg on Friday May 31st. On saturday June 1st George was buried by the military custom. A great number of people were present—Funeral sermon preached by Rev. Tobias followed by Rev. DeMoyer.[4]

JONATHAN W. W. BOYNTON PASSES FROM FARM BOY TO SOLDIER

Jonathan Boynton's reminiscence of how he came into the Union army is an interesting study in change. He passed from the carefree life of a farm boy to the dangers of soldiering, from the comfort of his home in upstate New York to the hard and strenuous life in the army, and from the approval and praise of Northern civilians, cheering him on, to the sullen stares of Southern civilians, who resented his presence.

I was born on the twenty-third day of June, 1843, in the town of Smyrna, county of Chenango, state of New York in a log house erected by my father Jonathan Boynton. The farm was located five miles south-west of Smyrna village in what was known at that time as the Bartlett neighborhood. My mother's name was Luvan Loomis. . . .

I attended school in district number eleven summer and winter after arriving at school age until I was seventeen years of age. The winter of 1859–60 I attended school on Pigeon Hill, making my home with my brother-in-law, Robert J. Gibson, and doing chores for my board. The teacher was Adaline Bumford of Plymouth, New York. The winter passed very pleasantly for me. John Allen, a nephew of Mr. Gibson, made his uncle quite an extended visit. We passed the long winter evenings practicing penmanship in which John was quite an expert. . . . Robert owned a horse called George that was exceptionally hard on the bit and it took a good deal of muscle to hold him. Mr. Gibson did not venture to alow me to drive him, but with John I was allowed to ride. We made a trip to Plymouth one pleasant afternoon behind old George. John placed the lines under his arms around his back and as the sleighing was fine just let George go—at about a 2:40 clip. When he was going at top speed, a snowball flew from his hind foot and struck John in the forehead. John said, "Well that was a nice center shot." The winter passed all too quickly and, when the term of school closed, I returned home to commence the usual course of farm work.

The year that I was eighteen years of age and the War of the Rebellion had begun, 1861, I was anxious to go to the war, feeling that the Union must be preserved. Billy Griffin from Otselic, N.Y., came to father's home in the month of May to bid me goodbye and see if I would enlist as a soldier. Father and mother said I was too young, but in one year, if I wanted to go to the war, they would give their consent.

The year 1861 soon passed and I was still anxious to serve my country as a soldier. I was now nineteen years of age. On the eighteenth day of August, 1862, I placed my name on the enrollment blank as J. Wellington W. Boynton. I had worked in the hay field mowing by hand and had returned from the field to the house for dinner. Joel L. Jaynes, a citizen of Smyrna, drove up and said he was enlisting men for the war and he expected to be captain of a company.

He was able to secure only twenty-seven recruits and they were all consigned to company F, 157th regiment. The regiment was organized at Hamilton, Madison County, New York, and was known as a Madison county regiment. Phillip P. Brown was colonel of the regiment.

Our first camp was Camp Mitchell at Hamilton, New York. We were sworn into the United States' service on the nineteenth day of September, 1862. We left Hamilton for the scene of war about the twenty-third of September, 1862, by wagon for Canastota by way of Peterboro, N.Y. I rode with a Mr. Bisbe who was giving three sons for the war, all in my company. We arrived at Peterboro about noon where we were royally entertained by the good, loyal citizens of that town. Tables had been erected on the village green upon which were placed all the delicacies of the season. While we were doing justice to the good things before us, the band played patriotic airs and the Hon. Garrit Smith addressed the regiment. Among other things he said, "You are going forth in defence of your country and your flag, but you will not all return. Some of you will lay down your lives and will never return, but those that do return will be welcomed home again by a grateful people."

About 1:00 P.M. we were on our way to Canastota where we arrived at 5:00 P.M. Again we were entertained, this time by the citizens of Canastota. Tables were erected on the green and sumptuously loaded with the good things to eat that are the delight of a hungry boy. For we were all boys at that time, soon to take the position of men in all that went to make a soldier. About 8:00 P.M. we boarded the cars for New York City. Our arms were issued to us in New York, the Enfield rifle made in England and marked "Tower, London."

We were in the City of New York nearly the entire day and had ample time to see the city. We went by ferry-boat to South Amboy, N.J., and boarded the cars for the journey south. We were a jolly lot of boys, for our services up to this time had been like a picnic or pleasure trip. We arrived at Philadelphia in due time and marched through the city. Then once more we were on our way toward Baltimore where we arrived without mishap.

The citizens of Baltimore were not very demonstrative. No cordial greeting was given us, no wish was expressed for our safe return.

We arrived at Washington and had breakfast, consisting of bread and black coffee without milk or cream. We had issued to us our regular outfit, consisting of blanket, shirts, drawers, stockings, knapsack, and canteen. In the afternoon the march was begun to Arlington over the long bridge across the Potomac. It was a terribly hot day with dust flying, and a few of the regiment fell from the ranks completely exhausted. We went into camp on the historical Arlington plantation five miles from the city of Washington.[5]

SARAH BEACH CLARK DOES HER PART

Sarah Beach Clark was born in 1843 in New York state and was brought to live in Mansfield, Pennsylvania, at a young age. Her account gives a woman's perspective on the country's process of raising armies and fighting a war. Women tried to do what they could for the war effort, but that was limited. The "housewives" Clark and her cohorts made were in fact very useful to the soldiers. The nightcaps were not.

So early as May '61 the recruiting officer was abroad in the land and occasionally a Mansfield (Pa.) boy or perhaps two or three at a time enlisted and went to join companies that were forming in distant parts of the state; but it was not until September when an entire company was recruited in Mansfield that the girls became imbued with the war spirit. School had opened at the old Seminary with a goodly attendance, but very soon failures to respond at roll call were of frequent occurrence on the boys side of the chapel and in explanation we would hear the word "enlisted." These enlistments were usually surprises to the girls because they were not of those who talked most or threatened hardest to go to war. The quiet fellows who thought hard and said nothing were the ones first reported missing. And often there were family surprise. A mother of two sons was constantly worried lest the younger should enlist for if he did he was so daring and reckless that he would wade right into the rebels single handed and would doubtless be killed. The possibility of the elder sons enlisting never occurred to her. The daring fellow stayed at home but one day the quiet one after fastening a flag in the top of a tall hickory near the house said to his mother, I've enlisted to fight for that flag and when it floats free from Maine to Texas I'll come back if ever. Four years later when he returned from Andersonville the storm torn remnants of the flag still floated from the old hickory tree. As the enlisted became more frequent the girls caught the enthusiasm and gave encouragement,—Being unable to become heroes, they wished to be the sister and sweethearts of heroes, and in their ignorance considered the glories and not the dangers of war, for those who know nothing fear nothing. We found that the ladies down town were trying to assist in a small way in the equipment of the home company, so for several days they went to help when lessons were over and were set to making what they called housewives. These were strips of morocco lined with silk or flannel and finished with pockets for holding thimble, thread, and buttons and filled with needles and pins, and it was said that occasionally a girl slipped in a piece of paper with her name in it so that the soldier who got it would know who made it. Our late townswoman, Mrs. Hollands who was supposed to know most about the needs of soldiers as her eldest son enlisted in May, superintended the work, and when the housewives were finished she said, "Now girls every soldier must have a flannel night cap for they sleep on the ground and they'll freeze their ears if they don't"—Someone said it was so warm down south that there would be no danger of frozen ears. "If its warm," said Mrs. Hollands, "they'll need them just as much to keep the bugs out of their ears." So the night caps were made.

Each man was provided with a testament on the fly leaf of which was written, "Presented by the Ladies of Richmond" [i.e., Richmond Township, Pennsylvania]. I have one that came home tho its owner did not.

The last gift was a beautiful company flag which was presented at a banquet, given the company on the eve of their departure, at the Seminary. Members of Company B will recall that memorable occasion. Speeches were made in the chapel—I think Hon. S. B. Elliott made the presentation speech which was responded to by J. S. Hoard, then Captain of the Company which had been named the "Tioga Mountaineers" [The name lasted till they joined a regiment when it gave way to the military custom of numbering regiments and lettering Cos.]. At the close of his remarks Capt. Hoard came to the front of the platform and shouted "Tioga Mountaineers, three cheers for the flag," and the cheers were given with a roar that made the windows rattle. Captain Hoard promised that that flag should be returned with not a bar dimmed or a star effaced. The late captain of the company was asked what became of that flag. He said the last time he saw it was when in the hands of his captors at Plymouth [North Carolina] he was taken to his late quarters and saw a burley [Rebel] sitting before his rifled trunk reading and chuckling over his private correspondence and that rebel's foot was on the flag the ladies gave. The banquet was served in the dining hall with the girls for waiters and some of the boys there ate their last meal in Mansfield for years and some of them forever. At 12 o'clock conveyances came to carry them to Troy where they took next mornings' train for Camp Curtin.

After this notable exodus school life was rather monotonous though somewhat enlivened by correspondence. When a girl was seen with a letter the envelope of which was embellished with pictures of flags, boys in blue, tents and other military devices that looked like one of these, one knew she had a war correspondent and felt privileged to ask her for the latest news from Camp Curtin. These letters written in a cramped, boyish hand 35 years ago are priceless.

Occasionally a soldier came home on furlough, and soon the stay-at-homes charged the girls with undue admiration of army blue and brass buttons. But the girls saw changes that were not confined to dress. The wearing of the blue developed a latent manhood that even the wearer was before unconscious of. When we heard of the enlistment of one boy—a neighbor and schoolmate, we thought because he was modest, diffident and rather undersized that in him was not the stuff of which soldiers are made.

But when we heard his comrades tell, himself would never have told it, of his unwavering fidelity to duty, of his unflinching courage, of how at Plymouth he was sent out on picket in front of the enemy and lay all day between two rows of corn stubble under direct fire and without a drop of water, how the smoke from his rifle as seen from time to time through a spy glass, was the only signal that told that he was still alive, and how after dark he came in with his cartridge box empty and his face completely powder blackened, we confessed that we had not know him, Ezra Ripley.

Sometimes a soldier on furlough thought it no harm to stimulate his mother's pride by enlarging on his adventures. Going from a country school to her boarding place one day a schoolmarm stopped at a house where a son was enjoying his furlough to get tidings of Co. B. The soldier was not in but his mother was. She said that the furlough was very short because there was no getting on without "Jimmie" at the front. The Captain always asked his advise, the men looked up to him, and the colonel noticed him and once when they put him on guard cause he was so brave and trusty a lot of rebels tried to take him, but he just made 'em—now she had forgotten what it was that he had made them do, but it was something they awfully didn't want to do only Jimmie made 'em.

The schoolmarm guessed. Was it surrender? No. Lay down their arms, right about face and double quick? No. Every term military and civil that would seem to fit the occasion was tried in vain, and the schoolmarm left without knowing what Jimmie made the rebels do.

Returning next morning the schoolmarm had almost passed out of sight of the house when hearing a call she turned and saw Jimmie's mother beckoning. "I know what it was Jimmie made the rebels so. He made them skeedadgel." Skedaddle was a new word then though it has since appeared in the dictionary, and it was some time before the schoolmarm knew that Jimmie made the rebels flee. In the summer of '62 the consequences of war began to be felt and the Sanitary Commission called for lint and bandages.

Several large boxes were sent from Mansfield. The pupils of the Rory Creek school were asked to bring old linen with sissors for cutting and old case knives for scraping and both girls and boys cheerfully gave up their play hour and rolled bandages and scraped lint, making a package every few days to go with the box from Mansfield.

Too soon we learned the severe lessons of war. The anxieties and forebodings with their awful fulfillment. We can hardly trust ourselves to speak of them even now. No one who had friends at the front could escape from an ever haunting fear. Though the story is told of one mother who was a philosopher. One day the old lady sat comfortably smoking by the fire when her daughter ran into the room crying, "O Mother they say Tom is killed!" The mother smoked quietly on. "Mother, Don't you care?" Then she removed her pipe and said, "Kathy, maybe Tom's killed and maybe he ain't, but I ain't going to pucker up and cry till I know the particulars." The sequel justified the old lady's apathy, for though Tom was missing he returned safe and sound after the war was over.

In '65 when the flag that bears our stripes and stars over every land and sea, with its glorious stars and rainbow bars waved only over the free, the boys in blue came home. Then the old charge of partiality to the uniform was revived against the girls, and the girls plead guilty. Sir Walter Scot in *Marimon* showed how "the laggard in love and the dastard in war did not win the fair young Lochinvar," but when the conquering heroes came the girls surrendered. That is why the girls that were left behind in '61 are soldiers wives and as long as the Grand Army of the Republic exists they will be camp followers.

On January 3, 1866, Sarah Beach married Col. Melvin L. Clark.[6]

NOTES

1. John C. Reed Memoirs, Alabama Department of Archives and History, Montgomery.

2. Michael Cunningham Letters, State Historical Society of Wisconsin, Madison.

3. David G. Fleming, "Historical Sketch of Company G, 8th Georgia, CSA," *Hawkinsville Dispatch*, July 10, 1879. The full text of Fleming's reminiscences of the Civil War, as originally published in the *Hawkinsville Dispatch* in 1879, can be read at www.mindspring.com/~jtfleming. This excerpt is used by courtesy of the owner of that webpage, Joseph T. Fleming.

4. Wesley W. Bierly Diary, U.S. Army Military History Institute, Carlisle Barracks, Pennsylvania.

5. Jonathan W. W. Boynton Reminiscences, U.S. Army Military History Institute, Carlisle Barracks, Pennsylvania.

6. Melvin L. Clark Papers, U.S. Army Military History Institute, Carlisle Barracks, Pennsylvania.

Chapter 4

Early Exuberance Gives Way to Steady Determination

As the months passed and the men in uniform learned what it meant to live in squalid camps far away from loved ones—as the loved ones at home learned more of what it meant to wait and wonder whether their soldiers would come home—the country moved from its initial exuberance to a steady, fierce determination to fight on to victory. Each side remained highly optimistic about its ultimate triumph, but as time passed and battles were fought, they came to realize that they might have to wait much longer for that ultimate triumph than they had ever imagined before.

Closely related to their confidence in final victory was each side's confidence that its cause was right, that God was on their side. The hard blows of war had not yet compelled many to do much soul-searching on that subject.

As reflected in the writings of the five men and two women ex-cerpted in this chapter during the period from the late spring of 1861 to the early spring of 1863, both sides also wanted a vigorous pros-ecution of the war—the harder fought, the sooner ended. And they were beginning to wish the war would end—soon.

JAMES DAWSON AND ELODIE TODD HOPE FOR EARLY
CONFEDERATE VICTORY

James Dawson was a young lawyer and widower of Selma, Alabama. He was also captain of one of Selma's several volunteer companies, the Selma Cadets. Along with the Selma Guards, the Cadets became part of the Fourth Alabama Infantry Regiment and left for Virginia in the spring of 1861.

Elodie Todd was a Kentucky belle, recently moved to Selma, and the half-sister of Mary Todd Lincoln. Despite her relationship to the president, Elodie was a bitter Rebel. Shortly before the Cadets' departure, she and Dawson became engaged. Excerpts from their year-long correspondence appear below. Dawson wrote like a thoroughly lovesick swain, once stating, "The rehearsal of my love must have become tiresome, as it has been the burden of at least fifty letters." Elodie once asked him to burn her letters after reading them, but he assured her no one else would ever see them. Dawson, Todd, and the modern reader will rejoice that most expressions of devotion have been omitted from this edition of the letters.

Dawson and Todd repeatedly expressed their hatred of the foe, confidence that the South was in the right, and assurance that God was on their side. They mixed expressions of personal regard for relatives in the North with angry words and wishes for their speedy demise. They deplored imagined Northern war crimes, or willingness to commit them, such as the remark attributed to Col. Elmer Ellsworth but never made by him or any other Northerner, that the North's war-cry should be "Beauty and Booty." Ellsworth himself was a twenty-four-year-old colonel of Zouave troops, famous before the war as an amateur drillmaster and a good friend of the Lincolns. He was shot May 24, 1861, by an Alexandria, Virginia, hotel owner.

Throughout the period from April to July 1861, Dawson and Todd's constant refrain was their hope and expectation that somehow Southern independence would be secured quickly, without major fighting. After the great Southern victory at Bull Run (Manassas), July 21, 1861, Elodie gave up such hopes, replacing them with a fierce determination that the South would still win in the end.

James Dawson

Dalton, Ga. April 29, 1861. We reached this place, my dear Elodie, last night at two o'clock. Our passage from West Point, over the whole route, was a continuos ovation to the troops. At Atlanta we were received very hospitably by the citizens, and in the evening one of the prominent citizens addressed and welcomed our company. I replied, and in reply to an allusion made to our beautiful flag . . . stated that it was the creation of two ladies nearly related the hostess of the White House, and had been presented to us by the fair women of Selma. The announcement was hailed in the long and loud cheering.

Elodie Todd

[May 1861] The deplorable state of affairs in Kentucky has made me sad. Our dear old state is poorly provided with Arms and Ammunition, and all attempts to supply the deficiency thus far, has proved a failure for what they ordered has been seized by the state of Ohio; another trouble is the division in political sentiment. What is to be the fate of home I cannot divine and will not think Kentucky, whose name has been written with pride and honor on History's page, must now be dimmed and dishonored, untrue to herself and her noble sister States.

The Blues are making more music and commotion about going to the "War" than when you left. The Church bells ring two or three times a day to call the ladies together in order to form arrangements concerning the making up of 110 uniforms for this Chivalrous Corps, who are so determined to fight their Country's Battles, that rather than remain at home, they intend going on their own Expenses and responsibility. I hope you and your Company will soon do your fighting and make way for this noble band, who I doubt not will return their brows crowned with Laurels.

James Dawson

Camp near Lynchburg Va., May 8th 1861. I do not know when we will be one, nor do I know our destination. Can't you prevail upon your brother in Law, A. L[incoln]. to change his policy & make peace—It would add greatly to our happiness. I have thought that in case of the continuance of the war, during the year, that, I might with your consent, during the summer, obtain a furlough, and return to claim your hand.

Elodie Todd

Selma May 9th, 1861. Last Monday night my mother and youngest sister, Kittie very unexpectedly made their appearance and it is needless to tell how

Mary Todd Lincoln, half-sister of Elodie
Todd and wife of the U.S. president.
National Archives.

delighted I was. . . . I am sorry that you are not here for I am convinced
could she but see you, some of her opposition to my marrying would be
more easily banished, ever since I can remember I have been looked upon
and called the "old Maid" of the family, and Mother seemed to think I was
to be depended on to take care of her, when all the rest of her handsomer
daughters left her and I really believe, they all think I am committing a sin
to give a thought to any other than the arrangements they have made for
me, but as this is the age when Secession, Freedom and rights are asserted,
I am claiming mine and do not doubt but I shall succeed in obtaining them.
    . . . Last night Kittie and myself went over to the encampment of the
"Blues" and spent a very pleasant evening dancing until 11 o'clock. The wit
and beauty of Selma were assembled and it was quite an interesting scene
to see the groups of young people scattered here and there, engaged in
lively conversation, others Dancing, while Mr. Woods and some others drew

an admiring crowd to be entertained by their music. Capt. Kent has invited the Ladies to come and dance every night and arrangements are to be made to make things more comfortable and pleasant. I hear they will certainly be moved off by the end of ten days. . . . Tuesday evening we all went over to the encampment of the Livingston Rifles, Tuscaloosa Guards, and Greensboro Artillery to the Parade. I made some pleasant acquaintances and enjoyed the fine band of music they had with them. The Greensboro Company is composed of the handsomest men I ever saw and all seem to be selected gentleman, and so happy and merry. But it made me feel unpleasant to think how few of the many there would perhaps return, and of course yourself and noble little band came immediately before my eyes, and first in my thoughts.

James Dawson

Harpers Ferry, [Virginia] May 10, 1861. We are encamped just in the rear of our line of battle, and will be very near the post of danger, should the enemy show his face in front. I am really indifferent to the dangers of battle. . . . I have great confidence in the justice of our cause, and have an abiding faith that fewer of our men will be killed, than the circumstances would indicate. You will notice that in all of our battles so far, we have escaped almost miraculously, while the enemy have suffered greatly in comparison.

Even now, with their large armies in the field, and all the appearances to the contrary, I do not think we will have a long war. The idea of subjugating us must be preposterous, and I think, if I could be allowed to have the ear of my future brother-in-law, I could persuade him to abandon the idea, if he ever entertained it. Can't you use your influence or get your sister Miss Kittie to use hers. I am anxious to know your sister, and more anxious to become her brother. Does she look like you? I hope her influence with Mr. Lincoln will save me the trouble of being hanged, should I fall into his power. Is it not strange that I should be so anxious to see Mr. Lincoln defeated in his policy, and at the same time, be so devoted to his sister in law.

Elodie Todd

Selma May 15th, 1861. Before our Tea was over in came two beaux to take us to either Camp or to hear Judge Campbell (of Mobile) speak. I declined going to either, at first, but was finally persuaded to go over to the Camp, where we can all enjoy ourselves dancing, altho' I was only a looker on and did not participate all evening having heard that Fighting had commenced at Pensacola and Harpers Ferry and tho' I did not place much confidence in the rumor, I could not think of enjoying myself in such a gay manner when those I was so interested in were in danger.

James Dawson

Harper's Ferry May 16th 1861. How singular that I should be engaged to the sister of Mrs. Lincoln. I wish you would write her to that effect, so that in case of being taken prisoner, I will not be too severely dealt with. Do you not think it was a very politic step in me to engage such an advocate at the headquarters of the Enemy.

Harper's Ferry May 18, 1861. This morning, for the first time, I was able to pull on my boots, and taking an escort of one corporal I left my quarters, intending to see some of the beauties of this celebrated spot. The lower town is built on the narrow and low banks of the Shenandoah and Potomac rivers which unite here, coming together almost at right angles, and from different quarters of the compass. The buildings are principally machine shops, in this quarters, and brick cottages, for the employees of the government, presenting a beautiful and regular appearance. Rows of black locust trees shade the single and narrow street, and add to the picturesque groupings of houses. A long street on the Potomac leads to the upper town, the residence of the better classes, and from the elevation of this street, the eye wanders over a beautiful landscape of water, forest, and mountain. Just opposite, across the Potomac to the left, are the battling heights of Maryland, now occupied by the Kentuckians, rising almost perpendicularly above the railway track. Across, and immediately in front, and to the right are the Virginia heights rising far above the upper town, and commanding the approaches on all sides. They are now occupied by the Virginia troops. There mountains are almost impregnable, and will be made so by the sharpshooters and riflemen, who will man them.

In a handsome stuccoed home, at the top of the hill, upon which the upper town is built, Col. Jackson, the commandant, has his headquarters. A Confederate flag floats from the flag staff and indicates our nationality. From this point, you have a lovely view of the surrounding country, fields and farms, while, just at your feet, the waters of the two noble streams, which break thro the walls of the mountains, mingle together, in friendly sympathy, after their rapid journey from their western source. I have seen much beautiful and sublime scenery, but I think this is next to the falls of Niagara, not so sublime, but uniting more of the beautiful, and for this reason, more lovely to me. In the distant fields, one sees flocks of sheep, and herds of cattle, browsing upon the rich clover and luxuriant blue grass. In a lower place and overhanging the bank of the Shenandoah, is the Jefferson Rock, from which you can see for one or two miles, the Shenandoah rumbling over its rapids, and winding thro the range of mountains. You look in another direction and you see, within a short distance, the two rivers running together, the waters of the Potomac distinctly marked from those of the Shenandoah, by their yellow color. . . . I visited the engine house where John Brown and his men were taken. The shot holes are still to be seen, and, at the corner of one house is shown the bullet hole made by the ball that killed Mr. Bukam. He was shot by old Brown. Other places of interest, connected with this raid, are pointed out, and seem from the number of persons examining them, to possess much interest. The town is crowded with soldiers clothed in all the colors of the rainbow, from red to blue. Most of the respectable families, anticipating a fight, have left the town, and the figure of a lady is seldom seen on the streets.

Elodie Todd

Selma May 19th 1861. The steamboat Selma caught fire just as it landed, but owing to the promptness of the Fire Company was saved with little difficulty; it was quite a relief to know that it was the Boat and nothing serious, for other fears generally enter our minds first, owing to the plots discovered some months ago, tho' I apprehend no danger myself. We have another company, or two indeed organized since you left. "The Selma Grays" Mr. Wetmore Captain, also the Dallas Rangers. Mr. Wetmore has declined going with the Blues for the War but is perfectly willing to go for a year.

James Dawson

Bolivar Heights, May 20, 1861. Mr. Averitt had service yesterday evening, and read a beautiful sermon. It was a touching scene to see the soldiers seated on the ground, listening attentively to the beautiful religious service of the Episcopal Church. I confess that it brought tears to my eyes, and all my thoughts turned to you.

Elodie Todd

Selma May 22nd 1861. This morning the Blues left for Richmond, leaving Selma a sad and desolate home for many, tears flowed abundantly from the eyes of men women, and children and I do not think there was an undimmed eye in the entire Company, it was truly a sad and impressive scene. I was thinking of a similar scene which transpired almost a month ago, one that separated you and I, and how little those around me knew that my smiling face was deceiving them and hiding from their views an aching heart. . . . but I . . . struggled hard and mastered [my emotion] that you might remember me as a Woman ready and willing to sacrifice her all if necessary to the advancement of so glorious a cause, one to save our country from shame and dishonor, to arrest it from a Tyrant's grasp and live as we have ever done a free and independent people. We could none of us ever be happy as subjects under King Lincoln, or wish to live if such was the case.

Selma May 23rd 1861. Pray do not think to inform Bro. Abe would do you any good, he would make you suffer for yourself and my being such a secessionist too.

James Dawson

May 25, 1861. We received news last night of the invasion of Va. by Alexandria and of the death of Col. Ellsworth, of the New York Zouaves. My letter was written in the afternoon, and it seems to have been strange that my allusion to him should have been so soon confirmed. I hope Miss Kate was not interested in him, more than in an ordinary acquaintance. You know he exhorted his soldiers to invade the south and promised the "Beauty and booty." Providence seems to have cut him off, as soon as he touched our soil, and it will not surprise me, if the army, led on by Scott, does not meet the same fate. There is great bitterness felt on our side, and we will kill all that we can lay our hands on. . . . I now fear that we will have much hard fighting to do. We are in the right, and this nerves me for the contest.

Harpers Ferry, May 26, 1861. . . . We heard last night of the attack of the No. and So. Ca. troops upon the Lincoln army, at Fair Fax Court house, and great rejoicings were had in the camps, over our success, I rejoice that the 7 New York Reg. was the first to be cut to pieces, and I hope a similar fate awaits all the enemies of my country. You will be surprised that I am so revengeful, but the invasion of Va. has stirred my blood, and, I think it will be a pleasure to meet our enemies in mortal combat. . . .We will now have a bloody war, and we intend to make it as destructive as possible. . . . Let us have trust and confidence in God, who doeth all things wisely. In the misfortunes that have befallen me, I have found relief in trying to take this view of them.

Elodie Todd

Selma May 26th 1861. I was very busily engaged sewing on an oilcloth cloak for the Cadets yesterday when your letter was handed me, altho I was thinking of you at the moment, it had not occurred to me that the mail had arrived. Today upon my return from Church I received another, you do not know how relieved and comparatively happy I feel whenever I am the recipient of a letter from you rumors were afloat yesterday here, that fighting had commenced and altho I tried to banish such thoughts, I could not, and felt sad all day and your letter was not calculated to improve my feeling, as you wrote so much of your dying. do pray cease that strain. I think often enough of the worst, and that I shall never see you again, yet I cannot regard it as you do, calmly and am far from being prepared for it and I hope God will never call upon me to bear it, for I believe myself to be perfectly incapable of doing so.

Selma May 27th 1861. . . . Ella Watts came over just as I commenced the last time, and as she was very disconsolate I was occupied some time in cheering her, often saying, I did not think we would have any war which would cause her face to brighten and much to my silent amazement she would exclaim, do you really think so, in a tone that expressed that she had more confidence in what I was saying than I had myself. A few days ago I met several girls with their faces and eyes crimson with the tears they had been shedding and they all acknowledge how many hours they indulge in tears for the departed Blues. I know I must be considered heardhearted but I return the compliment thinking they are very silly to show their grief to public eyes and think those who say the least oftener feel the deepest. I regard my grief as too sacred to be seen by every eye and am selfish enough to enjoy it entirely alone when I have the inclination to indulge which I very seldom do, as I think matters will not be improved and I have a great dread of an unhappy person who is a tax on any one, and you know the habit might increase. I am afraid of being like Mrs. Hardie, not only miserable myself but causing those around me to be so too. but I do pity her poor creature.

Kittie is writing to Sister Mary [Mrs. Abe Lincoln] and I requested her to mention the fact of my being interested in you and should you fall into the hands of the [enemy] hope you will be kindly received, presented with a passport to leave King Abe's Kingdom and returned to me with care, but I am fearful since Ellsworth's death that the Southerners will fare badly if they get within their clutches and hope you will keep as far as possible from them.

Selma is so quiet that one passing thro' would imagine it was ready to be inhabited, the town finished the carpenters and builders departed. Kittie declares it to be the last place in the world and I think is perfectly willing to leave now for some other place more congenial to her tastes. The gaiety of Springfield and the extreme dullness of this place must indeed be striking but I imagine it is the same everywhere now. I could not mingle with gay society and feel grateful that all is so quiet around me, and I am not worried with Company for the Ladies are working or grieving I think, as very few visits have been paid in the last week.

James Dawson

May 30, 1861. I hope by the time Congress meets that better and wiser counsels will rule the cabinet of Mr. Lincoln. Do you write frequently to Mrs. L. If taken prisoner you must get me released on parole, and I will return to you.

. . . I am very prudent and careful and temperate. On your account, I have given up smoking, of which I was very fond, and seldom touch anything stronger than coffee. This is done for your sake. Our engagement has made me a better man, as it has given me something to live for, that I have not before. See what a mission you have to fulfill and how well you have begun?

Harper's Ferry May 30 1861. It is night, and the camp is quiet and still. An occasional peal of laughter, with the music of a violin, ascend upon the air, and awakens in many bosoms the sweet recollections of home and absent friends. The hour of nine is just reached, and your miniature is before me, recalling, if memory had not left their features too strongly impressed to be forgotten, the sweetness of that face, which has made the future an elysium of hope and happiness to me.

Elodie Todd

Selma June 2nd 1861. I . . . am happy to say most of the ladies are aiding in sewing and a day or two since, there was completed 183 oil cloth caps, more than a hundred of those caps, and a box of goods being cut out. so you will soon receive some boxes, and from the lint and bandages I believe they intend all Guards and Cadets to be wounded twice over. . . .

Col. Ellsworth was only an acquaintance of Kittie's, but one with whom she was thrown much last winter, and being agreeable I think they were excellent friends, nothing more, but had she then seen him in his true light, she could not surely have entertained even that feeling. Nothing but contempt and scorn would have been the emotion of woman for such a man.

James Dawson

Harpers Ferry, June 4, 1861. I wish one grand battle could be fought in sight of Washington, to decide the war. I still have an opinion, for which, however, I am hardly able to assign a reason, that our difficulties will be amicably settled. . . .

While you have much to distress so sensitive a nature as yours on account of the division in your family, you should reflect, my dear Elodie, and derive consolation from the fact, that you are pursuing the only right path, and have given your brothers and your sympathies to the cause of your country. In after years, when these troubles shall have become historical, the bearing and conduct of your family will be a source of great satisfaction. . . .

I have just conversed with a Va. officer since closing this letter. He says Gen. Beauregard and Pres. Davis are at Manassas junction, 35 miles from Alexandria, and that a large army will be concentrated there to march upon Washington. I hope this is true, as it will do much towards peace. As soon as we show that we are able, we will conquer a peace without much bloodshed.

Harpers Ferry, June 8, 1861. I am writing you, probably for the last time, perhaps on the eve of battle tomorrow [none occurred]. . . . I feel calm and prepared for anything, being confident that I am in the keeping of an all wise Creator, and an all wise God, who doeth all things well. I am willing to fall for the cause of Liberty and Independence.

Elodie Todd

Selma, June 12th 1861. Today was appointed by our President for Fasting and prayer. My intention was to attend church, but as the morning was warm concluded to go this Evening and just as I was ready to start company came in and prevented my doing so. Mother promised to do my share tonight while I remained at home to write to you. Willie today heard me say I was going to church this Evening to pray for the soldiers and came and put his arms around me and begged to go with me. I promised provided he would add his prayers and tell me what he intended to say, he replied immediately, Aunt Dee I'll pray to God to give Mr. Averitt Bread every day and Captain Dawson Butter.

James Dawson

Harpers Ferry, June 12 1861. You should have seen me in my tent, today, with one of my lieutenants, mending the only pair of pantaloons that your captain now has. Excuse me for mentioning this circumstance, as it illustrates how little baggage we have. When one of our officers wishes to pay a visit of ceremony, he borrows a blue coat from some brother officer.

Elodie Todd

Selma, June 16th 1861. I am so far from being a Spartan, that if you were here and I could influence you to remain at home, I would not hesitate to do so. I am getting selfish, and do not see why some should be called upon to make so many more sacrifices than others. There are even some

here who have all left to them that they possessed before these troubles
began and whose mind or happiness is not disturbed by the absence of a
very dear friend, and they think every man should go. Alla Parkman remarked the same thing to me. I told her I notice those whose relations
remained behind generally spoke in that way but when the time came that
would cause her to part with Brother and those she loved then she could
not say the same. I had passed thro' the ordeal and knew and would be
willing to push the kin of others off to keep my own at home too. I really
felt angry at her for speaking in that way and knew she was not sincere in
doing so, for when Johnny spoke of going and you know he was not in
earnest, Alla nearly wept herself away when war was mentioned in her presence.

James Dawson

Winchester, Va. June 19 1861. I hope circumstances will yet allow us,
before the expiration of a year, to be married, as it is very trying to both of
us to be separated so long. I hope that Mr. Lincoln's congress will have
more wisdom than he has shown, and will agree to let us alone. Our preparations are so rapidly developing that we will then be able to cope with
them on equal terms, and they will certainly see the impossibility of subjugating us.

Winchester, Va. June 21, 1861. The Marylanders were sent to Harpers
Ferry yesterday to burn up the town. It seems that since our departure the
Union men have murdered several secessionists. Hence the reason of this
movement. The men sent are, of all others, in the army, the best qualified
for such an errand, and, I presume, have performed it reccurdem artem.
How terrible is war! If I live to return home, I will never draw my hand
again, except under the most pressing necessity.

. . . We hear all sorts of rumors here of Peace and war, and I have a sort
of presentiment that we are to have a short war. . . . I do not think now
that we will have to do any fighting until after the meeting of the Congress
of the U. States in July, when I hope reason will bring Mr. Lincoln to his
proper senses.

I went to Church on Sunday night, and was very much gratified. I felt
devout and I prayed for you, my own dearest Elodie. I hope that you will
be permitted to kneel with me at the altar, and that together our prayers
will ascend to the throne of Grace. Oh, my dearest, this is one of the wishes
nearest my heart, that you should be a Christian by profession. You are now
one, in all things, save the act of public profession, and I am glad to see
from your letters that you are inclined to be one.

Elodie Todd

Summerfield, June 27th 1861. Last week the Ladies gave their Concert in Selma and everything save Dr. LeCompte's lecture passed pleasantly. He was hissed and all manner of ridicule made of him which of course made us feel badly. The cause enabled us to go thro with our parts well and the applause which greeted my singing the Marseillaise, more than repaid me for all the trouble I had in practising, and I believe Mr. Harman, who selected me to sing it, was more pleased at my success than I. The amount made was $175, and all were so pleased, that they speak of having another.

Selma July 3rd 1861. Mr. Hobbs called a few moments since to request me to assist in singing tomorrow. Mr. Alex White is to make a speech and they wish some music, the Exercises in commemoration of the 4th. I most respectfully declined to assist. There is also to be a Ball or rather Hop tomorrow night, but I have no idea of attending and think it decidedly out of taste and place at such a time to be indulging in such amusement and cannot myself when those so dear to me are far away and surrounded by danger. I will think of them, and pray that God may spare them in his mercy and grant a speedy and safe return of them once again to us. How dreadfully I would feel to attend such a scene and afterwards learn that upon that night, anything had happened to you or my brothers. I believe I would never forgive myself for it, and I think there are so many who feel as I do that the affair will be a glorious failure.

[Selma] Thursday [July] 4th [1861] what would we be without our liberty, the few left of us, a poor unhappy set who would prefer Death a thousand times to recognizing once a Black Republican ruler. . . . Altho' he is my brother-in-law, but as such there is not one of us that cherish an unkind thought or feeling toward him and for this reason we feel so acutely, every remark derogatory to him, except as a President. I never go in Public that my feelings are not wounded nor are we exempt in Matt's own house for people constantly wish he may be hung and all such evils may attend his footsteps. We would be devoid of all feeling and sympathy did we not feel for them and had we no love for Mary.

Selma July 7th 1861. Friday and Saturday telegrams were received giving us information of the Battle at Martinsburg, but none of the particulars made known, and consequently my anxiety has been and is still great, and for two days I have been unfitted for anything and cannot be the same until I am relieved either by a letter or telegram telling me of your safety for we were all in Selma of the belief that the Cadets and Guards were in the affray, and well I know fought well and bravely. You I know did your part as it should have been done by a brave Southern Soldier and will upon every occasion that presents itself. I have never doubted, but earnestly hoped you would not have an opportunity to display your courage and have hoped against hope for peace. I cannot tell you nor can you imagine, what I have suffered since hearing the War has actually begun and I feel now like giving up and away to my sorrow, I who up to this time have been complimenting myself upon bearing up so bravely.

The Ladies have not yet begun the fall work, and I hope the Concerts will prove so successful that there will be no difficulty in [raising] the money to procure the materials that will be necessary. A Concert is in anticipation for Friday night. I have promised Mr. Herman to assist him, but think five days too short a period of time to practice for it in. this to me is an agreeable manner of making money, and I enjoy singing for the soldier. I must say, much more than saving for them.

James Dawson

In Camp, Winchester Va., July 8, 1861. I had just mailed the [previous] letter, when news came of the advance of a large army under Gen. Patterson, across the Potomac, into Virginia, and of an engagement between it and about 4000 of our men under Gen. [Thomas J. "Stonewall"] Jackson. An order was immediately issued to march, and in an hour our Brigade was on its way to the seat of conflict. We started at 4 o'clock and marched to Bunker's Hill by 8, a distance of 12 miles. We bivouacked in an open field, having our blankets and the velvet earth for our beds. At one o'clock we were roused by the bugle, and were again put upon the march. How can I describe the beauty of the scene. On our right the moon shed its soft rays upon the column of armed men, while upon our left a magnificent comet, with its long nebulous trail, beckoned us onward, and threw around us the mantle of superstition. The soldiers all saw in the unannounced phenomenon, the "in signo vinces"[1] of the Southern cross, and enlivened their march by singing Dixie. At sunrise, we halted for breakfast, and after a scanty and hurried meal, marched on to the battlefield, near Darksville, and were drawn up in line of battle, awaiting the approach of the enemy. This was repeated Wednesday, Thursday, Friday and Saturday. And on yesterday, our army returned to their quarters here. During all of this time, we have been without tents, and with very scant rations. At night, I slept upon one of the capes sent us by our good ladies, with my shawl wrapped around me, with clothes and boots on. Indeed for one week, I did not pull off my clothes, as we expected an attack at any time, and had to sleep upon our arms. I laid my head upon a rock, and thinking of you, my dearest, I generally fell asleep and rested quietly.

Winchester Va., July 11, 1861. How grateful I am to know that you have such proper feelings in regard to amusements, at times when your friends are in danger. On the day of the 4th we were all day in line of battle, and on that night slept on our arms. It would mortify me to think that at such a time, you could enjoy the festivities of a ball room, or even sing with such a contemptible person as Mr. Hobbs. He has no standing with those who know him.

I am really glad that you have such feelings about Mr. Lincoln. I have never been able to entertain for him any unkindness, save as an enemy to my country. I have never believed the slanders upon him as a man, and accord to him the respect that is due a gentleman. It would indeed be strange if you felt otherwise, and did not love your sister.

Elodie Todd

Selma Ala, July 14th 1861. We are all anxiety to know what the Confederate congress will do more so than when the Federal met. I hope it will be impossible for the North to raise the means to prosecute this unnatural War or rather that God will in some yet unforeseen manner avert it. I cannot think it will be a general thing yet it is predicted that Battles be fought in Kentucky in another month. I am still hoping almost against hope for peace.

I saw from the Montgomery Mail last Evening . . . the death of my cousin Col. B. Graty Brown of Mo. formerly of Frankfort Ky. but as he was on the other side, I cannot say I grieve, but sympathize with his wife and the rest of his friends and as he is dead I am glad he fell so early in the fight. his turning Republican caused his Father great distress.

James Dawson

Winchester, Va., July 14, 1861. I feel at a loss how to write you. The rehearsal of my love must have become tiresome, as it has been the burden of at least fifty letters, and I am afraid that you either think me terribly in love, or else an uninteresting correspondent.

You know that even now, I think the war will soon end. Providence will bring it to a close. This is my belief, contrary to all the indications. . . .

Manassas, July 21, 1861. We have had a terrible battle today My Dear Elodie, but have achieved a glorious victory. Our Brigade was in the hottest of the engagement, and the 4th Ala. Reg. has been cut to pieces. I have had from twenty to thirty killed and wounded, in the Cadets, but thanks to a merciful Creator and your prayers, I escaped unscathed. A cannon ball struck a fence which I was crossing, and knocked me down, but the only harm done me was a dislocation of my ankle, which I do not think will give me much pain. We have taken all the artillery of the enemy, their baggage and stores. Their loss is estimated at 4,000 to 5,000. But over this victory we have to mourn the loss of many of our best and bravest men.

Elodie Todd

Selma, July 23rd, 1861. I wrote you a day or two since but I cannot refrain from writing to tell, or try to do, my joy and happiness that you have escaped unhurt. Early this morning I sent down Town a servant with orders not to return until he brought me news from the Battle, which we received intelligence of late yesterday Evening he has just returned bringing me the Telegram from yourself and Captain Goldby relieving by it the anxiety of many hours. I was surprised and distressed when I heard of a Battle being fought and you were engaged in it and could do nothing but grieve and anticipate the worst and trembled so violently that for several moments I was incapable of reading the dispatch until with a desperate effort I overcame it somewhat and opened it my mind prepared to receive the worst, but imagine the joy if you can which possessed me when I read of your safety, and the slight loss sustained by the Cadets and Guards, would that you could now return and escape further exposure from such dangers, and that this glorious victory, dearer to me because your noble heart and brave courageous Arm helped to gain it would satisfy our Enemies and woo gentle peace to diffuse her gentle smiles again over our beloved Country. Will they longer continue this terrible War more so to them than us, even when they and we must believe God is on our side fighting for us, against their wicked schemes and devices? Surely they have suffered enough and should be willing to cease hostilities.

. . . I see from today's paper Mrs. Lincoln is indignant at my Bro. David's being in the Confederate Service and declares "that by no word or act of hers should he escape punishment for this treason against her husband's government should he fall into their hands." I do not believe she ever said it and if she did and meant it, she is no longer a sister of mine, nor deserves to be called a woman of nobleness and truth and God grant my noble and brave hearted brother will never fall into their hands and have to suffer death twice over, and he could do nothing which could make me prouder of him, than he is doing now, fighting for his country. What would she do to me, do you suppose? I have so much to answer for.

Have you seen the speech of Vallandigham of Ohio and do you not like the courage candor and intellect of the man? I read some portions with interest and would have liked to have shaken him by the hand because he dared to speak his feelings openly and avowed his principles, and even let them know that Mr. Lincoln had acted unconstitutionally.

James Dawson

Near Manassas Va. July 25, 1861. During the first when the bullets fell like hail I thought of you, as far away, at church, on your knees, praying for my safety, and I was nerved and strengthened to do my duty. It seems a miracle that I was not killed, as several of my men were shot down at my side. I attribute all to the providence of God, and I trust that I will endeavor to appreciate the mercy.

I went over the field yesterday. The scene was awful. The dead Yankees were still lying unburied in many places. I saw as many as one hundred in the space of an acre, they belong to Ellsworth's Zouaves, who were reduced from 1100 to 200 men. God seems specially to have marked them for vengeance. They wore blue pants and red shirts, and are fierce looking fellows. They fought well.

We are encamped on the battle field, surrounded by all the evidences of the sanguinary contest, broken gun carriages, dead men, dead horses, and the graves of the dead. Every house in the neighborhood is a hospital for the wounded of the army, our own have been sent to Culpepper and Charlottsville. The dead Yankees will all be buried today. Judge Walker arrived this morning to take the remains of Lieut. Simpson, his brother-in-law, home.

Elodie Todd

Selma, July 28th 1861. Mother wrote me that she never witnessed such excitement and joy in her life, as at Nashville when the news was received. Cannons were fired, companies paraded and indeed every sign of joy that could be manifested. here there was no rejoicing exhibited for sadness for the young and Gallant dead filled our hearts, and we could not forget them to exalt in a Victory that closed their lives in nobleness and honor, and before they could see their loved country free from Northern Tyranny. God bless and be merciful to them, and all who fall in our glorious cause of liberty, and rest their souls in peace.

You write me to be more cheerful and look on the brighter side. I look straight forward as far as I can and all around and above and yet all looks gloomy and dark. I have never for a moment doubted that anything but success would attend us, but I have thought of the many who would and must die to purchase it. Tis true there is not a man among you who would not willingly prefer death to slavery, and you would yourself sacrifice your life gladly to gain it. Yet we who are left will find in freedom poor and sad enjoyment when those that are dear to us must die for it, and no matter how hard we try cannot reconcile ourselves to giving you up cheerfully for the cause. I do not now think of peace for a moment, fighting alone can accomplish our end and that hard and bloody. We are prepared for reverses, for we yet remember some lost Battles in a similar struggle and notwithstanding them, success crowned our efforts. And when we lose now we will push forward again with redoubled courage and determination and must and will conquer.[2]

James Dawson resigned from the Confederate army in the spring of 1862 and married Elodie Todd.

GEORGE PHIFER ERWIN SEES CONFEDERATE SUCCESS AS CERTAIN

George Phifer Erwin of North Carolina exhibits in these letters attitudes typical of Southern soldiers during the first year of the war. Concerns with making camp life more endurable—and thus requests for the home folks to send food, clothes, and a slave—as well as confidence in Southern fighting prowess and a victorious and early conclusion to the war.

Yorktown Va. June 27, 1861
Dear Father
For fear you did not get my last letter I make another list of things which I want—Three colored calico shirts. Send Ed to cook for me. Geo West & I will tent together. Give Ed enough of clothes before he leaves, as it is extremely difficult to get them here, & do not send him unless some one is with him for it will be almost impossible for him to come by himself. . . .
My present life seems to agree with me thus far. I have been in very good health, and the general health of the camp is very good.
Do not, my dear parents, ever forget to pray for me.
Your devoted son
G. P. Erwin
Anything in the way of eatables will be acceptable. Geo Wests sends much love and says tell Uncle Hamp he has written to him twice.

Yorktown Va.
July 1st 1861
Dear Sister,
Yorktown is one of the meanest places in the world. It contained, before the war, about three hundred inhabitants, but not one now, except soldiers, and there is not a house in the place that is under seventy five years old. Besides the sand is over shoe-mouth deep all through the streets. You can judge of the pleasantness of the walking. A good many of the houses have holes in them, shot by Washington's artillery in the days of the Revolution,

which holes exist now as they did when made. It is, in sober truth, the oldest, ugliest, most good-for-nothing town that I ever had the misfortune to be stationed in—only one store in the place and the highest ambition of that one is to sell ten cents worth of tobacco per day. nothing in it except ginger-cake, beer & tobacco.

No fight is looked for here at all. All eyes are anxiously turned towards Manassas and Washington. Beauregard is the centre of attraction and I sincerely hope he may give the Yankees a sound thrashing. That may give us peace. I understand that Beauregard has telegraphed to Richmond for all the Doctors & Surgeons who can possibly be spared. That looks rather ominous.

All my letters have gone by mail and I am not certain that you have received any of them. I want Ed to cook for me so you can have him sent immediately, if you haven't already sent him by Brown or McDowell. Tell Pa if he thinks he can come by himself to start him by himself right off. I will send that message until I know that you get it at home. I haven't heard a word from home since I left, except a few words on the back of a letter sent to me by Pa.

All here are comparatively well. I am so myself. Do write soon and often. Love to Pa Ma Sallie & Cousin Maggie Aunt Kate Cousin Julia and every body else

Your devoted brother
G. P. Erwin

Yorktown Va
July 7th 1861
Dear Mother,
You never saw so much sickness in your life as here. There are four hundred sick in our camp alone and about a like proportion everywhere else. but a large part of these are trifling cases.

There are some eight thousand troops here now (you need not mention it though) and the deaths average about three a day, a very small proportion considering the number of sick and time of the year. Both our surgeons are away Drs. Hardy & Baker, and Dr. Hines, the chief surgeon of the Regiment, is surgeon of the Post and performs duty at the general hospital, so you see we are rather in the want of Doctors. Temporary surgeons have been appointed and Dr. Hines, a fine Dr. by the way, manages to see all the really sick ones in our camp. . . .

To give you an instance of exaggeration, Genl. Magruder ordered a fire engine & some rope ladders from Richmond in order to form a sort of fire company here in case of a fire. For if this dried up old place were to catch fire it would all burn up and would inconvenience us a great deal because all the houses in the place are used for Hospitals or for Commissary stores.

The ladders have come but the engine not and I saw in today's Richmond Paper that Gov. Letcher had started for the Peninsular with a ladder company and a large number of ladders and it added somewhat significantly, that there was no telling where those things might be destined for. I have no doubt but that they expect that Fortress Monroe will be attacked and all, merely because two or three ropes were sent to Yorktown.

I wish you would subscribe for the Richmond Examiner even for a short time. It is a much better paper than either the [Richmond] Dispatch or [Richmond] Express or, at least, so it is considered here and much more reliable and ready to do justice to other than Virginians.

I do not like the Dispatch very much simply because it puffs Virginia to the skies to the exclusion of others sometimes, I know, more worthy, while the Examiner seems desirous of meting out a due reward to everybody. It is much more ably conducted and the editorials are written with more force. It is, in fact, a better paper.

I hope you will feel no uneasiness on account of my sickness at present. I may get sick but I will let you know immediately. Write soon & often. May God protect you all & me so that we may meet once more

Your devoted son,

G. P. E.

Yorktown Va
July 16th 1861
My dear Father,

Genl [Daniel Harvey] Hill is very hard on what he calls "scriblers itching for newspaper notoriety" and you may hereafter find it difficult to get news from here by means of the Richmond papers.

There has been a skirmish below here on Saturday . . . between a portion of our cavalry, numbering 120, and a detachment of Yankees variously estimated from 50 to 150. It was a sharp brush though nobody hurt on our side with the exception of a poor horse which was slightly wounded. . . . They captured some arms haversacks, canteens, &c. and eleven live Yankees, which Yankees were brought here and then sent to Richmond.

I had the pleasure of visiting them with Genl Hill and had a right pleasant time. There was one 1st Lieutenant, one 2d Lt and nine privates, and only the 2d Lieutenant could speak English, all were Germans.

Several others have been taken within the past week, in fact they are captured every day or two. A drummer, taken several days ago, was asked why he was fighting against the South. He answered "for sixty dollars a month." I suppose all are fighting for the same thing money, and that is the reason they get on so badly.

The Yankees seem to have a perfect dread of cavalry. In this skirmish a few days ago, the Yankees showed fight against some of our cavalry who had dismounted and were proceeding on foot, but the moment they found out that the cavalry was coming, they turned and fled. It was a perfect rabbit chase. The horsemen would select their men and run them down and capture them.

Yorktown Va
July 28, 1861
Dear Mother,
I hope your fears on account of our reverses in western Virginia have been fully cast away but the news of Beauregards victory—There are now 1200 prisoners in Richmond. . . . They are all together in some large tobacco warehouse in Richmond and strange to relate, some New York merchants who have made independent fortunes from the tobacco trade of Richmond are now prisoners of war in the very houses of which but a short time ago, they were the customers, and out of which they made so much money. War causes many strange incidents in many a man's history.

That was a glorious victory and will open wide the eyes of the northern populace, because the results are too extensive and too palpably evident to be escaped or avoided. The prisoners at Richmond say they've had enough of war and if they were at home Lincoln & his party might go somewhere else for fighting material. It will have an immensely cooling effect on the northern mind.[3]

WILLIAM HARDY FACES HIS FIRST BATTLE

William Hardy, of the Second South Carolina, wrote to his mother on the eve of the first great battle of the war, which in the North would be known as Bull Run but in the South as Manassas.

Bulls Run, Sunday
July 21st 9½ o'clock
My dearest Mother,
Upon this beautiful sabbath morning I am writing to you upon the eve of a battle. . . .
A few minutes ago Mr. Maynardie offered a most appropriate prayer in the midst of a good many of the officers. It was a very solemn scene and I assure you we all felt it. I looked in my text-book [in fact a daily devotional book] a while ago for the 21st of July and found the following Prayer & Promise—Prayer: "O let the wickedness of the wicked come to an end, but establish the just." Promise: "As for such as turn aside unto their crooked ways, the Lord shall lead them forth with the workers of iniquity, but peace

shall be upon Israel." They are from Psalm 7–9 and Psalm 125–5. Rest assured my dear Mother that whatever comes will be by the direction of God, at least I feel it to be so. . . .

Every one seems to think that this Battle will decide the war on the part of the enemy. If they are defeated they will be very likely to give up the War. Give much love to each & every member of the family and to all my friends. Remember this: Don't put the least confidence in the Newspaper accounts, especially the Telegraphic news. I will get Mr. Maynardie to telegraph if I am hurt. don't be alarmed if you don't get a letter soon again for I can't possibly say when I may have an opportunity to write.

Very affectionately dear Mother

I remain your devotedly attached son

Willie H. Hardy[4]

CAPTAIN R. H. BROWNE ADVISES HIS WIFE ON SELLING SLAVES

The core and most striking aspect of the difference in culture between North and South was the South's embrace of slavery. Occasionally a letter gives a startling view of just how stark that difference could be, as does this one from Capt. R. H. Browne of the New Orleans Response Battalion to his wife, Sarah, back in New Orleans. The growing pressures of war required some financial adjustments, and Browne advised his wife about how to handle them.

Camp near Corinth Miss.
April 2, 1862 Sunday
My Dear Darling Wifie,

I was very much delighted to hear from you yesterday. It was the first news from you and I felt that a great void was partially filled. I was very much pained to learn that you were not feeling strong. I am afraid you permit your mind to be constantly occupied with melancholy thoughts, if this be true, Wifie, try to throw them off; as such things are the greatest canker-worm of existence.

Let me talk about business, now, first thing, and then speak to you in my own way. As to Rebecca, suppose you go down to Cor[ner] Esplanade & Chartre Street and see Mr. Joseph Bruin, negro trader; tell him who you are; that I am the lawyer of Thos. E. Matthews (his old friend) (Bruin knows me well); and ask him what to do with her? Dress her up & carry her with you. Ask him (aside from her) what he can sell her for, and if he thinks he

"Auction & Negro Sales" reads the sign on the building of this Atlanta, Georgia, slave dealer's establishment. Slave dealing was a socially tainted but widely practiced and highly profitable trade in the South. Library of Congress.

could, would he not as a personal favor to me, sell her for you, as you are alone, and I am in the army. I would not send you (rather ask you to do this) if Peterson was keeping any negroes at all. Bruin is the only one who has had a large stock of negroes on hand this winter in New Orleans. If he could sell her for 15 or 1600 I would not mind giving him 75 or $100. Besides, if she was there, she would have to keep sober and straight all the time, and the kinks would soon be taken out of her.

As to John, while I am deeply sorrowed at selling him, yet if you think you have got him a good master in Mr. Beebe perhaps it would be best to sell. See, however, if Mr. Beebe would not be willing for you to repurchase at a reasonable price in a year or two, if you desire to do so.

I am at an utter loss as to the furniture. I hoped to get $800.00 for it—six seems a great sacrifice; but what does James think? and Mr. Geo. Hews next door to Flint & Jones—get him to look at it (he is an old and good friend of mine and really, Sarah, I place more confidence in his advice than I would in that of J. C. C.), and tell you what he thinks about it. I am strongly inclined to think that it would be best to sell out and leave N. O.—mayhap forever. I am glad to say that I trust a very great deal to your good judgment and shrewdness in the management of all these matters.[5]

HAMLIN CHAPMAN JOINS THE WAR

Recruiting did not cease with the end of 1861. Hamlin Chapman was too young to enlist when the first shots of the war were fired at Fort Sumter and had to wait until the third year of the war to begin his military service. Other than that, the story of his enlistment is in many ways typical of those who volunteered before him—the patriotic enlistment rallies, the excitement and eagerness to go, the beginnings of homesickness at leaving family and friends for the first time, and, at the assembly camps and during transportation to the front, the first hints of the hardships that lay ahead.

[I] was born in Youngstown Ohio Dec 13th 1845. In 1851 [I] removed with my parents to Milwaukee Wis, making the trip from Toledo, Ohio by lake steamer. [I] attended the Milwaukee Public schools until 14 years of age. . . . In 1858 [I] was an eye witness to the rescue of one Glover, a fugitive slave who was detained in the county jail on Jackson street. His owner had arrived in the city and was to take the slave south with him the next day. A mob headed by Sherman M. Booth broke down the jail gates, battered the doors and rescued Glover, and assisted him on his way to Canada.

[I] removed with my parents to Fox Lake Wis in April 1862. . . .

At the breaking out of the war my parents had promised to give consent to my enlistment after I was 18 years of age, little thinking at that time that the war would last until I had arrived at that age. The first opportunity presented was under President Lincoln's call for troops to serve for 100 days and under the call Wisconsin raised three Regiments, the 39th, 40th, and 41st.

On Wednesday May 18, 1864 I enlisted at Fox Lake with Capt. Allan Whittier a veteran who had served three years in the 11th Wisconsin Infantry. At the time of my enlistment my weight was 123 lbs. At this time "War meetings" were very much in vogue, where everyone goes fired with patriotism and a fierce determination to induce his neighbor to enlist.

My comrades from Fox Lake beside Capt Whittier were Solon and Herbert Nourse Wm. Van Buren, William Morgan and Peter Craigon all nearly of my own age and good companions.

The time intervening between the day of enlistment, May 18, and May 30, the date of going into camp at Madison was occupied with drilling, boat-riding, calling to take leave of friends &c.

Camp Randall, Madison, was one of the Rendezvous for Wisconsin troops and the recruits were housed in barracks while regiments were being organized. I had been anxious to enlist ever since the breaking out of the war but the change from a happy home where a kind father and a loving mother were ever solicitous for my happiness and welfare to the rough life with all its discomforts of a recruiting camp had for a time rather a depressing effect, for I fully realized that however hard the present conditions were, they would be very much harder when we reached the point of actual service in the south. This feeling, however, gradually wore away as I became accustomed to my surroundings and I even grew to like the military atmosphere.

On our trip from Fox Lake to Madison I had my first experience in riding in box cars. We had passenger coaches until Milton Junction was reached when a change to freight cars was made. On our journey our squad from Fox Lake was joined at Beaver Dam, Horicon, and other places by a sufficient number of men to make a company of Seventy men. Arriving at Madison at 6:15 o'clock P.M. May 30, 1864, we marched in regular order to camp Randall and were assigned to quarters in barracks which were very uninviting, being in an unclean condition. We made a supper of boiled meat, butterless bread, black coffee. Our first night in barracks was one never to be forgotten. No one was allowed to sleep although all occupied bunks. Songs were sung, jokes cracked, stories told, practical jokes played, and everything done to keep the drowsy ones awake and make a lively time generally.

Our stay at Camp Randall was destined to be short as the next day after our arrival there, orders came for our Company to leave for Camp Washburn [in] Milwaukee. Before leaving Madison an election of officers was held which resulted in the choice of Henry Travers, Captain, J. C. Sargent, First Lieutenant, A. J. Smith, Second Lieutenant. After arriving at Camp Washburn the noncommissioned officers were appointed. I was honored with the appointment of 5th corporal and during the summer was promoted one rank upon the death of the second corporal.

At Camp Washburn, Milwaukee, I met many of my Milwaukee acquaintances and school Friends and found they were members of Company A of the 39th, the regiment to which our company was assigned as Company K. On Friday June 3d 1864 we were mustered into the United States service. . . .

Much of the time was spent in company and battalion drill until June

13th when we left for the South. The Regiment had been supplied with the usual army clothing of blue cloth and Enfield rifles, haversacks, knapsacks, cartridge belts and other accoutrements were issued. While in camp in Milwaukee my two sisters had kept myself and some of my companions well supplied with eatables so that up to the time of leaving I had not depended on army rations. The regiment left Milwaukee at 10 A.M. June 13, 1864 the boys taking leave of many friends who had gathered at the station to bid them farewell. Our trip to Chicago was made in second class pasenger cars. Arriving in Chicago at P.M. we marched to the Soldiers House where a most acceptable supper was served by the ladies of Chicago.

Leaving for Cairo at 10 P.M. June 13, we arrived there at 2 A.M. June 15 after a tedious ride of 360 miles in grain and cattle cars, without seats, and so crowded that only a part of the men could lie down at one time. The ride was a very uncomfortable one and gave us a fortaste of what the life of a soldier was to be.[6]

ELISE BRAGG ADVISES HER HUSBAND TO WAGE WAR IN EARNEST

Elise Bragg, of Louisiana, was the wife of Confederate general Braxton Bragg. In this letter from the second year of the war she urged upon him the necessity of a vigorous prosecution of the war.

Bivouac June 8th 1862
Dearest Husband,

Mr. Tappan gave a disheartening account of affairs at Corinth [Mississippi]. He says our indefatigable enemy have brought their siege guns eighteen miles over roads we have been calling impassable, & will pretty soon shell us out of Corinth & oblige us to practice our strategic policy of falling back. Indeed it is now rumored that we have done so. A very bitter satirical article came out in the [New Orleans] Delta now edited by an agent of Butler called "The game of evacuation nearly played out." It states their intention is, "to drive us back to Montgomery, & there sink the misbegotten thing called Confederacy into the ground." They are doing so very fast. We hear all public property is removed from Richmond & we await to hear it is evacuated. Great Heavens, cannot southern bravery make a stand somewhere! Are we to lose everything & be called cowards too! We have trusted to everything but our own arms, & now flatter ourselves we will tire out Yankees! We who never had perseverance & they are famous for it. I do not like to write about it, for I see no gleam of hope.

Towson says you telegraphed Willie to return for me. As he has not come I suppose he saw you first & told you our determination to stand by our homes, & not be homeless houseless wanderers, if we can avoid it. When our position becomes unendurable we can take our carriages & go by land to Tangipahoa. The enemy have entire possession of the river, for I suppose the gun boats are at Vicksburgh. Our forces never hold out over two weeks. Some of us are fitted for a life of utter poverty, & by staying at our homes may save something. At least we are not incurring expense, or asking charity of friends. Mrs. Polk & family are in the City. They have got tired running. Mrs. Beauregard is there also. They are not disturbed.

It has been two months since we had any rain, but two light showers to lay the dust & you may conceive what our crops are. The corn was planted early on our old lands & is now tasseling, will probably make little or nothing. The cane nobody talks about. I have not been able to have rice planted or potatoe slips, waiting for a rain. The weather has been most delicious. never have I known such a season. so cool, with a constant northern wind, as to make summer dresses uncomfortable & no musquitoes. Heaven is certainly blessing our enemies. The City was never so healthy, no prospect of yellow fever, & little sickness among the troops. It is so healthy here, we do not need a physician & have not had one for months. . . .

If the enemy were wise, they would quit the country & leave our army alone. Starvation & disorganization will tell silently & bloodlessly. Of all the fatal mistakes we have committed during this war, none will prove so disastrous as a Fabian policy. what was done in the heathenish days of Rome will not answer in the nineteenth century, with R[ail]. Roads, rivers, steam navigation & all in the hands of our enemies. With the Miss. River, the Ohio, railroads in their possession, they can & will command any amount of provisions, pause at nothing, until we are subjugated. They have what avail more than mere brute courage: energy, perseverance, all the appliances of modern war. Memphis & Vixburgh must fall. Why not leave them to their fate since it must be & take our army round into Tennessee & then into Kentucky. You leave an enemy in your rear, true, but is not that better than an enemy in your midst, starvation? You are sick, Gen. Beauregard timid & desponding. I must & will see you & Gen. B. must get along without you for a time.[7]

Gen. Bragg took her suggestion and did take his army roundabout into Tennessee and Kentucky.

AURELIUS LYMAN VOORHIS SOLDIERS THROUGH
CHANGING TIMES

A Civil War soldier's life was hard, often boring, and sometimes very dangerous, whether due to sickness, accident, or enemy action. Reading stories of great battles, it is sometimes easy to forget that the soldiers were real people, young men with fond memories of home and hopeful plans for the peaceful future. Aurelius Lyman Voorhis was one such, an Indiana farm boy from near Logansport, born in 1841, and enlisted twenty years later in the Forty-sixth Indiana. This excerpt from his diary of service along the Mississippi River during 1862 and 1863 shows the thoughts and concerns of a common citizen-soldier in the midst of a war that was growing ever harder and more merciless.

Friday, March 21st [1862]. Cloudy and cold no rain. Have just returned from a long walk and feel rather tired. Still must write a little just to keep my hand in. Have been thinking of home and friends and my childhood (am not much more than a child now [he is 20]) when we young folks used to have our Debating Society and a good deal of fun generally. Also have been trying to lay plans for the future but it is not much use as everything is so uncertain in this world. Think my mind is settled on the mercantile business. If I am so fortunate as to get home safe, I shall go to school about a year to fit myself for the business. It will then be time enough to look for a situation. For I find that a good education and straightforward principles are about all a man needs to get along and get in good places. Here I am scratching away and don't know whether it is correct or not because I never studied grammar. Think if I had my time at school to live over again, I would try to improve it better than I did when I was small. All I thought of then was fun. Well I must eat a turnip now.

Saturday, March 22d. [1862]. Cold and disagreeable, regular March winds. Nothing of importance today the same thing over and over again, sour bread, slop coffee and soap grease for breakfast and then warm it over again for dinner.

Thursday, March 27th. [1862] The war still goes on. We received the news of another battle at Winchester, Va. Our troops victorious again. Our brave Indiana men made themselves conspicuous. Hoosiers will fight when they get a chance. I am getting tired of this barrack life and want to go where I can fight some too. I started for war and want to be at it.

Sunday, March 30th. [1862] It has been very warm all day. Wrote a letter home and read some in my paper. Got through with my work in the kitchen in time to hear part of a sermon. It was very good. The Sabbath has passed very pleasantly to me. This is a poor place to serve the Lord—May he take us safely through is my prayer.

Wednesday, April 2d. [1862]. Received a letter from New Waverly from a young friend with the news that another one of my comrades, A. Black, was dead. We were brought up together in a manner and it makes me feel very badly. I should like to know where and when he died but the letter does not say anything about that. It is so very solemn to think that young men start from home well and hearty and a few short months, they are laid in the grave, gone to render their account to God. Well, we must all go some time and we should try to be ready. There is nothing too bad for some to do, others try to do nearly right but there are a great many temptations in our way.

Sunday, August 31st [1862]. Last day of August and of course the last day of summer. This morning a man belonging to the 43d Ind. Regt. was drummed out of camp with the word Thief on his back. Being on guard I did not go out with the Regt. I believe I would rather die than be disgraced as that man is. . . .

Monday, September 8th [1862]. Chauncy R. Rogers, a member of our Co. died very suddenly. He was a very lively young man and I believe a general favorite with us all. His disease was congestive chills. His death has made quite a change in the men but it will not last long for we have got used to such scenes. I hope God will impress it on my mind forcibly. About sundown we started with the remains of C. R. Rogers to his last resting place. The men sent out to dig the grave had selected a very nice place on the Bluff back of the town. The usual salute was fired over the grave, a short, impressive exhortation was delivered by Capt. A. M. Flory. The grave was then filled up and we turned away with sad hearts and left Chauncy to sleep alone. Out of the twelve men that have died belonging to this Co. he is the only one the company has buried, the rest being left behind and died among strangers, except those that were taken home.

Sunday, Oct. 12th [1862]. Of course I was called for guard today. Special guard it was and I believe it was for we had to cross the river which we did about ten o'clock A.M. . . . We went down and landed on the Mississippi shore. Went out to a plantation, divided off into squads and examined the farm. We found plenty of corn, beans and some hogs. Our party got some long necked squashes (in the Hoosier tongue kushaw) as we got around first. Before leaving we also got some sweet potatoes, every man had something to take back with him. We are now on our way back to our post in the woods. The sun is down and we will have to eat dinner and supper together in the dark.

Tuesday, Oct. 14th. [1862]. On guard again today. That's nothing new, think I was lucky to get to headquarters and had nothing to do until night, so a squad of us went back about one and one half miles to a plantation, got a lot of honey and killed a hog and then returned at night. We were divided into shifts, had two hours to stand. My trick come on at eight and off at ten o'clock P.M. I like to stand on a post at night, it is such a good time to meditate. I often get in deep thought on what has passed and building air castles for the future and often remain that way several moments at a time, but some rustling in the leaves or dew drops falling from one cape to another arouses me and I find myself standing, watching all around me for what? A deer, no, a squirrel, no, a man, yes, in watching for men to keep them from getting the advantage of us. How strange about a year ago I enlisted as a soldier knowing about as much about soldiering then as a blacksmith knows about tailoring, and here I am way down in Dixie looking out for the enemy and almost wishing at times for a chance to shoot some of the men that are doing so much against our Government.

Friday, Oct. 17th [1862]. Started early on a foraging expedition. We went about ten or twelve miles. Filled the wagons with corn and then pitched in to the sweet potato patch. A. Adair and I got very near a bushel. On the road back, the train was stopped and three or four head of cattle fell a prey to our humble selves, hogs did not escape.

Monday, Oct. 20th [1862]. Washed some clothes today. Went nearly all over town to get a one dollar bill changed. There is considerable business done here now of most all kinds, everything is very dear. For instance, a pack of envelopes that can be bought in Logansport, Ind. for ten cents cannot be bought for less than 20 cents, more commonly 25 cents.

Sunday, Oct. 21st [1862]. I am well contented here but still would be glad to have the war come to a close so that I might once more see those dear friends that are so anxious for our welfare and that long to see us but we will have to wait the Lord's good time.

Tuesday, Oct. 28th [1862]. On picket guard today. Had a pleasant ramble in the woods, could not help thinking of the goodness and greatness of God in managing all things. I reflected sometime upon my own conditions, noted from what it was even one year ago. I had then all my life almost been among Christian friends who were constantly looking out for my welfare but now I have been a soldier for about one year and in that time I have been tempted and tried in many ways and I regret to say found wanting in many things, such for instance as the use of foolish and obscene language, the playing of foolish games, such as dominoes, checkers, chess and I regret to say sometimes handling the vile cards. But about a week ago, on the night of the 22nd of this month, while on duty I could hear someone singing an old familiar tune and it at once set me to thinking what I was, nothing but a poor weak man of the dust not fit to live and yet God was sparing my life. I then made promise to let all those foolish things go, to be merry and pleasant and always contented, to avoid quarelling with my companions. By the help of God I have done tolerably well so far, and I think by watching close and trusting in the Lord (not in myself) I can do better. I do not write this for show but to impress it more forcibly on my mind. It is on my mind considerably anyway and that gives me reason to think God is helping me.

Friday, Dec. 12 [1862]. One year ago today we started from Logansport fully of the opinion that we were old soldiers but now we find that we knew nothing about soldiering at that time. How changed we are now. Nearly one-half of the men that formed our company then have died or been discharged or sick at hospitals now. Our Captain at that time is now Major, Second Sergeant is now Captain, our first Lieutenant was dismissed but is back again. Fifth Corporal is now 2nd Lieut. and so the things go. Rain today. We were called out to review at half past ten but notwithstanding the rain but the general thought it wouldn't do to get wet so about the time the water was running through our clothes, he sent orders to go to quarters which we did with a good deal of will. Our quarters are good protection against the rain.

Tuesday, Jan 6th [1863]. I was not well this forenoon nor last night but exercise and a hot meal brought me about right again. A cold, raw wind blew all day, it was clear but felt considerably like winter. We had a game of ball notwithstanding. No duty but dress parade, about half a dozen orders were read, one to the effect that we are to have morning company drill of two hours and battalion drill of two hours in the afternoon. That will take up some of our ball playing time but it suits me.

Thursday, Jan 22d [1863]. Our boat run nearly all last night [in the Mississippi River] but towards morning a dense fog settled on the water and it became dangerous to run so we landed on the Mississippi shore and remained until after daylight, when the fog cleared away a little and we started again. . . . About ten o'clock we landed on the Arkansas side to take on wood. There was a small mound here of fresh earth, seven or eight feet square. On inquiry I learned that four union and two rebel soldiers that were wounded at the taking of the Arkansas Post, died on their way up the river and were buried here. Friend and foe in the same grave away from their dearest friends. . . .

Tuesday, Jan 27th [1863]. Cleared off early this morning and our colored gentleman put out a huge washing. Every person appeared cheerful and contented as far as our present conditions would admit. There is considerable grumbling done now about this negro-freeing war but it is only an excuse to have something to grumble at I think; as for me I will stick to it as long as the Lord suffers me to live.

Thursday, Jan. 29th [1863]. Tolerably warm today. The nights are very cold though and it froze hard last night. Jay Richardson and I made two excursions to the woods for poles to raise our tent so that we could dispense with the center pole. The first trip we got them too short so we tried again and succeeded. It gives us considerable more room, at least it appears so. A detail was made again to work on the levee. For a night or two we have had spelling school, using a dictionary that Lieut. Stevens got when we were up White River last spring. I think we will keep it up if we can. it is good exercise for the mind as well as pastime and is much better than playing games or light talking.

Tuesday, Feb. 3d [1863]. We were relieved from guard about nine o'clock A.M. The night was clear and cold. I only slept about an hour or so. I read the balance of the time except the two hours that I was on duty. It is now 3 P.M. I have been taking a ramble among the hills although I cannot go very far without interfering with picket arrangements. I have seated myself on the southern slope of a hill so as to have the advantage of what little heat there is in the rays of the sun. These hills are romantic to me and I like to ramble over them when the sun shines. The gullies run in every direction and every shape and the hills are of all sizes and shapes and in some places it appears only a step or two from the top of one to the top of another. Just back of me over the brow of the hill has been in the time of peace, a small farm but now nothing remains but some old cornstalk shrubs to mark the spot where some man had earned his living, but I must return to camp. . . .

Sunday, Feb. 8th [1863]. Sabbath Day how poorly spent, O why should we not repent. This has been a very mild pleasant day. Some indications this morning of rain but the day has passed off so far without it. I hope it will be fair weather for a while. It seems that the Sabbath is not respected very well here in the army for some are chopping wood, others hauling, while some are out shooting at little birds, while I have wandered away from camp and am here on a side hill dispatching down some of my foolish thoughts on paper but I expect it is as good a thing as I can do. Oh how I long for this war to close so that I can be at liberty to go when I please and stay where I please so that I can improve my mind with something more than war arrangements.

Wednesday, March 4, 1863. President Lincoln has now been in office two years and what a tremendous responsibility has rested upon him and is likely to rest upon him during the remainder of his term. Without doubt he is the right man in the right place and every loyal man should support him with their hands and voice.

Thursday, March 5th [1863]. I got two letters, both from home, they have been having a revival there, my brother A[binus] H[enry] Voorhis, aged 16 years, reports that they have had a glorious meeting. "About fifty have united with the church, sister Puss [Percina Ruena Voorhis] and myself among them, etc." That is good news, all the young folks and some of the aged has started in the good cause. I hope they will prove faithful Christians.

Tuesday, March 10th [1863]. About four o'clock a sad incident happened by which one man was drowned. Capt. Ryan (Gen. Ross' aide) was in a yawl with two men belonging to Co. I and one man connected with the Q.M.D. [Quartermaster's Department]. They were carrying orders I think when they ran along side the Ida May [a steamboat] and somehow the yawl was upset. The Capt. and the commissary man got out but the other two went clear under the Ida May, one of them swam out and held on to a bush until he was taken in by a boat, but Burnsworth sunk to rise no more. In the midst of life we are in death and we should all try to be ready for the great change for we don't know at what time it may come.[8]

NOTES

1. "In this sign conquer," words supposedly seen, along with a cross, in a vision of the Roman general Constantine, before the great victory at Milvian Bridge, 312 A.D., which made him emperor.

2. N. H. R. Dawson Papers, Southern Historical Collection, University of North Carolina, Chapel Hill.

3. George Phifer Erwin Papers, Southern Historical Collection, University of North Carolina, Chapel Hill.

4. George Phifer Erwin Papers, Southern Historical Collection, University of North Carolina, Chapel Hill.

5. R. H. Browne Papers, Southern Historical Collection, University of North Carolina, Chapel Hill.

6. Hamlin L. Chapman Reminiscences, State Historical Society of Wisconsin, Madison.

7. Eliza [Elise] Brooks Bragg Letter, Chicago Historical Society.

8. Aurelius Lyman Voorhis Diary, Indiana Historical Society, Indianapolis.

Chapter 5

The Warring Sections Persevere through Weary Months of Struggle

LAURA BEECHER COMER KEEPS HOUSE ON THE PLANTATION

In case one is ever tempted to idealize this era of history, there are people like Laura Beecher Comer. A cousin of abolitionist author Harriet Beecher Stowe, Laura Beecher first married in her native Massachusetts, but after the death of her husband she moved to Georgia and became a school teacher. Several years later she married Mr. Comer, a wealthy planter with several plantations in Georgia and Alabama and his chief residence near Columbus, Georgia. In contrast to her abolitionist relations back in the North, Laura wholeheartedly embraced the system of slavery—she only wished the slaves would work harder and be more reliable.

The life of a plantation wife involved a good deal of hard work, as Comer's diary reveals. She tended sick slaves and supervised slaves in preserving meat and other food items, preparing meals, and other tasks. She also mended and sewed and purchased such necessary items as fabric or finished clothing for the slaves or herself, and, because of the war, she undertook such additional patriotic/humanitarian tasks as knitting socks for the soldiers or sewing mattresses for the military hospitals. Yet at the same time she had leisure for an amazingly busy

Harriet Beecher Stowe, author of *Uncle Tom's
Cabin* and cousin of Laura Beecher Comer.
National Archives.

social life, visiting and receiving visits often at a rate of several per
day.

She also had time to do a great deal of complaining in her diary.
She complained about her neighbors, her husband, her slaves, and
the rest of the world in general. She could not see why her husband
was not more outgoing and was at an utter loss to explain why her
slaves seemed to lack motivation for careful and diligent work. The
underlying problem with all these people was that they so often
thought of their own happiness instead of hers, and she simply could
not understand such selfishness. This lends her diary for the year 1862
a large amount of unwitting irony and even dark humor.

Finally, Mrs. Comer's frequent and lavish expressions of religious
devotion are reminders that in that age, as well as our own, more

people professed religion than gave any outward evidence of its life-changing power. Ironically, the Comers' slaves seem, on at least one occasion noted by Mrs. Comer, to have displayed more of the sort of change in behavior of which the Bible speaks.

Diary—1862

Jan. 1st. Forty-four years, the 6th of last March, of my life have passed away; and it becomes to me an important inquiry how have these years been spent? Beyond the meridian of my days the star of my existence will soon decline and set beneath the horizon and time (with me) will be no more. The probationary season will be past & where will my spirit be? If I have the spirit of my savior, my life will then "be hid with Christ in God." but have I that spirit? O God—my God—my heavenly Father warm up my heart with love to Thee & enlighten my sin-clouded understanding, quicken my faith, strengthen my hope & help me by thy grace, O my Father, to press forward toward the prize of the high calling of God in Christ Jesus! Terrible as has been the struggle to my poor broken stricken heart to give up all and everything that was once so dear, dear to me and so closely bound by the cords of my heart—by faith I can now penetrate the gloom and I see: Thou hast done all these things in mercy; that at last I shall have everlasting life—be saved with an eternal salvation! Bless the Lord, O my soul, praise Him and magnify Him forever!

Jan 2d. The morning I spent shopping and completing some business arrangements. Drove around by Mr. Rutherford's; found Mrs. Lizzie Howard there & spent an hour with the afflicted family. I spent the evening at home, looking over papers and writing—one letter to Mr. Comer who is at his Plantations in Ala. and one to Mrs. C. C. Mitchel of Miledgevills Ga. . . . The day has passed off pleasantly with the exception of a terrible duty (to me) I had to perform this morning—to punish a servant—how can they be so perverse?

Jan 3d. This morning the weather was delightful! Willis drove the Rockaway around to the door about 9 o'clock & I first went down to the Palace Mills to ascertain the price of grains, make arrangements for the purchase of bran and Rye.

Jan 4th. It is astonishing how many little bills present themselves where one thinks he owes nothing! I do wish people would not keep small bills against us when we are anxious to pay our just debts! Just as we were driving out the gate in the morning, Mrs. Cary and her two children came. I asked them to go in & sit awhile, and I should return soon, but having to drive around by Mrs. Adams' to give Mrs. Everett some woollen yarn for Lt. Everett's socks, I was detained longer than I expected & when I came home, found Mrs. C. had gone. This morning early I sent Willis down with the package of socks bound for Manassas & hope they will arrive safely and keep many poor fellows feet warm. The great benefit of this war is it allows every one the luxury & privilege of doing good, of living daily in the exercise of active benevolence, unwrapping the narrow and stinted robe of selfishness and looking beyond and away from self for the welfare & good of others. . . .

After dinner, I took my knitting and went down to Dr. Ware's & spent an hour with Mrs. Willis. Mrs. Ware was not in. Came home, worked awhile upon the sewing machine, which was brought, the day before, from Mr. Cowdry's to whom I had loaned it, in my absence, but I could not make it work well and gave it up untill Monday. Spent the evening knitting; knit a sock after 3 o'clock P.M. before I slept. Now I feel like enjoying a fine night's sleep & awakening to enjoy the holy delights of another blessed Sabbath morning.

Jan 5th. Willis, my carriage driver is not attending to his duty at all & [I] prefer remaining this cloudy day at home alone in my private room & there serving God to being annoyed with him. O God with my Heavenly Father, enlighten the dark minds of these servants & give them obedient hearts, I beseech Thee—for in them how great is the darkness?

5 o'clock. . . . I have been able by having no cooking done at all & remaining quietly in my room to be at peace but if Mr. Comer lives a few years I am sure I don't know what any one can do with his servants about the house; in the field, where a man is with them, whom they fear all the time they will get along, but I cannot, nor will not, spend all these precious days of my life, following after and watching negroes. It is a terrible life! Who can appreciate or understand anything about such a life but a woman who marries a bachelor who has lived with his negroes as equals, at bed & board! What a life many poor wives have to live in uncomplaining silence. If they say one word, censure without measure is heaped upon them.

O Lord my God, I pray thee strengthen me or I fall—how much more can I endure? Give me patience with weakness & ignorance & enable me to meekly endure unkindness, insolence, disobedience & all these things which so sorely try & perplex me. How many envy me now, that if they really knew my true situation would pity me from the bottom of their heart!

Jan. 7th. Tuesday. Spent the middle of the day with Mrs. McClain. I greatly sympathize with her. How intolerable and almost unendurable is the brutal & selfish husband? Who can depict the miseries they can entail upon the wife?

Jan. 8th. This morning I spent attending to some business in the city. Called at the Perry House & passed a social hour with Mrs. Grimes & Mrs. Bacon in their room. Met Mrs. Perry cordially as old friends ever meet at the door. She is a constant friend and an agreeable woman.

[January] 9th. This has been the busy day of the year; making brine & putting up meat. Who should not be gratefull they have it to do? Fortunately at 5 o'clock P.M. the front door bell rang & not before Rena the servant announced Mr. Jerry Slade & Miss Janet Slade. I was really not presentable but could not forego the pleasure of meeting two such friends in my sitting room.

[January] 10th. Mr. Comer came in from the Plantation this morning after sending Willis & the carriage to the depo for him I sent the Carriage to Mr. J. Woolfolk's for cousin Victoria and family who are to spend a week with me. Before our cousins came I was busily employed finishing lard &c of yesterday. O that I had servants who would do a servants work! At 12 o'clock the carriage came & at 2 cousin James Winter dined with us.

At night I was much fatigued but the pleasure of meeting friends always counteracts fatigue with me & we spent the evening socially in the drawing room & retired to our respective rooms about 10 o'clock.

Jan. 11th. 11 o'clock, Saturday, I went into the Kitchen arranged for dinner & then with our little cousins Banks & Laura went out in the woods to direct Herbert and America about fense repairing. The children were joyous & delighted much in their freedom as children always do. After dinner Mrs. Cairnes & Mrs. Dillingham called and the residue of the evening I spent with Cousin Victoria very agreeably. Does not every heart know some pungent sorrow?

Jan. 12th. The duties of this past week having been very arduous & trying I feel perfectly worn out. What would I give for one good servant? I mean one who would take care or even do what they are told to do. My hands feel like clumps & my face and neck are completely burned over. I feel as if I had all the while a tremendous load upon me, a weight which I cannot lay aside.

Jan 13th. 10 o'clock. The evening has been spent in social chat around the brightly burning fire in our pleasant drawing room grate. How cheerful is light & wood fire? This morning I was very busily engaged until about 11 oclock when I took an hour for rest & was much refreshed. After everything was prepared for dinner, ready to cook I committed all to Letties care. She is invaluable to me! I could not keep house without her.

Jan. 15th. 10 o'clock P.M. Have spent all the day indoors socially with cousin and her children very agreeably. Since morning before breakfast I was sorely tried with Fanny my cook, a very dull, obstinate servant. I make our coffee every morning & then find great difficulty in getting her to get our simple breakfast. How terrible is laziness?

After dinner I took a refreshing nap, while Cousin Victoria was kindly showing her servant in cleaning and ironing a silk dress for me.

Jan. 17th. The servants are doing unusually well. Lettie is worth her weight in gold! May God enlighten & direct her in the right way is my constant prayer. . . . I went down town & shopped awhile & then returned home to dinner. After dinner; I went again to the city & purchased ticking for mattresses drove around by Mrs. Adams and sought out Mr. & Mrs. Everett who spent the evening with I hope agreeably.

Jan. 19th. Georgia seceded from the Union one year ago this day! May the struggle for Southern Independence soon be over.

[January] 21st. Spent all day laying off walk & working with two servants in the front yard. Am wearied out although the servants worked well.

[January] 22nd. Fanny as usual cooked miserably, the poorest Turkey dressing I have ever seen in my life, I think. O, if I had a good cook it would be a pleasure to keep house, but to have all the details of house keeping & cooking to attend to & a great deal of the work to do makes an onerous and tedious daily task. I spent the evening conversing with Mr. Comer and knitting for the soldiers.

[January] 23rd. Willis drove his horse out this morning in bad plight, poorly fed & badly groomed: I have just written to our overseer at the Plantation.

7½ o'clock P.M. . . . I have just written to Mr. Clemons & sent several prs of woollen socks to the 2nd Reg. Ga. Volunteers. How delightful is social intercourse? How can any one be a recluse? I am sure I do not at all comprehend the feelings of a selfish person!

[January] 24. Have spent this day closing the "financials" of the past year. Having been annoyed with old bills which had been already paid I determined this morning to go to every house where I had traded and take the names of those we do not owe! I have quite a formidable list! . . . In the morning Willis drove around and Mr. Comer & I took seats in the Rockaway. I went to Hughes & Hodges to arrange for selling two bales of cotton for Hospital mattresses & to purchase other things for hospitals.

Attended to some business, came home to dinner & on my way called and spent an hour at Dr. Ware's.

After dinner I found nearly all our meat was spoiling in the smoke house; took all the servants and went to work forthwith doing all we could to save it. A tedious job we had which consumed all the evening & untill after night. I came to my room completely wearied out, although not exhausted. After supper I repaired to an easy chair in my room made a soldiers sock, conversed, read news until felt very much rested and refreshed.

Jan. 30. Mr. Comer upon finding our meat here was injuring, left yesterday for the Plantations in Ala. When he returns I think we shall go to Savannah, Augusta & Richmond. Still we may be disappointed in our trip.

Jan. 31st. I love my home; it is to me the dearest spot on earth! In twilight I was out in the back field last evening, I was where the servants were burning brush and Lithe being at the house ironing gave the alarm that a man was trying to get in the house! We all ran, but before we arrived the scamp had gone leaving a visible track! I was wakeful all night anticipating some harm might be done before morning, horses stolen, or something. This morning however we arose & found all right & what grateful emotions filled my heart! I will praise the Lord for his goodness and mercy to both his children of creation and of His adoption.

Feb. 2nd. This morning I attended church & the communion was celebrated, a solemn and interesting feast! This morning I only gave my cook brown batter cakes to cook & then could not get good ones, while I boiled eggs & made tea for myself. O, may God soften the hearts & enlighten the understanding of these dark; heathen negroes around me. I have faithfully taught them for 12 years and it seems to me, with the exception of two or three, they are the same they were then—determined, obstinate and dark as midnight!

Feb. 9th. Sabbath morning. Every wakeful moment of my life the past week has been occupied. Every morning I have sent breakfast to soldiers who are attending a sick brother and friend at the Depo. Monday I was engaged laying off wash, directing servants &c &c.

Thursday Mrs. Guines & Mrs. Bacon spent the day with me. Sent the carriage to Depo for Cousin Katy Comer and her two sons, Wallace & Legree who are on there way to school up to Cave Springs. In the evening we all rode up to Col. Jones & found Col. & Mrs. Jones as kind and polite as ever. The ladies seemed to enjoy themselves very much. In the evening I excused myself from cousin & kept an engagement previously made to Mrs. S. M. Jones. Came home at 10 o'clock; found all had retired.

Saturday we were out all day, myself, carriage and horses were in service of Cousin Katy. Just before night we went up to the Columbus Factory to see about some Cords &c &c. . . .

How annoying it is to have the whole details of house keeping to attend to. I love home! but I do crave reliable faithful servants.

12½ o'clock, Sabbath day. Cousin Katy and myself attended at Paul's Methodist church & heard the Rev. Mr. Wright preach from Psalms 103: 13 & 14. "Like as a father pitieth his children so the Lord pitieth them that fear him. For he knoweth our frame: he remembereth that we are dust."

Feb. 12th Wednesday. Tuesday (or yesterday) I worked all day very hard filling mattresses for Hospitals! Have twenty done, ready to be taken tomorrow.

This morning. I sent my carriage and horses for 9 young ladies to come and assist me in arranging & finishing mattresses. . . . The ladies came about 10 o'clock & appeared to enjoy themselves well all day. After dinner we all went up to Col. Jones's and enjoyed the trip well.

14th. Feb. I have been very busy all day, looking after my domestic affairs. Now Herbert has gone to the Plantation the remaining negroes are so in-

Black laborers on a wharf, James River, Virginia. National Archives.

different stupid and dull it is almost impossible to have anything done at all. They are terrible except Lithe and Rena, two little girls I am raising. I am very tired, almost wearied out with trying to live & keep up a house.

Last evening I went to a poor neighbor's over the way with my knitting & set an hour. This evening I sent over a basket full of meat to them. Nothing gives me so much pleasure as to contribute to the happiness of others!

Feb. 16th. My life is an endurance! What a selfish monster—how little the world knows of that man who makes long prayers at home, eats and sleeps & goes to church & cries the, shall I say? hypocrite's tears. My heart is continually pained. Talk of prisoners of war! Am I not chained and bound to endure in uncomplaining silence unto the end of life. O my God, 12 long years have I endured this burden & can I much longer bear it.

Feb. 22nd. This morning I had intended to be very quiet all day in my room but to my sorrow I found it necessary to discipline the servants who had become so snarled up it took me nearly all the morning to untangle their knotty skein. O what a terrible duty it is to govern servants. Would that I had a husband to do it for me. How grateful and happy I should be!

The war news has been sad from Tenn. but cheering from Missouri. . . . The President has issued a proclamation for a "Fast" next Friday. . . .

Feb. 23d 3 o'clock P.M. The day is clear and delightful. Nature is beginning to put on the robes of spring & come out in her beauty & loveliness! And how much I could enjoy life if I had an agreeable＿＿＿but as it is how I am weighed down. I started to church this morning & before we arrived there he was so cross I was glad to return & seek my room in peace. I have not been out all day. A person who is dissatisfied with himself cannot be satisfied with another but are always ill-natured, snarly, crusty and short. How delightful is sociability. I pine for it in my own house. Day after day the recluse keeps in his cell only crawling out to walk & eat. When shall I enjoy social life again? I am daily imprisoned here. . . . I am so anxious to be useful. Can I spend my life isolated and alone. Will God lead me into paths of usefulness, peace & happiness here but above all I pray that I may be prepared for happiness hereafter, in Eternity.

March 1st. Yesterday was Fast day. At 10½ o'clock Mr. Comer & I went to the Baptist church & at 3½ to the St. Paul's Methodist church. The houses were filled to overflowing.

March 3. Early this morning I arose feeling much better than I have for several days & have cut and fit me a dress beside directing the servants in their business which is no small item of employment! I have cut and made my dresses whenever it was possible for me, ever since the war begun. I never labored harder in my life than I did last year and still I feel as if had accomplished but little of what should have been done. I have dressed very plain & cheap, feeling that I must be as frugal and equinomical as possible in order to be able to contribute to the comfort and relief of the soldiers in our Army & others who may be less fortunate than myself, in some things! I like to sew awhile, but if I was compelled to make my living sewing, it would be a poor living!

March 9th. Friday "Fast-day" proclaimed by [Georgia] Gov. [Joseph] Brown. . . . The Confederacy is in a sad condition on account of its unfortunate promotion of political leaders. Such wicked men as [Georgia politicians Howell] Cobb & [Robert] Tombs!!! How can a people be so deluded? Why leave one government to get out from under corrupt leaders & governors & then elect such men or worse for another? How can these things be? I thank the Lord for the privilege of a quiet home where I can retire from the world & all its tumult & stir. Am I not now rapidly approaching the first half-century of my probationary existence? And O my God, make me honest with myself & Thee! Give me I beseech thee more & more of thy grace purify my heart from sin, enlighten my understanding & give a right mind in all things necessary to do thy will upon earth, and at last fill my soul with faith, charity, & love & make me meet for an inheritance in glory—in eternal life for Christ's sake. Amen.

9th Sabbath Evening 11½ o'clock. The day has been clear and delightful. The servants behaved very badly this morning. At 9 o'clock A.M. Fannie had not cooked any breakfast at all either for me or for the servants! I do wish they would behave themselves on the sabbath. As I have no dinner cooked on this sacred day and very little breakfast it does appear to me they stand very much in their own lifts to be so indolent & trifling! At 10½ o'clock went to the Baptist church but I did not go out this evening at all. Since dark I have been reading writing & looking over letters & papers. I always have a mountain of work to climb before me while many persons are at leisure & nothing to do.

[March] 14th. Since the servants have so little to do, they do nothing at all, unless urged & pushed along, which to me is a very irksome task indeed & I never shall find it agreeable or an easy duty to perform.

March 21st. The servants have done remarkably well. The place has seemed more like a quiet peaceful home than any day I have passed in Mr. Comer's family although I have been in it since the 15th day of Aug. 1848. No tongue can express what my sufferings have been in that time!!! . . . This morning I mailed a letter and papers to Mr. Comer in Ala.

Yesterday I was very busy at home all day and have been today employed in making me a fine lace collar. Mrs. _____ offered to make them for me but when she sent one home to me by her little daughter and servant—it was enough! I would not wear anything so much out of taste. Offering & doing things—well—are two very different things. I ripped it in pieces & spent the residue of the evening and part of this morning completing a nice collar out of fine & beautiful material which alone, for two collars, cost me $48. Our home is the most delightful place in the world to me. I have always craved a house and now I am sure no one could feel more grateful for it or value its privileges and blessings more! . . . Every morning after breakfast, the servants come into my room for instruction prayer & singing. I have waited long enough for him who should lead a family—& be the proper head—but I cannot longer exist and govern a family without family as well as private prayer. May God endue me with strength and patience to endure!

Saturday morning the 12th [Apr]. . . . Stirring news expected from the war! Island No. 10 is passed by 3 gunboats. Fort Pulaski is attacked. I am anxious to hear from the east & the west! A few weeks must reveal great things. The immediate future is full of important events! . . .

Apr. 13th Sabbath evening. I have never known rain to fall all day more steadily. The water is running as a river over the yard. How grateful I am to be shielded from the pelting of the storm. Ft. Pulaski surrendered yesterday at 2 o'clock after a fight in which only four were wounded. What a terrible war this is?

April 16th. I shall retire early & rise early that I may press my work forward lest a battle might occur & I be called away as I intend to go & minister to the sick and wounded.

April 18th. In the event of a large battle I shall take a servant and go to the relief of the wounded & suffering.

April 26th. I have been unusually depressed for several days. Probably from physical causes. It is a great effort for me to go out & mingle in the world at all. . . . I think the weather has much to do in affecting my feelings at present. The political horizon is dark & forebodes evil! The horrors of civil war are hanging over us!

May 7th. Mr. Comer is in fine health. I have never seen him look better & I hope he will remain so, for both of his men [white overseers] have gone to the war & Mr. C has both plantations to look after.

June 1st. A terrible battle is now raging near Richmond Va. A cloud obscured the sky this evening and was accompanied by thunder & lightning rumbling afar off, as if all of Heaven's artillery was in motion. Solemnity seemed to pervade the very atmosphere! All my sympathies were and are aroused for the suffering soldiers on that awful battlefield! May God avenge the wrong & support the right!

June 2d. No news of battle today! The atmosphere has been flurried all day & everything has presented a gloomy aspect. The Lord reigns; therefore, let the earth rejoice but, the nation is under severe punishment.

June 5th. I have just aroused from a refreshing nap. Mrs. Randall Jones spent yesterday with me and Miss Mary Slade last night. Willis very carelessly broke our carriage tongue yesterday evening as Mrs. J. & myself were riding into the city. 5 negroes, servants of Wm. Harris were burnt & hung yesterday for murdering their master!! In what terrible times do we live? . . . I have offered my service & all the ready means I could command to the Confederacy & have done all I could to benefit the country & others have received all the praise.

June 10th. This morning the servants did not act faithfully but in confusion & annoyed me much to get my little work done and breakfast over. After breakfast the carriage was driven around & I rode up to see Mrs. Shepherd & had a pleasant call which I do usually there. She is very social. . . . The Guerrilla warfare in our army is most efectual. Stone-wall Jackson has had another victory! . . . Yesterday (Tuesday) I was sent for at the Hospital in consequence of a soldier's death named Smith whose father resides near our Nehee Plantation. At 4 o'clock I called upon Mr. Grimes & there had a pleasant interview on army affairs with him. He is an intelligent and genial youth. I feel deeply interested in the result of this war but am more calm & complacent than I was last year. I then felt Atlas-like, as if the weight of the Confederacy was on my shoulders! How earnest and sincere I was— but what folly for one woman to have been so completely absorbed!

June 16th. What careless things servants are. Who can account for them? . . . Yesterday morning we attended the Baptist church & also at night we heard a refugee preach. I was neither interested nor edified. His object was to get names signed to petition congress in reference to sabbath keeping.

June 25th Wednesday. News of a battle having begun near Richmond yesterday!

June 29th. Last evening about 6 o'clock I heard Adjt. James Ware was killed. I have not a better friend in the Confederacy to lose. He was such a pure, noble man! O what a pang is sent to that poor devoted mother's heart. I am very anxious to hear still further news from the recent battle! Upon hearing the news I immediately called for the carriage and rode down to Dr. Ware's, found the family greatly distressed, and why should they not be—a gem has fallen from the family casket of no ordinary worth!

June 30th. Rain is still generously falling. Great anxiety prevails here. Electricity so affects the wires they will not work & no dispatches have been received all day. Last evening I went down into the city & called at Col. Crawford's & Dr. Ware's. . . . Adjt Ware's corpse will be brought to Columbus. I rode up to Dr. Lockharts early this morning & found them in a great deal of distress about Henry who they heard was mortally wounded. I deeply sympathize with the afflicted family so many deaths in so short a time, husband, brother, father & if Henry dies the oldest son. How much can the heart bear? I turned away in sadness but not such a sadness as the base selfishness I often meet inspires. O, who can endure a narrow-minded selfish person? I cannot.

July 3d. The Battle that is raging near Richmond causes constant & deep anxiety. I wonder Mr. Comer don't send his wagon. I am almost wearied out with waiting. How selfish mortals are? . . . The corpse of Adjt Ware's expected home tomorrow evening.

July 4th At 6½ o'clock this morning Lt. James Ware's body arrived at the Depo under the care of Dr. Ware and Phil his servant. At 9 o'clock the funeral service was performed at the Presbyterian church. A large number of people were present. The services were the most interesting I have ever attended on such an occasion. Dr. Higgins preached an able & eloquent sermon & when he addressed himself to Phil the servant who brought on his masters body I think there was scarcely a dry eye in the house. The music was performed in slow time was well selected and appropriate. Dr. Ware's is a lovely family. They are all very dear to me.

July 5th. Capt. J. M. O. Jelks, of the Dixie Eagles, died in Richmond last Monday night of Typhoid fever. He was a good man & a good friend!

10 o'clock P.M. Cool & delightful! This evening I went down to the camp to carry cakes for the Nehee Boys and there met Lt. W. D. Emery, whom I met some years ago in Montgomery Ala. A pleasant gentleman. Then I went down to Rev. Mr. Deboties to get Testaments for the soldiers, called at Rev. Mr. Wrights door to leave a message concerning Mrs. hart whose funeral will be preached from St. Paul's church tomorrow morning.

July 16th. Oh, what obstinate things negroes are sometimes. Especially Bachelor's servants! It is killing to every social feeling to be in a family with the stupid & selfish. May one day bring deliverance to my captive soul.

July 20th. I shall leave for the Plantations sometime this week. Mr. Comer cannot come in and I must go out once more. I dread the Journey. . . . I fear my health will fail & I shall be compelled to go to a cooler climate. I prefer to remain at home although I have many perplexities & troubles; home is a dear place to me. It is passing strange that servants cannot see it is for their interest to do well! I cannot understand why they are so indolent, obstinate & willful. I know I offer servants sufficient inducements to servants to do well for I give money and almost anything else when they ask for it & often when they do not.

July 26th. Wednesday morning I came to Nehee [one of Mr. Comer's plantations]; Thursday heard Squire [a slave] was sick & I came to Cowickee [another of Comer's plantations], found him very sick with fever; all the other servants well. While not attending to Squire I have been very busily engaged attending to domestic arrangements, making starch. Ally has made some very nice & Martha is today assisting her to make more. We are also trying tallow, preparing Beef-feet oil &c &c., besides collecting our cattle together. At 5 o'clock we shall leave for Nehee.

August 3d Sunday morning. Tuesday we came to Columbus [their primary residence outside Columbus, Georgia]. . . . Arrived at our door about sunsetting having been out in a shower. Lithe soon informed me that our house dog was gone. We never have lost a watch dog when either Mr. Comer or myself were at home, but the servants have lost three valuable members of the canine family in our absence. Strange! The servants at Cowikee Plantation appear to be entirely changed. they serve cheerfully & well & what is more than all they seem earnestly seeking another—a heavenly home—eternal, & which will not fade away! The evening before I left, all the adults or part grown servants came up to our house & had a prayer meeting. Nero, and old Negro, and father of a large family made a fervent & heart-touching prayer & gives evidence of a great change although he has been a great sinner!

Aug. 9th. Our plantation overseers are both gone to the Army, & Mr. Comer and myself have our hands full of business. I have considerable of writing to do & some calls to make this week especially.

Aug. 10th. Saturday evening. Very warm but Mr. Comer came in this morning & was so poor. I think he sinned greatly! How comfortable, how delightful is a grateful spirit, but how sordid and unhappy is a selfish spirit. Rich poor people must suffer exceedingly—if we judge them by their words and actions. . . . The servants were doing well & everything going on well untill Mr. C. came with his unsocial & fault-finding spirit, since which a cloud has fallen. How can one be so unreasonable and perverse? I cannot tell! . . . Everybody seems to have a heart full of sorrow & care—some real & others imagination! For my own part a heavy weight is upon me always, bowing my head like a rush & nearly crushing my spirit down.

Aug 23d. What a pleasure or what a pain servants can be? Who can know them? Is not the negro a mystery? I am sure the African is a peculiar being, a remarkably indolent being. Many duties are now pressing upon me. I have been all the week very anxious to go up to Dr. Lockharts & hear from their sick family but my heart and hands have been full at home!

Aug 29th. Mrs. Jones spent last evening with us. After tea we all became quite interested in conversing about the War! Our servants have been very lazy, obstinate & willful ever since yesterday morning from some cause unknown to me: I hope they will soon pleasantly resume their labors again and render a cheerful obedience. How unhappy the selfish, ignorant & willful are. . . . How terrible it is when servants have their fits of obstinacy & indolence! The negro is certainly not more than half-civilized.

Sept. 4th. How indolent servants are. They really sometimes seem inert— as matter both in mind and body. Fannie my cook & Lithe my house servant have been very willful & obstinate for the last three days & seem determined in that obstinate course. It is a terrible task for me to govern these semi-barbarous, half-enlightened beings. How can I endure it. O God strengthen me! Tuesday morning I went into the city engaged 800 yards of Osnaburgs, enjoyed a call upon Mrs. Lee & one at Mr. Slade's very much. Mrs. Peck was at Mr. Lee's & she is a very pleasant lady too.

Sept. 28th. The excitement of the day is over, the servants are in from work (save one who . . . turned lower than the beasts and has been out in the wood two days), Rena is bathing my feet & preparing me for bed. . . . Something is always occurring in a family of servants to disturb and annoy unless we rise above it. The negro is a dark ignorant being, consequently obstinate as all ignorant beings are. Oh, how perverse the human heart can be!

19th Oct. Came home after a pleasant ride about sunsetting. Had the poorest biscuits for supper I have ever seen, & I thought I had seen those that were poor enough before these, but Mary has certainly excelled all cooks I have ever seen or known in getting up the poorest biscuit!

[October] 29th Found everything as I had feared I should under Fannie's pretended care but real neglect. She is a poor apology for a servant. She may do well for others. I have hired her out. She has had too much leisure with us & she shall try another house.

Nov. 2nd. Sunday attended the Baptist church & then communed at the Episcopal at noon. A sectarian gate is too narrow through which for my continually expanding & enlarging soul to enter heaven. Last evening I spent a pleasant social hour at Dr. Boswell's.

Nov. 6th. Last Evening Miss Ella Boswell made her first call upon us. I am delighted that Dr. Boswell & family live so near!

[November] 9th . . . Yesterday morning I rode into the city and came home to repair a bonnet. Milliner's prices are to extravagant these wartimes for me. I will make my own bonnets & dresses before I will such a price for so little.

Dec. 3d. Cloudy & raining. Warm for the season. The past month has been spent mostly in arranging for the winter. It is no small job now, at the exorbitant prices, to provide for a family of servants, nevertheless, ours now have their usual supply, minus a portion of their shoes, which will soon be forthcoming. . . . Last Saturday evening I came out to Cowikee & remained until Tuesday morning then called upon Mrs. Brown, Mrs. Suche & went to the shoe-shop to get shoes made after which I rode on to the Tannery, then called upon Mrs. Smith, Mrs. Covington & Mrs. Willis. Purchased a few articles at the store, arrived at the Nehee Plantation about dark, found Mr. Comer and all the servants well.

Dec 5th 9 o'clock. I returned from Nehee Plantation about 3 o'clock last evening through rain, mud & water calling upon Mrs. Walker, Mrs. Jelks & Mrs. Brown. I found the plantation house in very neat order which made me feel quite at home but how often sorrow tread closely upon the heels of joy & thus it was last evening. I called up Edmund a little [slave] boy who had never before told me a story [i.e., a lie] & punished him for telling me a lie and a shocking temper he showed. This was my model good little boy! Oh the depravity of the human heart!! Today I shall spend repairing Mr. Comer's clothes & in the morning leave for Columbus.

[December 16] Lithe has acted very badly since she came in from the Plantation. I am afraid visiting her mother has been an injury instead of a benefit to her. Oh, it is terrible to be weighed down with a large family of these ignorant creatures! When shall I be delivered from them. Care & perplexity of these miserably obstinate creatures has consumed 13 of the best years of my life! And I would gladly now be free from them forever! I love my home but it is continually clouded by these wilful & disobedient servants. How much longer can I endure? I daily pray God that my back may be strengthened for the heavy burden I have to bear. . . . I am enjoying by a delightful fire a little waking repose while Rena is rubbing my feet, which by the way is quite a luxury!

Dec. 19th Prices are very high. I paid $1.00 for a doz. of Apples. $4.00 for a pair of kid gloves. Common muslins are 2 dollars per yd!!! Whew. whew. Up to this time we have not sold anything for a high price, but we shall be compelled to sell or exchange our produce at corresponding prices to what we have to buy or we cannot live at all. I think we shall decide to sell to traders at the market price & to families at a lower rate. I know of no other way to get along.

[December] 20th In the morning I went over to the Depo for Mr. Comer who came in looking rough as any old farmer one would see & gruff as rough! We rode over into the city, after sundry decisions and changes of mind he left the carriage & went to see the town! . . . How terribly awful is a sullen sulky disposition. May not a wife sit beside a corpse as well as a husband who sits & speaks not nor stirs these long winter evenings? A self-ish, unsocial companion weighs down, oppresses the spirit almost to the extinguishing life itself.[1]

EMILIE QUINER TENDS THE SICK AND WOUNDED

Emilie Quiner was a young school teacher in Madison, Wisconsin, when the Civil War broke out. In the summer of 1863 she went to Memphis, Tennessee, to serve as a volunteer nurse in the Union military hospital there. Military nursing was still largely performed by men at that time, but female volunteers like Quiner did good work and at the same time helped begin the process that would make nursing a predominantly female rather than male profession. Her diary of July, August, and September 1863 gives us a glimpse of life in the Union hospitals and of Emilie's own feelings about the tragedies in her ward and the fact that while these young men's lives were ending, her own went on.

Wednesday 8th [July 1863]. Started immediately after breakfast to see Dr. Previn, Surgeon General of Hospitals here, he immediately engaged us for hospital duty, and gave us our papers, We visited the Jackson Hospital and afterward the Yazoo, where we were engaged. We found Mrs. Wemb, a Wisconsin lady, and Mrs. Green a sort of under-matron here very pleasant. They told as some very discouraging things and for some time I felt rather blue over the prospect. The surgeon in charge, Dr. Hartshorn, came in and assigned us our wards. Fannies is next to mine on the same floor. The wards are long rooms containing from fifty to seventy beds. Each one has a surgeon, a ward-master and four nurses besides a female nurse. Dr. Nelson the surgeon of my ward seems to be a very pleasant man. There are some very sick men in my ward, and being an entirely new business to me, I start at it rather awkwardly I expect but I shall soon learn how to work, I hope.

Friday 10th [July], Dreaded to go to my ward this morning, the air is so bad there. There are some very sick men here, and they require my constant attention. I already feel very much interested in some of them, some who are very sick. Wm. Clark a boy of about 19 who has chronic diarrhea I am afraid will never get well. I feel very badly about him and shall do all in my power to help him. he is very low however, and there is but a bare possibility of his recovery. There are several other cases of the same disease all doubtful.

Nurses and officers of the U.S. Sanitary Commission at Fredericksburg, Virginia. These were civilians who, much like Emilie Quiner, had gone to serve the needs of the suffering soldiers in the war zone. Library of Congress.

One man Alfred Kent about twenty I should think and from Ohio is very low with fever & debility. I am afraid that he cannot recover. I was very tired to night.

Saturday 11th [July], In my ward early. Clark better today. I talked to him a long time about his home and friends, told him I thought the doctor would give him a furlough and send him home as soon as he was able to go, he seems to feel discouraged, and, though he listens to my plans for him, and acquiesces in them yet he seems to think that he shall never see home again. I am afraid he won't, poor fellow!

Monday, 13th [July], Rained this forenoon made it very cool. Went to my ward as usual. Men getting along very well. Did not go out tonight. One of my men very sick. He cannot live. He is an Ohio boy. he is a very fine fellow, about 20 years old. I would almost give the world if he could live.

One ward of a Union army hospital in Washington, D.C. The facility in which Emilie Quiner served was probably not this nice. Library of Congress.

I wrote a letter to a cousin of his in the army at Vicksburg telling him how he was, and asking him to write home, and inform his friends. He is very grateful for anything I do for him, and though he never says much, his eyes follow me everywhere. He is very home sick. How my heart aches when I think that this is the way that the flower of our country's youth are perishing in this cruel contest. I am thankful that God has given me the opportunity to do some good and pray that he will give me strength to do my duty faithfully in the fear of His Holy Name. Tired out tonight. went to bed, with a heavy heart, almost expect to find Kent dead tomorrow morning.

Tuesday 14th [July]. Kent is better this morning. Ate quite a breakfast. I do wish he would get well. Clark is getting better slowly. I think he may get well. he seems to be in better spirits.

Wednesday 15th [July]. Warm today. In my ward all day. Mr. Smith & Dr. Sweetland of the Adams Hospital, came this afternoon to have us go up to the Officer's Hospital to see a Wisconsin captain. I did not go; the rest of the girls did. I feel too anxious about my men to go anywhere. there are three or four that may die any hour. Kent is very low tonight. I have sat by him all the afternoon. he is very quiet. It seems as if I could not bear

Clara Barton, pioneer female nurse for the Union
army. National Archives.

to see him die. the Doctor will not let me tell him that he must die for
there possibly may be a chance for his recovery he says. [In the nineteenth
century it was considered very important that a dying person should be
aware of his impending death so that he could leave any final messages for
loved ones and make any final preparations that might still be needed.] I
have no hopes of it. God pity his poor old mother, and God pity all the
mothers whose hearts will ache through the terrible consequences of this
unnatural war. Went to bed tired enough.

Thursday 16th [July]. A warm day, it rained about noon and cooled the
air somewhat, a real tropical shower it was. The rain coming down in sheets.
I enjoyed it, but I guess some of the boys who lay under the ventilator
didn't for the rain came right through. In my ward all day. Kent has been
torpid all day. Had no appetite for food, could hardly rouse him to take his
wine. I feel very bad about him. he will not live through the night, I fear.
God have mercy upon him, poor fellow. I would do any thing in my power

to give him back the lost life power but alas human arms are too short, and human effort too weak to help in such cases. There is another man in my ward whom I fear will die today. I wrote to his wife yesterday.

9 o'clock P.M. Kent is dead. He breathed his last a half hour ago. I closed his eyes. they prepared him for the grave and took him away. I shall never forget the sorrow I felt for his death. he was so young, so patient, so lonely and homesick, and so grateful for everything I did for him. I shed as bitter tears over his dying bed as I ever wept in my life. it is so hard to see our noble boys die here alone so far from friends who would give their lives almost to have been with them in their last moments. I shall write to his mother. The saddest duty of our position is this, breaking the tidings to anxious loving hearts at home. God give you strength to bear it, poor loving mother. My ward will seem lonely after this. I have watched him and fed and cared for him so long that the sight of his poor pale, face on the bed seemed a part of my life. poor fellow; so they die.

Sunday 2d [August] In my ward all the morning. Dr. Nelson asked me why I did not go to church. I plead want of time, but fear that want of inclination might also have formed a good part of my excuse. I have lost all my energy of late, have not the least ambition increasingly to do anything which is out of old routine of ward duty. I can neither read, write nor talk, as I used to do. I have almost despised Southerners heretofore, for their want of energy, but shall never do so again. This southern air is depressing beyond belief and I do not wonder that sick men do not recover for many months in this climate.

Wednesday 5th [August]. There are quite a good many Rebel officers in this Hospital and we met a huge number of ladies from the city with baskets and I presume all manner of good things, bent on deeds of charity to the secesh [i.e., Rebels]. It made my blood boil when I thought that it was such as these who had caused and were still causing all the misery that we were encountering daily in our life in the Hospital.

Sunday 26th [August]. One of my men is very low. I do not expect him to live more than a day or two. I wrote to his mother on Tuesday, telling her that she had better come to him, as he was very anxious to see her. I expected her yesterday. I fear she will not reach here before his death.

Tuesday 28th [August]. A warm day. We went up to Mr. Smith's office to get some things from a box which came from Wis. The man whose mother I wrote to last week, died today, he was not quite sensible when he died. He wished very much to see his mother. I expect she will be here soon.

Wednesday 29th [August]. In my ward early. Immediately after breakfast the ward master came to tell me that there was a lady below who wished to see me. I went down and found it to be the mother of the man who died yesterday. she was almost inconsolable when she found that he was dead. I had to undertake the task of comforting her, with poor success I fear, for who can comfort or console such broken hearts. he had died without a word for his friends and she an old lady, had come this long distance to see her only son and found him dead. I could not find words of comfort for her only begging her to look to God for consolation in her hour of bitterest need.

Thursday 30th [August]. In my ward all day. That old lady went home last night. Mrs. Brown, wife of one of our sick men in my ward is here taking care of her husband.

Monday 20th [August]. Fanny, Louise, & I went to market this morning and we see a great many queer things. I enjoy it very much. This morning I saw an old market woman coming in on a mule with a straw hat upon her head the brim of which was at least half a yard in width and her face was so browned and sunburned that she would have safely passed muster among the Winnebagoes. . . .

Saturday 15th [September]. I went to market this afternoon. There were a large number of people present. It was very warm indeed. These Saturday afternoon markets are a great curiosity to me. There are so many things to be seen which are wholly characteristic of the South. After we had made our purchases we met one of the boys in Lou's ward who invited us to have some ice cream. This conveyed an idea of coolness and we consented, standing and eating our cream in one corner of the market where every moment we were jolted by the crowd, it was delicious, and I think I never enjoyed any thing more in my life. We went home, and just this side of the market met my wardmaster and one of the nurses who wanted us to go back and have something. We assured them that we did not need anything, but they seemed so much hurt and disappointed that we told them they might get us any thing they chose. On our arrival at home we found awaiting us, two huge melons which they had brought from market. I had four invitations to go and get ice cream tonight. I could not accept them all, so went with the first one who invited me. We had a grand time altogether got some ice cream peaches and ice water and came home rather late and very tired.[2]

ELIZA WILCOX GRAVES OBSERVES THE WAR'S IMPACT ON THE SOUTH

Eliza Wilcox Graves, a Northerner, went to live in Little Rock, Arkansas, some time before the war. She remained there until late 1862, observing some of the grim results of war in that Southern community and relating them in this letter, probably written in December 1862, to her relatives George and Elizabeth Greenleaf Wilcox, of Wisconsin.

It is a long time dear brother and sister since I wrote you from Arkansas and as you never answered it (or if you did I never received it) I am going to write you again. Perhaps you thought of us as belonging to those awful rebels and would not own [us] as friends. But we have come out from Rebeldom, escaped as it were by the "skin of our teeth." We were over three years in Little Rock fast stuck in and under such military dicipline by Gen Hindman's & Gen. Price's orders that we could not write or recieve letters, Newspapers, etcetera for nearly two years except some came through by private soldiers subject if found out to severe dicipline. Every article of Food or clothing was very scarce. We paid 25 dollars for a pound of Tea, 18 doll. per pound Soda, $150 for the two last barrels of Flour we purchased, 300 hundred for both! and everything else accordingly, 6 doll for little roasting Pig, 6 for a Turkey, 50 cents pound for venison, 10 doll for pound of Coffee. Flannel 16 doll. per yd. Calico from 5 to 7 doll. cotton muslin for shirting 5 to 7 doll. per yd. Linnen. Fine teeth combs 5.00 doll. Paper pins 5.00, Needles 3.00 a paper. Bonnet Ribbon 12 doll. yd! and every thing else like that. Hoops 40 doll. Gaiter Boots 40 doll a pair, spool cotton 2.50 apiece. I had a good supply and could let my neighbors have some of mine of almost everything and I could give some to the poor suffering ones in the prisons and Hospitals. I never was out of anything. . . . So by keeping up good courage and economy good cheerful spirits & happy temper myself I helped to keep up others also and by taking such cheerful views of our surroundings and pointing out the bright side of those around us that the weak and fearful the desponding and fainting run to me to think for them how they had best conduct their affairs. In this way both myself and husband were enabled to do much good aside from our schoolroom duties. We had a large school up to the time of our leaving them and such earnest begging of us to prolong our stay as we left no one to take our school of 80 or 100. But just as soon as we were in our good minds after the horrors of the Battle of the 10 of Sept we took our departure. Have you ever been in a battle? If not, you have one set of feelings that have never been called out. We were in one for twelve hours and had to run out of one house that was taken by the Feds and ride as fast as we could with the retreating army for three miles up to the City only to be penned into that and stand two hours of Cannonading and shelling before the Mayor would be allowed to hold up the Flag of Truce!! The Confederates were determined to hold on to the United States Arsenal there or burn the City to its foundations. That was why we went down to the Plantation to stay. Thinking we should be safer there than in the City. But the Federal Army crossed the river below us and came rushing right through our dooryard,

A refugee family leaving a war area with belongings loaded on a cart.
National Archives.

garden Corn field killing everything right and left. We were a most desperate
people and nothing but desperate measures could make us come to anything
like decency.

We were Union all the time but dare not say one word even to ourselves.
For you know in Arkansas neither Law or Gospel has much influence when
the voice of some few people together can call together enough to take
Lynch law into their hands. We saw and knew of much that would make
you all have open mouths and eyes for some time if I should tell you all but
I will not. Enough for you to know we had all our house set in order and
we left something like the children of Israel journeying through the dessert
not knowing what a day might bring forth. If we were living at night a band
of Guerrillas might break in before morning and lay us all low. If living in
the morning a bullet or Bowie Knife might take us in our houses or in the
Public Street and we go without warning or forethought to our final account.

When we saw a gentleman of our acquaintance one hour we almost ceased
to be surprised if the next one came to tell us he had been assassinated in
his house or on the street. It became to us as you may well think a time of
horror. We looked and longed for the Federal army to come and release us.

We had a most excrutiating day for we were momentarily expecting death from balls or shells. Such screams and shrieks as we heard that day! such fainting and Fits among mothers who had their husbands and sons in the battle. Such agonies among all classes can only be realized to be understood. More babies born than a few. Time or not time made no difference. And those with babies a few days old running into the streets begging for some one to take them to a place of safety from those horrid shells as they came shrieking through the street and over our heads. Every man in the city was forced into fighting and only Mr. Graves and another gentleman who had both been very sick were allowed to stay with a city full of women and children. Some ladies went from one fit to another until they died. But why tell you of these horrors? You are safe up among the hills of Wisconsin I suppose and we are once more among our Green ones safe and sound. We travelled in ironclad cars and were in constant danger from Guerrillas from the shore and incendiaries on board of the steamboats on the river until we reached Cairo [Illinois] and then we breathed freely from human hand. God shielded our heads in the day of battle and we were brought safely out among civilisation to bless Him with a loud voice once more.

I was grieved to know you had been called to give up dear little George. But oh so much better that he went with a mother's and Father's & sisters arm about him to give comfort than to die upon the battle field or in the Hospital. So many I have seen going to the grave away from all who even knew them that I have come to know it is a blessing to have our dear ones die with us. . . . One or two more battles must end the struggle we think. We have been behind the scenes and ought to know.

I send you our Photographs dear brother. You see we have grown old outwardly but our hearts are just as warm and young as ever and we love you all as much as formerly. We wish you to write us a good long letter telling us of your troubles & joys and let us keep alive the remembrance of each other on earth a little longer and be every hour, day, and year preparing to meet in our all loving Father's home that is waiting for us whenever our work is done for which we were sent hither.

ever yours truly E B W Graves[3]

AUGUSTA KIDDER OBSERVES THE NORTHERN HOMEFRONT IN 1863

While attending Cherry Valley Female Seminary, Cherry Valley, New York, during the late 1850s, Augusta "Gussie" Kidder, of Eau Claire, Wisconsin, made the friendship of fellow student Olivia A.

Brown, of Chattaqua County, New York. They continued to corre-
spond afterward, and Gussie Kidder's letters provide a glimpse of the
Northern home front. In contrast to Eliza Wilcox Graves's harrowing
picture of what it could mean to be a civilian in the South during the
war, Kidder's home front is relatively calm, with the war nevertheless
a grim reality just beyond the horizon of everyday events but still
threatening the lives of friends and loved ones.

> Eau Claire, Wis.
> April 25, 1861
> My Dear Ollie,
> There is an immense excitement here over the war news and of course it
> is the same where you are. Isn't it dreadful? There is to be a great Union
> meeting tomorrow eve. I mean to attend. . . .
> Your old school friend,
> Gussie Kidder

> Eau Claire, Wis.
> May 18, 1862
> I had a real good letter from Sara Clark today, and have also heard the
> sad news of my cousins death, Darwin Willard of Jamestown. How sad it
> is. I know we cannot lose our friends in a nobler cause still it is just as hard
> to lose them. and my poor Aunt, to lose two sons in so short a time! I hope
> you still hear steadily from your brothers and that they are well. Is the one
> who came for you at C[herry].V[alley]. in the army? I shall hope and pray
> for you and your friends as I do for mine. My brother is not in the army.
> he gave it up some time since, the regiment that he was to join not being
> called out of the state. I am very glad of course. I thought him too young
> to go and it seemed to me that there were no more soldiers needed to crush
> the rebellion than we had already in the field. What glorious news we are
> having (only saddened by the thought of the mourning hearts somewhere).
> I only wonder now that they don't lay down their arms at once, all of them
> and submit. They must soon do it and why don't they do so now and save
> further bloodshed. I do so long to see this war end.
> Your old school friend,
> Gussie Kidder

> Eau Claire, Wis.
> March 8, 1863
> My Dearest Ollie,
> So you have been teaching this winter. I am not so very much surprised
> after all, for it is very fashionable here. Nearly all the young ladies here teach

school at least one term in the year. I have a very pleasant school, only small scholars, and some of them sweet little ones to whom I am already quite attached. The term is nearly over. I fancy I should not like the occupation as well in the summer, but I may possibly try it again when summer comes. Father and Mother are willing, for they say it keeps me out of mischief. Encouraging! isn't it? If mischief means what occupied me last summer, teaching or other devices will hardly keep me out of it. There is no chance here for extensive flirtation, for it is here, as you say it is at your home, the young men are all gone away. Many to the battlefield and when those will come back who knows? We have quite a number of photographs of "soldier boys." and when I have a photograph album which I hope will come very soon, my army friends will claim a good share of it.

Tuesday eve. [March] 10.

We have had a gayer winter than I anticipated. Surprise parties have come in vogue again and with as good success as ever. Few of them were voted among the best parties of the season. Oh! such fun! I wish you had been here. Old fashioned spelling-schools too have been revived. Several "loads" [i.e., large sleighs loaded with passengers] (as well as sometimes single cutters) have been out a few miles into the country to a spelling school, and had real sport, and then we invite them to come down to ours and spell us down. But our sleighing will soon be gone if this sunny weather lasts much longer, and the season for parties will soon be over. I wonder how we have had so pleasant a winter with such a dearth of young men. The very few (not half as nice as the absent) who remain with some old bachelors and widowers who are too selfish to join the army but who are fair subjects for flirtation have done double duty.

Our family are all at home . . . I cannot be too grateful that we are all spared and kept together to enjoy so much happiness. If only this war were over so that all our friends might lay down their arms and once more return to a peaceful life.

Your old school friend,
Gussie Kidder

Eau Claire, Wisconsin
Sunday P.M. August 30, 1863
My Darling Ollie,

I hope that your brother is entirely restored to health by this time. How much care and anxiety you must have suffered.

There is but little sickness here except among children and that not alarming, generally. Our family are in excellent health as usual. I'm glad to hear that your brother has returned for I know from experience how you will enjoy his society after so long an absence. He must be thankful for the comforts of home after two long years of camplife. When will this cruel war end? My Uncle, who is at Vicksburg thinks we are very near the end but says there are a few more heavy blows to strike first. He has been wounded but not dangerously and we hope he will be spared to return soon to his family.

Your old school friend,
Gussie Kidder[4]

JOHN AND WILLIAM BARNEY MARCH THROUGH DIXIE

By late summer of 1862, it was clear that the North would need more manpower in order to fight the war through to final victory. Accordingly, Lincoln called upon the governors of the loyal states for another 300,000 volunteers, and in a final surge of volunteer enlistment, the country responded and filled the new regiments. It was a patriotic outpouring that Henry Clay Work celebrated in his song, "We Are Coming, Father Abram, Three Hundred Thousand More." One of those new regiments was the Twenty-ninth Wisconsin, and in its ranks were two brothers, William and John Barney. Born in Waukesha, they had moved with the family to a farm near Hartford, Wisconsin. William became captain of Company I, and John a corporal in that company. They wrote frequent letters to their father, to their brother Sam who had stayed at home, or simply "to all at home." The letters describe the scenes they were passing through, the operations of their army as it tried to take the Confederate stronghold of Vicksburg, and their feelings about the war.

Camp Randall, Madison
Wisconsin Oct. 5th 1862
Dear Father,
This morning I went with the rest of our Regt to hear the Chaplain of the Regt preach. I can tell you it was a funny sight to see 1000 men assembled out of doors to hear a sermon preached. you didn't see men there viing with each other to see which could dress the best, but every one there was dressed as we always dress at home, only I suppose that some of us were not quite as clean as we would have been, had we been at home but we were clean enough I guess. We were marched up to head quarters at 9 o'clock where we found the Chaplain waiting for us. When it was time to commence the services the Chaplain got on top of a cannon (a twelve pounder) and preached a *first rate* sermon. The sermon was preached to the

men, advising the men to give their families a part of their wage, at least ten dollars [by means of an allotment system involving pay-roll deductions]. Almost all of the boys are going to send $10 home, but I think I shall send home $11. . . . We have not received our uniforms yet and more than that we don't know when we *shall* receive them.

John J. Barney

Opposite Helena on the Miss. shore
November 14th 1862
To all at home:
We have been here just one week and we now begin to feel ourselves quite old soldiers. We have seen everything there is to be seen except a battle and that we are waiting for very impatiently. . . .

John J. Barney

Opposite Helena on the Miss. shore
November 14th 1862
To all at home:
They all pretend to be Union men here every man but I know better. One man here, the man we took so much property from and then returned it to him because he said that he was a Union man, rides back and forth through our lines seeing every thing he wishes to when I know well enough that he is "secesh" every whit. The old reprobate says that he is worth one million dollars in real estate and I have not the least doubt but that he is worth one half of that and perhaps the whole. He must own four or five sections of land with good improvements. I passed through one of his fields of cotton of not less than 200 acres and I should think it was first rate too. . . .

John J. Barney

Camp Salomon, Mississippi
December 5th 1862
To all at Home:
Our foraging parties instead of making a regular steal of it as they used to are conducted now as they ought to be so that nothing is taken except that, that the Col. orders them to take. . . . The foraging party that was sent out yesterday . . . bought all the beef and pork they wanted and then went to forageing on their own hook. The plantation which they visited was descrtcd, but old boards, shakes, chairs, tables, stands, brick &c., were in abundance and all the wagons that were not loaded with meat were loaded with this stuff. . . .

John J. Barney

Camp Steel Mississippi
December 17th 1862
To friends at Home:
I think the general health of the Reg't as good as when we came here.
Three men have died in the Hospital since last Sunday and there is one in
our Co. that is very doubtful whether he ever lives to see Wis. again. . . . It
seems very strange that the Surgeons or no one else hardly know what ails
some of those that even die in the Hospital. Jennings has no fever but seems
to be gradually dropping away and the Surgeons say they don't know what
ailes him although all three of the men that have died seemed the same as
him. Harrison in the first place was taken with ague and after the fever and
ague was checked he was taken with the diarea that he now has whatever it
is. . . .
I don't want to fight any more than any one else but compromise is out
of the question now and there is nothing left but for us to fight it out and
the sooner the fighting is done and the soldiers sent home the better I shall
like it. . . .
John J. Barney

Camp Steele, Mississippi
December 21st, 1862
Brother Sam:
We are now some distance from home, just how far I cannot tell, but it
is some ways to say the least, but I cannot comprehend that we are further
off than when we were encamped at Madison. There is one difference however which you would realize if you were with us,—the weather is like a
warm Wisconsin Autumn. I do not doubt but that you at home are having
huge times in the sleigh-riding line. . . . But John J. concludes that he will
not take to this climate as readily as you may think I have by my expression;
he says that when this war comes to an end the people down this way can
take a last look of him as he shall be sure never to visit them again.
I wrote in my letter in the morning something about the great expedition,
I believe. Since that time vessels have continued to arrive until the river is
full as far as you can see with steamers loaded with troops and supplies. As
I write I can hear the dull, heavy puffing of steam tugs a few rods from my
tent, and the shrill whistle of the "little corporals" as they go on their work
of conveying signals to the fleet. These "little corporals" are boats that go
with the gun-boats and convey messages at all times, let it be in a fight or
otherwise. Seldom if ever are they hit. They are painted a dull lead color,
about the same shade of the water in the river, and are so small that at a

distance of half a mile it is hard to draw a true bead upon them even with a rifle. . . .

Your Brother,
William K. Barney

Friars Point, twelve miles below Helena
December 26th 1862
To all at Home:

We are stationed at one of the prettiest towns in the South. I believe it is at any rate. The place looks more like some of our Northern towns than any I have seen since I came South. It is the County seat of this County. The houses here South look no more like the houses North than our barn looks like our house. They are all low houses with a hall passing through the middle, the same as some of those log houses there used to be in Hartford. The people all look pale and sickly, although they are as healthy for all I know as we. . . .

Today I was strolling around town when I came to a house where there was some trees that I never saw before and I asked the owner what they were and he said that they were fig trees and that they raised a good many figs the past season from them. The owner of this place was a *very* wealthy man and one of the most *bitter* secessionists I have seen and yet as soon as we came here, guards were placed over his property to protect it from our soldiers and I'll warrent that not *one bit* of it will be taken for our soldiers, although it would add *greatly* to our comfort were some of the things taken for us. There are some turnips growing near where we are encamped and *they* are not guarded. Do you believe that we have turnips to eat? Last night some of the men on guard killed a small pig and while they were cooking it Wm. came around and asked them what they were cooking and they told him that it was a rabbit that they killed. I guess that Wm. didn't try *very* hard to find out whether it was a pig or rabbit. Just as I am writing Orderly Gould pokes his head in at the door and calls for a volunteer to go and butcher some of the hogs our boys have "*confiscated.*" Al says that *he will* "*confiscate*" the living and *I'll bet he will.* . . .

John J. Barney

Friars Point Mississippi
December [January] 2nd 1863
To all at Home . . .

A year has opened to me with very different prospects from any I have ever seen, and from any I ever expected to see. . . . Although things look dark now; Burnside's defeat at Fredricksburg, Grant's retreat in this State north of us and other defeats we have had, tend to make our prospects darker than they were before, yet I *hope* that this war will terminate before three years and terminate too as we want it to. I sometimes lose all faith in *all* our officers when I see some of the *stealing* that our officers are doing. One of our Capts, the Capt of Co. K. a few nights ago went out privately with his company to one of the plantations nearby and stole two loads of cotten and sold them to a Capt. of one of the boats on the river. As a natural consequence the planter when he saw that the cotten was stolen from him by one of the officers he marched down to the picket line and fired at our pickets. The next morning Wm. was ordered to take a squad of men and burn all the buildings on the plantation. Just as they were burning the last building, the Col. heard the circumstances and he had Capt. Delmeter arrested. He is now under arrest and I hope that he will suffer. I'll tell you what I *know* about this cotten speculation. I know that salt, calicoes, and cotten cloth, the *very things* the South most need, was sold to them at *outrageous* prices and in return took cotten at 40 cents per pound and then I know it is sold at Cairo for 52 or 55 cents. Now where is this leak? The cotton is certainly sold at Cairo again and somebody pockets the profit. There is no one of the officers that pretend to deny but that almost all the officers are speculating in cotten in this Department of the Army. . . .

We are stationed at one of the worst places in the South. At this place the negroes say that men were headed up in barrells and then rolled into the river and that men have been tried in a large Post Office there is here and when convicted of being Union men they were either hung or rolled into the river. I have heard the negroes say this and when just such stories were circulated through the North about this time I cant help but believe them. . . .

John J. Barney

Devalls Bluff, Ark.
January 18th, 1863
Brother Sam:
War is a terrible game, but you at home can illy understand with what indifference a soldier comes to look upon events which concern so vitally his welfare. If you were to tell the 29th, and they were to believe you, that tomorrow they would be in the hardest battle of the war, most would lie down and sleep as well as if contrary news was given. . . .

Your Brother,
William K. Barney

Camp near Helena Arkansas
February 15th 1863
Sam:
Since I last wrote three of our company have died. . . . Three *good* soldiers are gone that we hoped to take home. Who is next? Is all this sacrifice of

life for naught, are we to come down here and throw our lives away for nothing? I expected at *least* that the North and our army were ready to fight and see this thing through. But now instead of helping us they [antiwar persons in the North] even protect deserters and *help* them desert. . . . Desertions are nothing but what happen daily. It is nothing for a Reg't to lose fifteen or twenty at a time. And there is no reason for it except some of the northern papers howling about the emancipation proclamation and fighting to "free niggers" and of course some of the soldiers are ready to catch at any thing that they think will help them out of the army. I would like to help mob some such papers as the News and those of like stamp. . . .

Al Herrick . . . is our cook. He can cook anything from heavy dumplings to burnt beans We have to draw about a half ration of flour and Al said one morning that he would make some pan-cakes that the women's at home wouldn't be a circumstance to, and I thought he told the truth. He made a kind of paste of flour and water and then took some soda and dissolved it in some water and stirred it all together and baked them. They looked "yaller" I tell you, and tasted—well imagine how. After a while he put a quart or two of vinigar in them to sour the batter. they were not quite so "yaller" as the others but they were like "Aunt Jemimah's plaster" or *some* like father's Johney cake. But we have the choice of two evils, eat them or go without. About a week ago Al said that we must change diet, so he volunteered to make some dumplings. After taxing his wits he made some that he pronounced good, but you know the old saying of "the proff [*sic*] of the pudding &c" well this saying came forceably to my mind after chewing on one end of a *dumpling* full five minutes without making any impression on it. Orange had the advantage over the rest of us for he swallowed them as a hen would gravel stones. I wish you could take one meal with us to see how we cook. Al is chief of the Cullinary Department. He goes into the fine cooking and we do the coarse. . . .

If our army were not so dissatisfied I should expect to be at home now soon but as it is things look dark. . . . The weather is very pleasant here now. As Orange has just written to Mrs. Thomson. "The toads commence to holler and the trees are most leaved out." If that isn't going into the sublime then I mistook the meaning of the word. This is the time they commence to plow here. The weather is warmer now than it generaly is North in May.

John J. Barney

Helena, Arkansas.
February 17th, 1863
Brother Sam:
. . . Sam, be careful that you do not write in any of your letters to anyone things or words you would not be willing to have anyone see in after years.

Letters may live, and you should be careful what you put in paper and ink. . . .
Your Brother,
William K. Barney

Camp at Helena Ark.
March 2nd 1863
To all at Home:
Last Sunday we started through the "pass." The pass is about 5 miles below Helena. Our men blew up the levee and then there was nothing to prevent the water from the Miss. flowing through a natural channel into the Coldwater. We encamped five miles below Moon Lake and about twenty from Helena on Gen. Alcorn's plantation. The plantation is one of the prettiest I ever saw. His house was surrounded by evergreen trees, with some Magnolia and China. I am going to enclose some of the China tree seeds in another envelope, together with some kind of vian [vine] he had to cover an Arbor. . . . The pass where the fleet has gone down is full of trees, nearly as thick as they are in our sugar bush [grove of sugar maple trees]. It looks almost impossible for boats to pass through but they do. I hope that they will succeed but if they do not, I am afraid they will see hard times before they get back. The Guerrillas can fell trees after us and blockade the river so that it will be impossible for the boats to get back. But that's speculating. Hope we will fight our way through at Vicksburg and then all's well. . . .
John J. Barney

Camp at Helena Ark.
March 2nd 1863
To all at Home:
Wm. and I, I hope will be home some time and I want to find you on the old place [there had been talk of his father's selling the old home place] where it will seem like *home* to me. I used to have some ambition for something, I hardly know what, now the only ambition I have, the only goal I want to reach is *home*. Then after this I'll be content. . . . I don't want to go home till this war ends as I want it to and then I want to go, and more than that we are going to make it end in less than *one year just as we want it to*. And then I want to come North and kill *one half* of the Democrats there just to show how the soldiers appreciate their efforts to comprimise a peace, bought at the price of eternal dishonor of the North. Isn't it a shame? . . .
John J. Barney

Helena Arkansas
March 13th 1863
To all at Home:
Since my last three of our company have died in the Hospital at Memphis. two from the effects of the measles and one from the Typhoid fever, I think.

. . . They were . . . as good boys as I ever knew and as good soldiers too. How much misery is caused by this awful war. Today another boat load of sick leaves this place for St. Louis. . . . Henry Calkins has the dropsy and will probably receive his discharge as soon as he gets there. I forgot to mention that Herbert Gould is one that is going also. He with the others I *hope* will get discharged. They have all got so they seem almost like brothers, especialy Henry Calkins who is my tentmate. . . .

John J. Barney

Camp at Helena Arkansas
March 20th 1863
Brother Sam:
I wish Uncle Sam would arm the negroes and let them fight instead of sending them to such places as St. Louis where they have nothing to do but cook rations drawn for them from Uncle Sam's storehouse. There is no doubt but they would make the *best* of soldiers no one denies that. . . .

John J. Barney

Smith's plantation Louisiana
April 26th 1863
To all at Home:
Perhaps the next you hear of the 29th you will hear of their figuring in a fight near Vicksburg. Don't think that either Wm. or I will be killed and worry about us as I am afraid you do for some are going home and perhaps Wm and I are among that number, at any rate it is no worse for us to die than anyone else. I expect to go back to Hartford with Wm yet and hold plow. Perhaps Wm. will drive. He is tough on a march and I can see no good reason why he wouldn't make a good driver. . . .

John J. Barney

Perkins plantation two miles
from the Mississippi April 28th 1863
To all at Home:
We left Gilberts Bayou yesterday morning and after marching all day in the rain and mud we arrived at this place, somewhere between Port Hudson and Vicksburg. . . . Last night orders came to issue one hundred rounds of cartridges and two days rations and be ready to march again this morning at five. We are still here but presume will march *somewhere* before night. There are good reasons to suppose that we are either going to Port Hudson or Vicksburg in either case we shall see what we enlisted for, fighting. . . .

John J. Barney

Camp between Port Gibbson and Grant Gulf, Mississippi
May 5th 1863
To all at Home:
We *thrashed* them *good* and are still after them to give them another one.
I hope we shall be kept on the move until this war ends, be it one year or
three. It looked some like ending this war when we seen a dead *rebel* in
every corner of the fence. I suppose I am hard harted but it cant be helped.
I wish more had been killed than there was. We are now waiting for the
provision train from the river which we expect tonight when we shall make
another move. I expect it will be to the rear of Vicksburg. Wherever it is I
hope we may thrash them as nicely as we did this time. . . .
John J. Barney

Camp two miles from Black river
Mississippi May 9th 1863
To all at Home:
Wm and I and the whole company in fact, never were in better health
than now or more ready for an active campaign. . . . Gen. Grant passed us
yesterday. All the Regt's were ordered to fall in and we gave him three cheers
with a will. . . .
John J. Barney

[printed form—the underlined words are filled in on the printed blanks]
I certify, on honor, that <u>John J. Barney</u> a <u>Corp</u> of Captain <u>O. B. Bissell</u>
Company <u>(I)</u> of the <u>29th</u> Regiment of Infantry Volunteers, of the State of
Wisconsin, born in <u>Waukesha,</u> State of <u>Wis</u>, aged <u>19</u> years; <u>5</u> feet, <u>8</u> inches
high; <u>dark</u> complexion, <u>black</u> eyes, <u>brown</u> hair, and by occupation a <u>Farmer,</u>
having joined the company on its original organization at <u>Hartford Wis</u>, and
enrolled in it at the muster into the service of the United States at <u>Madison
Wis</u>, on the <u>27th</u> day of <u>Sept, 1862,</u> . . . for the term of Three years and
having served HONESTLY and FAITHFULLY with his Company to the
present date, is now entitled to a DISCHARGE by reason of <u>Death on the
16th day May 1863</u>. . . .

in Rear of Vicksburg, Miss
June 14th, 1863
To all at Home:
I send three dollars in money which was John J.'s It seems almost mar-
velous that he should have left it so I could get it. The morning before the
fight he gave it to Lloyd Nawscawen, as his pocket book had got wet some
way and he was afraid it would spoil the money, so he said. Place it in safe
keeping, these same identical bills, as no one of them could be bought of
me for three thousand times their value. . . .
William K. Barney[5]

FIVE CONFEDERATES FACE INCREASING TROUBLES IN THE SOUTH

Meanwhile in the Confederacy, the situation continued to deteriorate. These letters from several Confederate soldiers and one civilian during the middle part of the war illustrate the effects of growing pressures on Southern society.

S. B. Thornbrough

In this letter Confederate soldier S. B. Thornbrough writes to his brother, R. W. Thornbrough. Both are Confederate soldiers. The February 1862 fall of Nashville has led Thornbrough to begin questioning the ultimate chances of Confederate success.

Big Bottom Ark. March 2nd 1862
Appreciated & Ever Dear Brother
The presant opportunity affords me much pleasure to write you a few lines in answer to yours of Date Feb. 15th 1862. I came up home to day from Camp McCray and glad was I to find you letter here of late date. . . . My health is good at this time. Pa is complaining some. he had a chill on yestarday out at garners though he was able to ride home to day. sister Betty is sick to night though not dangerous. I hope she has a seviere head ache and some fever. the rest is as well as usual. P. M. Stark is complaining some though he can go about the rest of his family is well and I hope these lines may come to your hand in dew time and find you enjoying good health and able for duty. Robert I do not want you to go into camp before you are able to go for it may through you back again, and I want you to take the best care of your self that you can for the best is bad anough. you would like to hear something about Camp McCray. it is at the cross roads or Starkville you wished to know the No of our Regiment it is not a Regiment yet but a Battallion it is the first Battallion of Arkansas Sharp Shooters and that is all that I can tell you this time for all of the companies has not got in yet and we are not nombered yet though I expect R. S. Hill company will be company C. though I dont know yet how it will be and I dont know how long it will be until we march I suppose we will go to Jacksonport from here when we leave unless we have orders to go some where else. Robert you never have seen such times as is in ark at this time. I suppose the Northerners is in this state and marching rapidly, and it looks like every body is gone now that could go but they all have to go now for the malitia

is called for and every body that can shoot will have to go. and then I do not think it will take long to wind the ball or unwind it, one. I heard to day that the south had given Nashville up without the fire of a gun and retreated back to Memphis and if that be so I fear it will be a hard struggle for us and probably one that will prove to be a death stroke to the Southern Confederacy. So I will just say for you to look sharp and not let them get you and I will try and not let them get me Robert. we have plenty of clothing at our camp for our soldiers all has drew clothes that wanted them. I have drawed a coat, cap & blanket. and could get more if I wanted it but I have got plenty of clothes to start with Robert. Russell Turney, Isaac Dillen, Polk Hunt & Jack Bailey all come home last wednesday night from your company but they could tell nothing but they left them in Nashville and that is about all they know. they say they are sick but they dont look verry sick. well Robert I will have to come to a close. . . . I will write to you a gain soon and tell you where we are and where to direct your letter to and all about it in general &C. So I will subscribe myself your Brother as ever.

S. B. Thornbrough[6]

W. W. Grissam

In this letter Confederate soldier W. W. Grissam writes to his uncle, J. Monroe Fich.

Durhamville, Tenn. March 16, 1862
Dear Uncle Monroe:
I hope you arrived safely at home in due time; if you did, I guess it was with a "squeeze and a grin," for I learn there has been stiring times up that way lately. The railroad is now under military controll and passports are required of passengers. The times are closing down upon us, and it may be that in a short time we will not [be] permited to pass out of the limits of our own neighborhood.

We have just received a letter [from] Finis, he reports himself well, and at Humbolt [Tennessee] at time of writing but says he suposes the Regiment was then under marching orders as he had learned that one hundred rounds of cartriges were to be distributed to each of the soldiers. Finis complains of not receiving any letters Weakly [i.e., weekly]: he does not consider the fact that no one knows where to address him.

Half of the male hands [slaves] in all this country have been sent to fortify No 10 [a Confederate stronghold on the Mississippi River] but I am afraid that it will be of no avail. I learn that New Madrid is in possession of the enemy, and will they not cut off our supplies by river? The main dependence.

We have but about two hundred militia men in this City none have yet gone to answer the last call most of the districts will make up the number by volunteering. Ours (the 1st) received proper credit and not included; it only musters 17 men, 16 having joined the army: all that were considered unable or ineficient have been discharged from the Regiment myself included.

We would like for you to write to us and let us know how all are getting along, and whether you have any interruption of the mails.

I may or may not come or go up to see you soon. can't tell anything about it. don't know one day what will be done the next.

This leaves us all well. Nothing more at present.

Affectionately Yours

W. W. Grissam[7]

Wiley White

In this letter Confederate soldier Wiley White writes to his wife, children, and parents from another Confederate stronghold on the Mississippi River, Fort Pillow, located north of Memphis. Wiley is already starting to lose hope of Confederate victory.

[Fort Pillow, April 1862]

My Dear Wife and children Father and Mother

I am well at this time hopeing these few lines may find you all well I have nothing strong to write to you. at this time the health of our company is tolerable good. Rebeca I want to see you and the children very bad tho the prospect semes bad now, tho I think I will get back home agane. Rebeca you must do the best you can for I no your chance is bad. you must take as good care of your self and I will do the same. I am in hops [hopes] the links [Lincoln soldiers, i.e., Union soldiers] wont hurt none of you. I am afrade when tha start down the River they will do damage. I am in hops they wont get out as fur as your house. I was very sory to here of Mises Harrell's Death tho I here of many evry day. I would be glad for this war to come to a close so we could come home to our familys one more time. I think we would do more good at home than we are doing here for the prospect is bad for us to gane our indepence at this time. if they whip us at Corinth we are gone, for they have whipt us at number 10 [Island Number 10]. Rebeca i want to see you and the children the worst I ever have since I have bin out in the survice. I think I will be at home after a while. Mary you and Cornelius must be good children. I want to see you very bad. Mary i think of your pore criple arms very often you must write to me as often

as you can. there is letters comes here by male [mail]. no more. good by,
Wiley White to B. R. B. White and Mary and Cornelius White[8]

L. M. Beckerdite

In this letter of Mississippi militiaman L. M. Beckerdite to his
friends "Mr. Wesley King, lady, and family," Beckerdite mentions the
presence of Union armies in much of the surrounding territory as
well as the shortage of goods, such as imported fabrics, due to the
war. Yet he takes a more optimistic tone, expressing continued confidence in Confederate success.

Waterford [Mississippi] May 17th 1862
My much esteemed friends
It is with great pleasure that I attempt to address you now. I must ask of
you one and all to forgive me for not writing sooner. I have penned several
letters to you, but their are so many reports relative to the yankees having
possession of the Rail Road between here and Jackson Tennessee therefore
I never mailed any of them. I do not know whether this one will get thorough or not, but I shall try it, as I cannot come to see you now nor will I
have the opportunity to till this war is decided should I be so fortunate as
to come out safe I hope to come up and see you all and spend some time
with my acquaintances. I did intend to come up and see you this spring,
but could not as the yankees were advancing so fast upon our State that I
thought it became evry one to stay at home or in his State and be at his
post should he be needed, which now seems to be the case for if the time
ever was that evry man that can leave home and go to the rescue of his
Country it is now. let us be victorious again at Corinth and the northern
army will never make another stand this side of the Ohio river and if our
army should be victorious in Virginia we will soon be done with this war
we must gain our independence if there are men enough in the South to
gain it. We now see what the northern Congress has done. they have passed
the Emancipation bill, "that is to set all the negroes free wherever they
should be victorious."[9] then this is enough to satisfy us that they are intending us all of the harm that they can do us. There is no excitement here
about the result of this war for those that are at home have all the confidence
in our Army at Corinth. There is little skirmishes at that place evry day. Our
forces are strong enough at Richmond, in fact anywhere in Virginia. we
have an army ready and anxious to meet them any day.
I would like to see Thomas and Monroe. I know they have a great many
amusing tales to tell. I would like to hear from them very much. I have
never received but one letter from them in 12 months which I answered

the next day. I do not know whether they got it or not nor do I now know where they are at. I was not in the fight near Corinth. my Regiment was disbanded a few days before. there were near a 1000 men in this county (marshall) that were anxious to go when they heard that the yankees could be got at but our Officers at that place would not suffer any more to come in side of the lines. Therefore we could not go. my company is now at Holly Springs in this County. There are a great number of troops in the State now ready to meet the yankees when needed.

Crops, owing to so much cold rain this Spring, do not look well. there is little or no Cotten planted this year here, but something to eat seems to be the aim of all farmers now. I have many fears for our wheat. Oats are quite sorry. . . . Mrs. King I expect that you often think what the girls do, as all of the calico is out, well, they who have cotten cards and spinning wheels are using them. I wish Mrs. King that you would buy up about two thousand pair and come down. you could make a fortune at it. homespun of any kind is worth 50 ct per yard here and very scarce at that. this war is doing one thing. it is setting a great many girls to work that did not know a spinning wheel when they seen it. Tell William that I received his letter which assured me that I was not forgotten by my old friend, give my kindest wishes to him and Lady and if this letter gets through I will write to him next, my best Respects due to all who may see fit to inquire after me, to Luiser, Rebecca, Charley and Limmy remember me and reserve to yourselves the kindest hopes of your friend. L. M. Beckerdite[10]

Alex Stevenson

South Carolina farmer Alex Stevenson had three sons in the Confederate service. This letter tells something of the concerns of the parents of the soldiers, who kept the home fires burning and wondered how their boys were faring in such far off places as Virginia and Tennessee.

Abbeville C. H.
Southcarolina
July 5th 1863
Dear Son
Those lines wil in form you that we are all Wel at presant hopeing the same may find you injoying the same blesing. I received yours of the 11th ult we were truely glad to here from you and to here that you was Wel I received a letter from Henry yesterday he was wel, But we cannot here anything from Franklin it is over 3 Monthes Since we heard from him he

was better at that time than he had been for sum time past, you wished to know how to direct a Letter to Henry, he was when he wrote last at Petersburg, Va, but was under Marching orders but did not know where they were going, but for me to direct my letters to Petersburg Virginia and the[y] would be forward on to him, if you wish to Write to him direct your letters to, H. W. Stevenson Company A 2nd Regt Rifles S. C. V. Jenkins Brigade, Petersburg Virginia.

there is fine Wheat and oats Crops made here this year and a good prospect for corn, your cousin Robert Yeldell Wrote me a letter wishing your Mother and me to move out there as he had a good place there for us, do you think we had better go or not, the frends here is wel as fare as I know, your grand Mother was in feble helth when I last heard from here but as wel as she is for comen, I Wrote you a letter to Pollard I expect about the time you left there but dont know wether you received it or not, I wish you would Write me the letter of your Company and how to direct a letter to you I would be more perticular in Writing if I was Sure that I directed my letters right my paper and pen is so bad I dont know Wether you can read it or not, we cant write to Franklin as he is on the other side of the yankee lines, Lizza is going to school She sends her love to you, your Mother was very much disapointed She hoped you would have came to se her before this She sends her best love to you, So fare you wel my son

Alex Stevenson[11]

SOPHIA BISSELL WITNESSES THE SACK OF LAWRENCE

The most bitter and implacable part of the war was west of the Mississippi, in Kansas and Missouri, where a guerrilla conflict had been flaring off-and-on since 1856. Bushwhacking, assassination, and massacre were standard tactics for such Confederate raiders as the vicious William C. Quantrill and his brutal henchman William "Bloody Bill" Anderson. Quantrill's band of desperadoes included Frank James. After the gang split up in 1864, Frank's younger brother Jesse joined the band led by Bloody Bill Anderson and rode with it for the rest of the war. After the war he led his own gang.

One of the most infamous of the atrocities perpetrated by the Quantrill gang was the sack and massacre at Lawrence, Kansas, August 21, 1863, in which Frank James took part. Sophia Bissell here gives her eye-witness account of that event. The scenes were obviously still fresh in her mind when she wrote this. Her handwriting occasionally becomes illegible and her narrative is not always coherent, but it does give a vivid impression of the fear felt by helpless civilians in the face of war.

Lawrence Sept 8 1863
Dear Cousin,
We were very happy to receive a letter from you last week and were gratified to think you felt such an interest in our welfare. The twenty-first of August was an awful day in Lawrence and one never to be forgotten by her inhabitants. I presume you have read most of the marked circumstances of the day and as you requested us to write the particulars I will endeavour to give you some idea. you may be aware that ever since this war began, every few weeks, it would be reported about town that Quantrell was coming, that he was so many miles off. Horsemen would come rushing in saying he was coming and sometimes it would be [Confederate general Sterling] Price that was on the way. Well we got accustomed to these reports and did not believe them. Last fall however after our return from the East one night the militia were called out and a great many of the citizens packed their trunks and made various preparations for their coming, but that was a false alarm. Five or six weeks ago Genl Ewing [Union general Thomas Ewing, Jr., commanding the District of the Border] or one of his staff sent word to Mayor Collamore that Quantrell was getting together a force eight hundred strong for some place and we better be on our guard. The mayor sent to Leavenworth for troops and they came, a large number of citizens were placed on guard every night for a week or more. A great deal of sport was made of our "big scare" and of our nervous mayor both here and in Leavenworth, so much in fact that the troops were sent away and the guard given up. Quantrell had his spies here all the time then it seems and knew just what we were doing. we as a family had it a little more to heart than most of the others: a great deal more than ever before. We arranged our money and papers and talked over what we should do, putting said papers in a safe place, there they remained several days unharmed. as we all did, and so it went on until the fright was entirely forgotten. Time passed on until that Friday morning. Quantrell did indeed come to Lawrence.

Henry and Robert our black boy rose early that morning as they were going up to the farm to work. It was between four & five: They were in the yard when Robert looked up on some rising ground just a little ways from us & says who are those! They are "Secesh." They have no flag. Arabella called to me to look out of the window at those men! I ran threw open the blinds & then I saw a large body of horsemen trotting quite briskly along just then they turned a corner coming nearer us and we heard them say. Rush on, rush on for the town, and they did rush on, but did not stop for us at that time we hear pistols firing and looking back of us saw the Horsemen running from house to house & we knew who had come.

[A portion of the letter here is illegible] Then another came & wanted Henry. He went out to him. He wanted money. H gave him five dollars & he left. Then we saw the bands collecting as if to move off & soon they did, passing directly in front of our windows. We could hear them ask from time to time if they should come up. Something would be said & they would pass on we began to take long breaths and think we were going to escape. when looking towards town we saw five coming rushing & yelling directly for us. Then we knew our time had come. They came on horseback right up to the front door. The leader forcing his horse up on to the Piazza. Matches, matches said one [illegible] up stairs. the others ransacking the house up stairs & down. The leader called for the man of the house. Henry went out to him. Your name! Bissell! You from New York! So said I, from Vt. worse yet. Worse yet. Our trunks we had got into the yard although they forbid our doing it. Then they began breaking them open, throwing them into the air & letting them come down & stomping on them till they did come open. I ran to the leader & begged him to spare the house, pleading and telling him we were quiet peaceable people! will you not spare the house? said I. it is now on fire. Oh then I cant save it

so we took in a faint sense of what it was to be surrounded by guerillas we immediately buried our papers & money excepting a little which we left and to appease them put our silver in the [illegible] & disposed of our watches and jewelry & waited for them to come. And oh to hear the yells & hear the firing & to see the people running black & white old and young and the Fiends charging after them firing as fast as they possibly could. Oh it was perfectly awful! The only wonder is there were no more killed. The last ones that came to us drove us to the back door, two men, asked for the man of the house, Henry went to the door, say they your name! Bissell! Do you belong to Mr. Lawrence? No Sir. If you had told me you did I would have shot you dead. Your money. Henry handed them ten dollars. They turned towards the barn. Where are your horses. They looked in and saw the one (we had given the black boy a pistol & sent him to the country with two other horses. He was chased & fired upon was obliged to let one go but escaped with the other) then said they take everything out of the house! You are not going to burn us are you! Yes we are. They then left! we began in good earnest to take the things and another came & wanted water & said we were not agoing to be burned. we took a little courage then & stopped to look towards town. we could see Moss St. all in flames & the houses of our friends and acquaintants here & there all in a blaze. All the houses of the first settlers were burned & of [illegible]. The leader relented again ordered them all on their horses & be off. They tipped their hats and bade us good morning. we returned the salutation, trying all the time they were here not to irritate them at all. We rushing into the house put out the fire down stairs & carried water up stairs time & time again, time to throw the things out of the windows nearly suffocated & left to burn. we found the barn all on fire, got the carriage & harness out & sat down on the Piazza in despair. not saying a word or shedding a tear. Just then a man from Franklin rushed into the house up the stairs by a good deal of exertion put out the fire. So we have a house to live in. Henry was not seriously injured. Mother had been sick all the week, sat up day before for the first time but she worked like a trojan. Mother had lost a thousand dollars by the raid. Arabella the next worse. They taking a good many things from her trunks, among other things her last silk dress. Henry next & I least. I cannot begin to tell you all that was said and done. Oh we faired so much better than a great many others. Some had their houses and stores burned & were killed leaving their poor wives widows & penniless. [illegible] thought there were between seventy and eighty widows & between two & three hundred made orphans that terrible day. Nearly every house has a story to tell, although some were not molested in the least. we have packed a trunk of linen which I think we shall send to you tomorrow for safe keeping. we do not feel secure yet. May God in his mercy spare us from again being invaded is the constant prayer that ascends from this poor af-flicted people. . . . [It is] very painful to think over & especially to write what occured that dreadful day. . . . Yours affectionately

Sophia L. Bissell[12]

RICHARD E. CARTER REFLECTS ON THE LOT OF THE SOLDIER

Sgt. Richard E. Carter of the Fifth Wisconsin was obviously in a waggish and facetious mood when he wrote this letter to his married sister comparing the hard lot of soldiers in the field with the comforts of civilian life back home.

Camp No. 21 in the field Va.
June 19th or 20th 1862
My Dear Sister,
Behold a finely tinted sheet of note paper upon which is very fine writing written in a very fine hand by a very fine young man indicted in a very fine country under very fine circumstances. I wonder if that old man of yours isn't now in a raging fit of jealousy. I wonder if his dark eyes aint shooting forth a strange light as you are reading this. Let me imagine—You are sitting

down to tea as he hands you this. Your position is immediately opposite his at table. As you open this, the strange paper, the fine writing, the look on your face all tends to perplex him. His features assume something of the same grotesque appearance it used to assume when Hattie didn't do as he wanted her to. The appearance at the tea table will compel an insidious comparison. You have on your table for instance some nice bread, clean nice looking butter, cheese cake puff or otherwise, tort—those nice little pillows that Bill and I couldn't eat because we did not like them—tea, cream or new milk, sugar it may be some garden stuff onions Lettuce, cucumbers &c. All having a cleanly appearance. At the table commencing with yourself sits Byron to your left, next Kate, next Miss Skishasky, Miss Powers, then comes the incorrigible, next George, next Sammy, all with an air of content, no fear of having to hurry, you read this to yourself, grin at the absurdities, laugh at the oddities, thinking meanwhile that Dick had forgotten to play fool anyway. Well change the scene. About three quarters of a mile from a stream running through a tremendous flat that is rightly named a swamp although the stream is promoted beyond its qualifications when it is dignified by the name of River. It is however called the Chickahominey. I say about ¾ of a mile from its banks encamped in the edge of a piece of timber it being on the edge of another swamp lies a Regiment honored by the name of the 5th Wis. About 50 yards to the rear of the color line are the Line officers' kennels about 20 steps to their rear are the tents of the Field & Staff. Here you will first discover the undersigned. The glorious old Sol [i.e., the sun] is drawing near the horizon shedding his lustrous rays alike on the evil and the good. A smooth-faced rosy cheeked prepossessing youth steps around & says—supper's ready—allow me to conduct you to the table. hush it isn't dirty, its our mess chest with the lid thrown back & taps fitting in to the body that it may serve as a table. This was done by the rosy cheeked youth, Henry Watty, ladies & gents, a Pennsylvanian by birth & a good young man. He belongs to the mess. I tell you we have no table cloth you must be content with the bare boards. Let me commence. At the corner left of the lock, sits Dr. Wilber on a Camp stool, the personification of good nature. on his left sits Dr. Crane, . . . he sits on a bag, sometimes containing corn, some times empty. on his left sits John G. he sits on a chair. on his left sits Lt. Langridge on a Cartridge box. on his left sits_____the Qr.Mr. [Quartermaster] Sergt. [i.e., the writer] on a large wooden pail open top up the picture of despair. you know him. on his left sits Lt Ordway. . . . on a cracker box on his left sits Capt. Emerson. he sits on his calves usually on his left sits Lt. Cook on a cracker box. on his left sits Serg. Cole on a box he always carries with him. on his left—I guess I am around. How large—It is a little over 3 feet long by two feet wide, makes when open about 4 feet by 3. Crowded? not at all. Then the table. Tin plates before every man, earthen cups & saucers before about half, tin cups before the rest, knives &

forks to each two silver forks, one to each Dr. Usual fare. For breakfast Coffee—would & could conveniently carry a wedge—sugar a good article in a tin dido. Large table spoons. Hard crackers, ("boiled horse") salt beef. Dinner, Boiled horse, Hard crackers & coffee. Supper. Hard Crackers. Boiled horse & coffee. Luxuries—tonight for instance. Hard crackers. Pickled tongue. Butter—you know how you used to fix for our buck wheat cakes, last winter, only yours wasn't streaked enough, thus you want to put it in your grease pan that you use for frying cakes—that's it. then two bottles of Tomato catsup—one bottle of pepper sauce, one bottle of London Club sauce, a dish of dried apples—oh its huge—luxurious—Explanation: Sutler's just come. Dr. Crane is our caterer for this moth & he's something of an epicure. Well we are seated at table now for something to eat. Every man for himself. See how anxious every one is. It's about the time firing usually commences at evening. You must not think the anxiety is caused by desire for fight, not at all. It is for fear—fear he'll lose his supper. Three minutes all are through, save the two Doctors & clark. they never get excited, not at all. Then commences the second table. Yes we keep a small hotel. Well how does the thing compare. Tomorrow we have salt mackerel—if we're here—Hard crackers—you know what they are—That's a fair description. For a day or two past we have had potatos. They are delicacies.[13]

MICHAEL CUNNINGHAM LOOKS AT THE CHANGES THE WAR HAS BROUGHT

In these letters, Cunningham laments the cost and hardship of war as well as its destructiveness to civilians in the areas where it is waged. Yet he remains convinced that the Union cause is right and is worth the cost of the war.

Memphis Tenn Oct 3 1863
I hope and trust that I may be permitted to go back home when this cruel war is ended and live in a land of peace It is hard to look at the country through which we have passed this spring and summer five years ago it was the pride of America and was the homes of her most wealthy sons and daughters and now those homes are heaps of mouldering ruins and the owners of them fill an unknown grave I hope and pray that the day be not far distant when our glorious old flag shall wave free to the breese in every city town and hamlet in the United States. And the din and tumult of war be heard no more in our broad land. . . . We've had a hard time since we

have been here no tents and no blankets to cover us and its rained very hard and is very cold and nothing to eat except hard tack I would sooner eat sawdust if it was salted than to eat them I tell you a soldiers life is a hard one just now But there are some pleasant spots in it when we look at the mighty stake that we are fighting for the preservation of the union it nerves us on and gives us new courage but it has cost the lives a great many brave men and is likely to cost a great many more.

Glendale Miss Oct 9 1863
My Dear . . .
I compare the past with the present and it almost makes me shudder to see the change that a few years have made in this Nation. Three years ago we was the most prosperous nation on the globe all nations looked up to us and now we are fighting and killing each other as fast as we can and the other Nations laugh at us for doing it.[14]

NOTES

1. Laura Beecher Comer Papers, Southern Historical Collection, University of North Carolina, Chapel Hill.

2. Emilie Quiner Papers, State Historical Society of Wisconsin, Madison.

3. Eliza Wilcox Graves Papers, State Historical Society of Wisconsin, Madison.

4. Olivia A. Brown Papers, State Historical Society of Wisconsin, Madison.

5. William K. Barney Papers and John J. Barney Papers, State Historical Society of Wisconsin, Madison.

6. Miscellaneous Confederate Letters, State Historical Society of Wisconsin, Madison.

7. Miscellaneous Confederate Letters, State Historical Society of Wisconsin, Madison.

8. Miscellaneous Confederate Letters, State Historical Society of Wisconsin, Madison.

9. This may be a reference to Lincoln's April 10, 1862, approval of a joint resolution of Congress calling upon the states voluntarily to enact programs of gradual emancipation. If so, Beckerdite has badly misconstrued it.

10. Miscellaneous Confederate Letters, State Historical Society of Wisconsin, Madison.

11. Miscellaneous Confederate Letters, State Historical Society of Wisconsin, Madison.

12. Henry Asbury Papers, Chicago Historical Society.

13. Richard E. Carter Papers, State Historical Society of Wisconsin, Madison.

14. Michael Cunningham Letters, State Historical Society of Wisconsin, Madison.

Chapter 6

The War's Concluding Phases Bring Triumph and Sorrow

J. N. DeFOREST AND EDWARD JENNER WARREN TAKE CARE OF BUSINESS, NORTH AND SOUTH

It is easy to forget that amid the suffering of the soldiers, the destruction of war, and the anxious waiting of the soldiers' families back home, America was also a nation of thriving business during the war years, particularly in the North. In the South, business faced the peculiar problem of trying to function in a society that was collapsing. These letters from two businessmen, J. N. DeForest in the North and Edward Jenner Warren in the South, each writing to friends in his own part of the country, give a glimpse of what was on the mind of that sector of society during the Civil War. Their concerns range from taxes, to investments, to politics, to relatives in the army. The bounties to which DeForest refers are enlistment bonuses aimed at recruiting troops. The conscription of which Warren speaks is the ubiquitous Confederate draft, theoretically universal for all males ages 18 to 45.

J. N. DeForest

Windsor [postmarked Madison, Wis.] Feby 14 1864
Dear Cousin [Mrs. J. H. Delavan, Patterson, Putnam Co., NY]

Yours of 3 inst is at hand and I reply though I shall have to retain this letter and mail it at Madison as I have no govt stamp to put on note. I am making an effort to effect a compromise with the party that is holding our Rail Road from being completed and spend about half of my time in Madison trying to obtain relief by the Legislature if I fail in what I am trying to bring round.

I enclose you my note drawn at one day after date payable with interest for one hundred & thirty five dollars bearing interest for 3 years on Mr. Estabrooks Mortgage to Feby 1st 1864. I also enclose a receipt for you to sign and return to me for him. Mr. Estabrooks thinks he will be able to pay one half of the mortgage another year and perhaps the whole. Still he would be glad to keep the money if you was willing to let it all remain at 7 pr ct interest and I promised to ask you when I next wrote. Of course he will expect to pay interst promptly every year.

We have letters from both the boys in the army. Both are well Newton is anxious to engage in growing cotton upon some confiscated plantation but the war department will not acept his resignation. I think it probable both will go to Mobile when it is decided to attack that place. The liberal bounty offered by Govt and our local bounties are filling our quota rapidly with volunteers. The present call filled will give us an army that ought to make short work of it when the next campaign opens. The south already begin to feel very anxious to be subjugated or rather as John Van Buren expresses it they want Jeff Davis subjugated and the South made free. In view of the waning hopes of the south it was remarked that it was strange that Jeff Davis & his friends did not sue for peace. "I will tell you why they dont," said a person. "God Almighty wont let them until slavery has been fully abolished and these men have wrought out there own destruction."

Our cold weather has entirely subsided and we are having delightful winter weather with 3 feet of snow on a level. All well and desire remembrance to all the friends.

Very Truly Yours

J. N. DeForest[1]

Edward Jenner Warren

Greenville [North Carolina]

Sept 9, 1864

Friend Willard:

I got home on Thursday after I left you, & now my health is pretty well re-established. . . .

I am glad to inform you that the collection of the taxes has been suspended in Beaufort until 30 days after the meeting of Congress. I think we will get up such a memorial to Congress as will induce that patriotic & independent body to remit them altogether.

What say you to the Chicago nominations & platform [the 1864 Democratic party convention]? I confess I see no prospect of peace in it. I regard it as a most conclusive proof that the North will never consent to a separation. I believe too that one single fact, not to speak of any others, will insure the defeat of this movement at the North—the fact that the platform recognizes no peace men, no supporters of the constitution, no enemies of Lincoln & despotism outside of "the Democratic party." There are hundreds of thousands of good men at the North who will not stand this. But time will soon put an end to all speculation on this subject.

What do you think of my being a candidate for speaker of the Senate? Turn this thing over in your mind & will talk about it when you come down.

Mrs. W. says she would like to have about 30 yards of shirting, say a bolt. I want you to understand that when you send it you are to send your bill. I do not intend to be entirely overwhelmed by obligations.

Truly yours

E. J. Warren

Greenville

Oct. 25, 1864

Friend Willard:

Yours of the 15th came today—only nine days from Hillsboro. It is a wonder to me that I got it at all, as I believe my correspondence is now pretty thoroughly [illegible] by the rascally postmasters.

I have been expecting you here for some days, & am surprised that you say nothing about coming. I shall continue to look for you. This will be my only chance of seeing you before the legislature meets. That will be on the 3d Monday & I have courts both the 1st & 2nd weeks.

Some of my friends have led me to think of the Speakership. I do not think it is likely I shall be a candidate—certainly not unless my election is certain. About this I can form no opinion until I get to Raleigh. . . . With my views about this war & its probable termination, I should hate very much to step into Tanner's shoes. In my estimation the honor would be far too dearly bought.

I see no hope of peace & am almost sick of speculating about it. I think it is almost certain Lincoln will be re-elected, & that will prolong the war indefinitely. It is hardly worth while to consider what will or can be done in the event of his defeat.

I was in Washington [North Carolina] the 3d week in Septr. Whitehurst was not there, having gone to Columbia, as I understood. I hope you have seen him & given him such authority & instructions as you desired. I un-

Peachtree Street, Atlanta, Georgia, 1864. National Archives.

derstand your home has been stripped of the sash & blinds by the military for hospital use. It is in such conditions that I hardly think you will be able to induce any body to occupy it.

We have rec'd the cloth.

Truly yours

E. J. Warren

Raleigh Dec 21/64

Friend Willard:

I have your letter of yesterday.

The Revenue bill has passed & it is too late to act upon your suggestions.

Your case is different from that of farmers. They pay a tithe & you do not. Still the tax is very heavy upon you. I sent you the bill as soon as it was printed & hoped to hear from you before.

I shall go directly home from here. I must do so to make arrangements for next year.

Truly yours

E. J. Warren

Greenville

Dec 29/64

Friend Willard:

Yours of the 26th came today.

You can qualify at any time after the clerk receives the certificate of your appointment, but will probably not be exempted from conscription until you qualify.

It will not be possible for me to leave home before I go to Raleigh again. I have not yet got any pork for next year, & fear I shall have a difficulty about getting it. I want to go down into Beaufort & Hyde, but see very little prospect of finding any sort of comestibles. I can get what I want there.

Truly yours

E. J. Warren

Raleigh Jany 18, 1865

Friend Willard:

I have just got your letter of the 17th, & am sorry it is out of my power to go to Hillsboro now. I am laid up with rheumatism today—unable to get about.

Please let me know what you can do for me by way of a loan for a short time. I think I can invest a considerable amount to advantage. Please sent me what you can conveniently spare & are willing to lend by express, & let me know at what time you will want it returned. I should be glad to have a long & confidential talk with you.

There is another thing I want you to do for me. I have a brother in Columbia as a prisoner of war. His name is John W. Warren & he is a Lieutenant in Co. "C" 1st Wisconsin Cavalry. He writes me on the 18th Dec & I have rec'd his letter since I came here. This is the first intimation I have had that I had any brother in that service.

He says nothing about his condition or how he is faring. But I wish you to write to some friend of yours in Columbia to see him & supply him with whatever he wants for his comfort. I know nobody there, & perhaps could accomplish nothing if I did. Can you tell me how to communicate. I want to know all about him, & if necessary, I will go & see him.

All this is, of course, confidential.

Truly yours

E. J. Warren

Raleigh Jany 26/65

Friend Willard:

I have just learned from S. Brown that he can invest in 50 or 100 bales [of cotton] at $3.25 provided he can have the money immediately.

Please let me know at once whether you wish to go into it. I wish I had known this when you were here.

Truly yours

E. J. Warren

Raleigh Feby 5, 1865
Friend Willard:

I have determined not to keep more than one half of the money I borrowed. I do not know whether I shall be able to invest all the balance advantageously or not, but think I can. I will be able to tell better when I get home. I leave $2,500 in the hands of Tucker for you. As to the investments of which you speak in the West, I cannot form any definite judgment, but I have an idea that such investments are among the best you can make.

I have not time nor means here to investigate the question you put about taxes, but will do so as soon as I get home. I leave here on Tuesday.

Please let me know how soon you will want the money.

Truly yours

E. J. Warren

Greenville
Feby 18, 1865
Friend Willard:

. . . I am sorry your health did not permit you to go to Columbia, both on your account & my own. I fear the prisoners have been moved from there to Salisbury, & that is almost certain death. I sent my brother before I left Raleigh, two flannel shirts, a pair of pants, a buffalo robe (I could get no blanket) & some books. These were all the articles I could get. If you know anything of the removal of the prisoners & their present place of confinement, please let me know. . . .

Truly yours

E. J. Warren

Greenville, Mar 5, 1865
Friend Willard:

I have yours of the 25th Feby. I had rec'd your balance sheet &c. It shows well & I sincerely hope it may not all slip through your fingers. I am much inclined to think now, as I thought a long time ago, that it would have been a good plan for you to invest in specie, & it is my opinion that you had better sell your spring cotton for specie. In this I may be mistaken & undoubtedly your judgment in such matters is better than mine. I will only make this further remark—that, in case of enemy raids, you can take care of your specie more easily than you can of your cotton.

In the raid here we were not troubled at all—in fact no private citizen was, except that they took all the good horses they could find. I was at my house & remained there. No one set foot on the premises. The business of the raiders was to capture a company below here (Capt. Gray's) & to destroy the commissary stores in town. they had strict orders not to enter private houses, & for allowing their men to violate these in some instances along the route the officers were imprisoned after their return to Newbern. On the whole the people here have every reason to be thankful that they got off so well. Of course you have heard that the distinguished Maj. Denilbe was captured.

My brother was in Raleigh the other day on his way to Wilmington to be exchanged. He wrote me from that place where he says he found some of my friends & was kindly treated by them. I had sent him before I left Raleigh, directed as he instructed me, a buffalo robe (I could get no blanket) two flannel shirts, a pair of pants & some books. He did not get a single one of the articles. This is Confederate honesty!

I hope you suffered no serious loss at Columbia. Sherman seems to have turned towards Cheraw & Fayetteville, as I always thought he would. If his plans do not fail there will be an advance from Wilmington & Newbern to cooperate with him. In fact there is a rumor here that [Union general John M.] Schofield is now in Fayetteville. I hear also that your military authorities do not expect to make a stand at Goldsboro. I hope & believe we shall not be troubled here, but if all this takes place, we shall be virtually in the enemy's lines & shall be cut off from all communication with the interior.

Do you notice that Col. Hoke of Charlotte does not advise the people to insult the Yankees & spit in their faces as we of the East were expected to do two or three years ago? I do not object to some people understanding what war is.

I shall be glad to see you. You need have no fear for your safety here.
Truly yours
E. J. Warren.[2]

FRANK AND NAPOLEON BARTLETT SEE LIFE AND DEATH, NORTH AND SOUTH

Frank and Napoleon "Poly" Bartlett were two brothers from a farm near Morris, Illinois. Poly joined the army while Frank, the younger, stayed and worked as a hired hand on a farm not far from that of their parents. The letters they exchanged, along with one to Napoleon from his mother and one from his company commander, show something of the mind of the North as the war passed its mid-point and victory seemed to be in view. Despite the improving outlook, much suffering and loss still lay ahead.

Steamboats at the levee at Vicksburg, Mississippi. Library of Congress.

Vicksburg May 24th [1864]
Brother Franky
I received your good letter of the 17th inst. I was very glad to get a letter from you. But you must write a longer one next time. I am well now and enjoying myself here in camp near vicksburg. I have been out on a long march of 18 days. your letter came here very quick it is the latest one I have by 10 days. I got a lot of letters when I got in from the march. And a newspaper. Franky you must send me a paper when you get one with a good story in it. This morning they put me on as cook for the mess for one week and longer if I wish there are 13 men in my mess. Do you remember G. Brennan Mrs. tremains husband. he is in my mess. I was just giving out my dinner when the Capt brought your letter to me. I tell you what it is franky you laugh if you were to see how we live for breakfast we have coffee & hardtack for Dinner we sometimes have Beans & sometimes Peas & hardtack. for supper we have coffee & meat with the hardtack. But I am getting fat all of the time but the hotest of the weather has not come yet by a great ways. I would like to have all of you here for a week or so to see how camp life goes. Every morning & night there is a gun fired at sunrise & sunset. It is one of the 13 inch siege guns which has a but as large around as a

barrel. You must know it makes considerable noise. I had to smile while reading about your fracas with the jackson Boy. You must keep out of all quarrels & let such boys entirely alone. You say they had a large war meeting in town & are recruiting Can you tell me who is getting up a company in Morris. I have had 2 letters from Johnny since I came down here. It will be 2 months since I enlisted but it seems as though it had been 6. but time flies faster now. Franky you must take more pains with your spelling than you do. practice writing all that you can. If you do hate to take up the hour or so which you would spend in fishing you never will be sorry for it. Tell johnny that I dont know of any one who wants a good horse unless it is a general & he would like to get a charger like johnys colt because he could see the position of the enemy so well. I was sory to hear of Old Mrs Waters death. I would like to get my photograph to send home but I lent my last dollar to Lieut. hichcock. Hick is sick now in the hospital. You must write soon.

Poly [Napoleon]

Morris [IL] June 6th [1864]
Brother Poly
I received your good letter of the 24th inst. [This is a mistake; Frank means May 24, "24th ultimo," not June 24, "24th instant."] I was very glad to get a letter from you. I wrote as long a letter as I could I had a little time to spare and so I thought I would write as long one as I could we are all well I must tell you that uncle Jasper folks have been down. Johny come down after me the same night that they came and Mr. Perry let me go home with him Johny had his colt down with him and I rode part of the way while we wer going home Johny was all the time braging about [how] large roy was and that he could take me in one hand and when we got home the first thing in the morning they wanted to know which was the stoutest and tried to throw me down but I downed him evry time and he got mad and bawled and went off and hid in current bushes and stayed there a long time I went to the panaramy [panorama—a show] the other night. I tell you it was a sight. the other day while I was looking up to the tent where the panaramy was the first thing I saw was James barr come tumbling out of tent and roll over about half a dozen times clear in to the midle of the street and a little while after wards I herd what was the mater mils and Barr wer both as drunk as they could bee when they come along the street went in when mils grabed up a drum and lifted up the sticks as if he was a going to bust it the Show man was in to carys Saloon then the little boy run in and told his father and he run in and was a going to lick mils when barr interfeared and the Show man nocked him heels over head in to the street then enock hopkins come and pushed mils and barr in to cays saloon he has put 4 men in to jail.
I forgot to tell you who was getting up a company. hanner has ben trying

to get a company after he had got up enough he started off and after a while back come near all his company boys not any larger than I bee and all that had places before they went they all lost them that boy in to Johnson went and they would not take him and now he is running around with no place. hanner tried to get Leroy and them to enlist and leroy has been talking all the time about it. I have just come down this morning and I have just got swept out.

I will be darned if I can think of anny more.

Franky

Vicksburg June 28th 1864
Brother Frankie

. . . Your letters Frankie are quite interesting as they come from a place I know so well. But if they came from any place that I did not know they would not be as much so. . . .

Poly

Vicksburg June 28th 1864
Brother Frankie

. . . They dont drive teams here as they do up north. The country is so rough that a lumber wagon such as they use up north would not take one load to market. The 2 horse wagons have springs like Mr. Briants. But they Drive 6 mules most generaly in fact about all the teams are 6 mules & they dont drive them with 2 lines to a team as they would in Morris but they drive them all with one line. The driver rides the near mule of the hind team which he calls the wheelers and he has a large line that goes through rings in the harness of the near mule of the second team which he calls the swings because they are on the end of the tongue and do the turning. the line goes to the bit of the near mule in the lead team when he wants them to haw he pulls the line if he wants them to turn to the right he jerks the line & says gee. It is considerable work to drive one of these teams & a man has to tend to his business. . . .

Poly

Rose Hill, July 31st 1864
Poly
My Dear Son & Soldier Boy

It has been a week & three days since we received any tidings from you. It seems a month. What can be the matter? I hope nothing serious. Your letters may have miscarried. I have not written you for a long time I have been very unwell, kep my bed a week. The babe has been sick also, but we are quite well at present. I have a large stout Irish girl but cannot tell how long she will stay I am going to keep a girl here after the work is altogether to hard for me.

Now I shall have more time to read & write I am owing a number of letters I must write two or three today if possible Pa & Johnie have got the timothy about half bound it is just about as it was last year. Pa cut Jack Willsey's oats it took him just a week fifty acres at one dollar & a half an acre & find himself & team we are out of corn for the horses & they begin to show it but there is a fair prospect of more soon our corn never looked much better at this time of the year. Our potatoes look fine & buckwheat of which we have eight acres if it amounts to anything we shall have plenty. Now for news items.

First, Mrs. Barr has a little boy three weeks old. Billy Filkins was drafted & got exempt on account of his big toe that he got at Uncle Rufus by cutting it with the axe. There will be a draft here soon if they do not volenteer. Here comes Frankie he is such a good boy. we miss him very much; he comes home once in two weeks. Mr Perrys people think that Frankie is about perfect he tells me that he is going to begin school soon. You know where Uncle Theodore lived last winter, well the lower part of that house is fited up in a school room & Mr. Borce & a young Lady whom he employs as assistant teaches. The school has a good reputation. . . . Pa Arabelle & Jessie have gone to town to church Johnie & Frankie have gone to Unckle Rufus & the girl has gone home & so you see that I am here alone with the little ones Leroy Josie bob & baby Roy & Josie are reading newspaper The baby asleep & bob where do you think he is? under my hoops asleep the flies plague him so & it lightens & thunders & rains just about as hard as I want to see it & looks as though it would rain all day I forgot to tell you how the sugar cane looked it is fine & lots of it pa had some seed sent to him from the Pattent Office & it looks very nice. . . . The prospect is now that we shall have plenty of pancakes & lasses. Frank Burgess is discharged from the army his time is out a great many are returning. Frank told me that he did not like it well enough to enlist again he is as tough as a pine knot Charles saw Charlotte in Chicago last week one day she said that she had just received a letter from you she is coming out soon O Charlotte is a very good girl but well you know just how it is with them, but she is a queene by the side of the one I have at present she will lie faster than a horse can run & steal anything she wants but she is a good girl to work. we pay two dollars a week I dont mean to touch the work the girls help night & morning. Poly I suppose you were in real earnest about the black girl you had found, well I dont care how much you love them if it is at distance I should hope that you would be able to find girls of your own color to associate with I would like to get a good black girl to work for me one that understood cooking & washing & ironing. There must be some good girls down there; send one along by some of the boys. we have sold

14 pigs at two & two & a half dollars apiece. Johnie goes to haul oats for Jack Willsey to morrow & will haul three days & then he is to haul hay to Morris for stage two dollars ½ a ton; Pa got Johnie a new pair of boots four dollars. send any thing Poly in the shape of clothing it can not come amiss. Mr. Turner preaches here this afternoon. Try & get a position as clerk if you can you will not be so much exposed to danger. send your photograph my child. they say Poly looks like his mother. I can see a resemblance in our photographs. Well good bye I hope you are well

Mother

Morganzias Bend [Louisiana] Aug 24 [1864]

Brother Frankie

It is now a long time since I got your letter but I have not had a chance to answer it until now. But then I guess you can stand it to wait a while any way. I got a letter from Johny a little while ago which I have not answered yet. I wrote to Johny a few days ago though. Johny wants me to send him some soldier clothes but I dont think that I can this fall. next spring I culd send any amount I suppose. But winter is coming on & we want all the clothes we have got & can get. I think that he said you were going to commence going to school in town soon. Well then I supose you will have a bully time this winter wont you. Getting into little sham fights every day. But I guess there are a few boys down town yet that can whip you yet if you do feel pretty big. Johny says he is going to ride his colt down and back every day. How does Johny's colt look any way has he changed any since I saw him. I am sorry to think that all the boys that write to me say our folks have let the horses get so poor. Jackson says that he never saw Pa's horses look as bad as they do now. but the corn is getting hard enough to feed now isn't it. Every[thing] is very Dear [i.e., expensive] now I suppose. How is it now is everything getting higher all the time or have they got to a stand still. You need not send me any more store gum nor Buffalo hide. I have got a chew of prairie gum in my mouth now & Johny & roy are going to send me some. We are now camped on the bank between the levee & river. You may not know what a levee is. Well the folks have built a long turnpike from 6 to 10 feet high along the river to keep the water from flowing over their farm in high water & they call this a levee. We use the river water altogether. bring it up at night and let it settle. The Miss[issipi] River is not like the river by Morris [the Illinois River] clear and fine but is very roily all the year round. The regiment left here this morning on a scout down the river & are going to be gone some 6 or 7 days I suppose. I am pretty well south now & when I come to look at the map only about 200 miles from N. orleans. The weather is not so very warm here. the nights are quite cool one or 2 blankets over me is not 2 much. I got a bully lot of stuff from home when Col. Nomes came back. My onions will be the best thing of the eatibles. We are in a bully place for fishing can have fresh fish when we feel like it. I have not eaten any meat for 3 months and I dont care for any feel tip top this morning.

Poly

White River Ark Sept 11th/64

Mr. and Mrs. Bartlett

I am sorry that I am under the necessity of writing to you the fate of your Son Napoleon. He has been sick for some time. We left him at Vicksburg when we left there. He got better and came to us at Morganzia Bend La. and came from there to this place with us. He seamed to think that he was getting better but has not done any duty lately. He has been around camp all the time and last night he went with some of the rest of the Brig[ade] to the River and got a canteen of water. he said that he felt better than he had for some time but he was taken worse this morning about four oclock and died very sudden. It caused a great feeling in the Company as he had become a favorite with all that knew him. He was well liked by all. We have just returned from barring [burying] him the Company all turned out and barred him with all the honors of a good soldier. His things I will send home if I can.

Yours with much Respect

Lt. H. F. Hitchcock[3]

GEORGE PHIFER ERWIN SOLDIERS ON THROUGH GOOD TIMES AND BAD

The letters of Confederate soldier George Phifer Erwin to his family back home in North Carolina deal with the latter part of the war from a Southern perspective. Southerners remained remarkably optimistic, choosing to focus on such of the war news as seemed more encouraging and putting the best face on the rest. "Providence," to which Erwin refers, is an eighteenth- and nineteenth-century expression for God, intervening actively in human affairs. Such belief was all but universal among Americans of the Civil War generation, both North and South. As Erwin expresses, many Southerners believed that though their cause was right and just, God was punishing their various sins by allowing the wicked Yankees to wage war against them so long. The Northern election of which he speaks is the 1864 presidential election, pitting Republican Abraham Lincoln, running on a hybrid "Union Party" ticket that tried to reach out to Union-loyal Democrats, against Democratic candidate George B. McClellan, an unsuccessful general who promised that he would pursue the war to final victory, despite the fact that the Democratic party platform declared the war a failure that should be terminated immediately, without victory.

Finally, Erwin's letters reveal regional differences within the South and an amazing amount of merry-making and good eating even in the last desperate winter of the war. Much depended on where in the South one happened to find oneself.

Hd. Qrs. 60th N.C. Regiment
Dalton Apl. 29th 1864
My dear Father,
. . . It begins to feel like Spring—warm, balmy days, the woods becoming rapidly clothed with green and birds singing joyously. Just such weather as will prepare the roads for active operations. They must soon commence, and I tremble when I think of the mighty results depending upon the hazard of two great battles now imminent. Should a kind Providence favor us a little further as has been the case in the opening of the Spring, we may look hopefully forward and see Peace not far distant. But if it is necessary. That our beloved South should be still more severely chastised, we can only bow the head and receive inflinchingly and with awe, the merited punishment of our shortcomings. I trust that, before the present year is closed that we all may be permitted to return to our several homes with the assurance that bright Peace will shelter our loved land and horrid devastating war will only be remembered among things that are bygones. Still we should not build our hopes too high, lest we suffer by their fall. Everything is so uncertain. We cannot at all times read aright the dispensations of Providence, nor understand the various fortunes of war—why we gain a victory here, lose a battle there. To human eyes it does seem as if victory was our due now. The chances are for us, our generals skilful, our soldiers enthusiastic, our numbers nearly equal to that of the enemy, but it is a worn out theme, speculating upon the probable course of events. . . .

Madison Ga
July 1st 1864
My dear Sister,
Yesterday morning, the newspapers brought the unexpected and distressing intelligence that a party of raiding tories [i.e., Southern Unionists] was in possession of your & my home, that the bank had been robbed and that a train of cars had been burned, only a very unsatisfactory telegram. And

judging from the amount of plundering robbing & burning usual in such cases my imagination can somewhat anticipate the terrible circumstances in which you were placed, the indignities heaped upon our citizens who have not before felt the horrors of war. I am in a terrible state of suspence. These miserable tories, home yankees, are to be more feared, when they get possession of a country, than the Yankees themselves. The paper also stated that an ample force had been sent up to rout them. This is the only thing that, in any degree, relieves my mind. I know they, even if they remain only a few days, will do immense damage to our homes and citizens generally, and if allowed to remain will utterly ruin the country. I hope to heaven they may be captured and meet the reward their merits so richly deserve.

I shall be miserable till I hear and I know you will inform me as soon as you are able. My greatest fear is that their anger will be directed against Father on account of removing the money from the Bank, and reek their vengeance upon him and family. It makes my heart ache to think of the possibility of your being turned out from your home and witnessing its destruction, though thousands of our true southern men & women have suffered the same fate. And knowing that we suffer for our beloved and harassed country will nerve us to bear privations for her sake.

Tuscumbia Ala
Nov 5th 1864
My dear Sister,
The Yankee election will be over before this reaches you. I hope that, whomever is elected, this campaign [i.e., current military operations] will teach him the folly of prosecuting the war any longer. I have hardly a preference for the Candidates, don't care much one way or the other, but lean a little towards Lincoln, believe he is the less of two evils, decidedly the biggest fool, which will be to our advantage. However I believe that Providence will overrule it to our advantage and wait with patience for the final result.

In Camp near Columbus Miss
Jan 7th 1865
My dear Sister,
I am boarding with several other officers, with an old North Carolina lady Mrs. Willis who was a Miss Wood & is an aunt of Dr. Tate's first wife. She is one of the kindest old ladies I ever saw and has taken a great fancy to me. We get along admirably together. While I feel very sensibly the loss of a Christmas frolic in the old North State you must not think that I am sitting quietly & continually moping about it. On the contrary we had a gay time out here during the Christmas holidays. At this time before the war, it seems to have been almost a part of the religion of the people in this

neighborhood each one to give a party. Of course latterly it has been partly discontinued and only those who are best able to afford it, adhere to old customs. There were only six in the neighborhood this winter. The old lady as we call her, Mrs. Willis, gave the most magnificent one & the best of it, it was given especially to us her boarders. There were about one hundred present and we had a glorious time. Whiskey was so scarce that nobody could get tight [i.e., drunk] & everything passed off quietly. I wish you could have seen the table. It did not present much idea of starvation & then I wish you could have seen how the substantials disappeared before the onslaught of the fair sex. We did not have any of your city belles who cannot bear anything more substantial than [illegible]. I verily believe they, and of them, could eat there half a pound of meat as well as any soldier in the Confederate Army. Our bill of fare was, one roast pig, one roast shoat, one roast kid, three or four hams boiled, three turkeys, grated ham chicken salad, cakes of all sizes, shapes & qualities syllabub, boiled custard, charlotte russe, apple float, . . . jelly of all kinds, coffey, tea, both pure, biscuit, butter, & everything else. It was the most magnificent supper I've seen since the war commenced. We danced from dark, six o'clock, till three. The girls at home dont bear any comparison with these out here in the way of dancing. I don't mean in grace or any thing of that sort, but in endurance. Some of them danced every set & we danced about forty, and appeared no more fatigued than when they commenced. They went at it with their whole souls & seemed to enjoy it more than any persons I ever saw. We had two sets of musicians, danced in two rooms & had a double set in each room the whole time. It was bitter cold, a misting rain but cleared off before we broke up, & the roads in a dreadful state. Some of the girls came six miles. Just think of it. In the evening I thought that our party would be a failure or only a very small one but pshaw! I didn't know them. I do now & I truly believe that any of them would go, party-rigged, on a dark rainy night, ten miles through a swamp, with water running into their carriages & every moment a risk of turning over & drowning, in order to see where a dance had taken place. Our party opened the season on Dec. 21st. After that parties followed each other in quick succession. I attended them all except one—Unfortunately two occurred on the same night & I could not attend both. I made the attempt however, staying at one till twelve o'clock & then starting for the other, but by the time I reached the latter place, three miles distant, the report of a Yankee raid had broken the party up & the guests were just leaving. . . .

Our country . . . is seeing, I hope, its saddest hours. Sherman in Savannah, Hood driven in confusion across the Tennessee with the loss of half his army & the loss of morale in the other half. Only our noble Lee with his glorious army, stands firm. It is a glorious band. I see no cause for desponding of the final results, but I mourn for the loss of life among our brave soldiers, the destruction of the country overrun by the enemy & the suffering which must follow to a large class of our poorer population. Our cause looks gloomy enough but there is no reason to despair. It only calls for greater energy and more extreme measures. I hope our Congress under the direction of our President will prove equal to the emergency & that the exigences of the times will call forth some statesman with sufficient wisdom to propose & carry through measures proper & suitable to our present situation.

In camp near Pickensville Ala
Jan 25th 1865
My dear Sister,
This is the worst country to live in I ever saw in the prairies of Miss[issippi]. In winter cant navigate at all, mud in the greatest abundance & no bottom to the roads & it is this way all winter. No moving about at all. Wherever you happen to be in the beginning of winter, there you have to remain till the warmth of Spring dries the ground. And yet in summer it is the most beautiful country almost in the world, fertile, everything grows in the greatest profusion and the roads are as smooth as a pavement (not our Morganton ones) & what is singular, not a particle of dust. Just imagine, On a cool summers eve, good buggy & horses, riding over a perfectly level road, smooth as glass, not a particle of dust, with a pretty girl, wouldn't it be delightful! . . .

Our prospects look gloomy, don't they? . . . Although such is the look of things out here I believe everything will come out right yet. Never despair while there is one Southern soldier left to bushwhack the Yankees & we have many a one left. Everything will work for our good. I don't believe it is written in the book of fate that we shall serve under the rule of the Yankees. We may deserve severe chastisement from Providence for our national sins, but it appears to me that the Yankees deserve it the most and I believe they will meet it in good time. We are suffering now; our time to see the Yankees in the same situation will come soon. The strong alone cannot gain the victory. A higher power rules the course of events. The enemy are the mere instruments. I believe our nation will rise purified & innobled by this struggle & march on to its destiny, the highest place on the role of nations. Hope on, hope ever, is my motto.[4]

EMILY ELLIOT KEEPS A LONG VIGIL

Denton and Emily Elliot lived in Wooster, Ohio. She was a school teacher, he the well-educated son of a farmer. They married in 1862, shortly before Denton went off to war as a captain in the 103rd Ohio, part of the "Three Hundred Thousand More" troops that Lincoln had by then realized would be necessary for putting down the rebellion. The documents that follow tell much about Northern home life during the war as well as what it meant to the families of soldiers to wait, and wait, for the return of the loved ones.

The first document is a letter from Denton to Emily, discussing their relationship and how they met. The next is Emily's diary for 1864, the first few weeks of which she was able to spend with her husband at the army's base at Nashville, Tennessee, while his portion of the army was in winter quarters there.

Tullahoma May 29th 1864
My Dear Wife,
I last evening rec'd a good long letter from you dated May 21st. It was begun a week ago yesterday and finished last Monday. It was of unusual length and interest. It found me enjoying my usual health and spirits. . . . We are still awaiting orders to leave for the Tenn[essee] river. The details of the first order were changed a little by an order rec'd last night. I take five companies instead of three to Dodsonville and the Col[onel] takes five companies to Bellefonte. I suppose we will surely leave this week. We have to make the trip through on foot instead of on the cars as first ordered. It will take three or four days to make the march. Part of the country will be pleasant and romantic to march through. We will cross the Mountains below Cowan [Tennessee]. . . .

You revert in your letter to the ever pleasing recollections of that summer you were teaching our school and I was at home. I did not suspect then that you were glad to have an excuse to come tripping down through the orchard. I was always glad to see you come and always thought it long between your visits. I dont know but I was half jealous sometimes when I found you had gone some where else instead of coming to our house. I was always very glad to have an excuse to go to the little white school house and sometimes when I rapped at the door I think my heart rapped as loud as my knuckles. The sight of a school house always wakens in me many pleasant memories of happy hours I have spent in them with you. We little thought then of our destiny. Truly "there is a divinity that shapes our ends rough hew them how we will." I little thought then that less then six years would see you my wife and me a Lt. Col. in the army. The army was the least I thought of then. How happy we will be to recur to those times when we sit smiling side by side hand in hand at the window of our own little home on a cool summer evening. The days of our courtship and honey moon will never be over, will they love? We will live and love and love deep love long as in those halcyon days of early bashful modest love. Our love will only grow stronger deeper truer as the years roll by.

Diary of Emily Elliott, 1864

Friday, January 1, 1864.

Finds me in Nashville. Came here three weeks ago. had not seen my husband for sixteen months. It is very cold today yesterday was quite warm but a sudden change took place last evening and it is as cold today as it often is at home. This is the first New years day I have spent from home. Wonder where next New Year will find me.

Saturday, January 2, 1864.

Cold again today. The Major [her husband] is "officer of the Day" and must ride all the forenoon. I'm afraid he will almost perish. I pity the poor boys who were out on picket last night. I sent five pairs of mittins to camp this morning. Must read some in my New Years present today—Lane's poems from Dr. Mitchell. Must dress for company. Don't like to have to live for fashion.

Sunday, January 3, 1864.

Sabbath. It is so cold and stormy that we will not go to church. Major will have to report at Headquarters. We will spend the day in readings. Afternoon. Read Longfellows "Children of the Lord's Supper" this morning. Like it very much. I read aloud to the major and this P.M. he has been reading Butler's Anthology to me. We enjoy ourselves so much. How anxious we will be to get settled in our own little home.

Monday, January 4, 1864.

Am now ready to sit down. Must try to finish "mendings" today. I want to get Dentons clothes all in good order for maybe I will not stay long. Living here is very expensive—extravagant I think. Hope we will be able to curtail our expenses. Denton is in camp. Mrs. Colt is here with me. P.M. George Burdett and Mr. Wilhelm were here to visit me. Denton will soon be home. How anxious I always [am] for him.

Tuesday, January 5, 1864.

Am going to camp today. Mrs. Patterson will go with me. It is very cold but we want to see the "boys." They always seem so glad to see a friendly face in camp. They have been from home now nearly 17 months. I am glad to find them so comfortable and so much less demoralized than I expect. If their officers were all "men" I think they would have a better example. But I am much pleased with the condition of the regt.

Wednesday, January 6, 1864.

Have been writing letters. Denton wrote to Lib and to Dr. Weaver this forenoon and I have been filing my part of the letters. I must go home soon. I cant think it is right for me to stay long—boarding is so very ex-

Coming to Nashville to visit her husband, Emily Elliott would have passed through this railroad depot. The Tennessee state capitol is visible in the distance. Library of Congress.

pensive. Denton says nothing of having me go and would like to have me stay but we may need what we are now paying for board. But I don't know how I can go. How can we part?

Thursday, January 7, 1864.

At home all day mending socks and repairing Dentons coat. Have my work nearly done. Fear our housekeeping arrangements are all frustrated. I must go home soon if we cannot lessen our expenses. Hope I will soon hear from home.

Friday, January 8, 1864.

Morning. Mrs. Patterson Mrs. Commel and myself will go over to camp. I want to get acquainted so as to feel more at home there. I don't wonder that Denton likes Dr. Mitchell. I believe I do too. Evening. Home again. The day passed very pleasantly. Denton was with me most of the time. Took dinner with Capt. Gody, then went to the Adjt's—found his wife with— staid about an hour—went back to camp and took supper with Sergeant Burdett.

Saturday, January 9, 1864.

Evening. We have not been living today, or at least have had no place to live. Mrs. Cage came today to move away the furniture. Took it all from our room but Mrs. Colt had more put back. Maria Cage is a real little rebel. She is the first one with whom I have had any acquaintance. Rec'd a letter from home today. All are well. The Oyster supper was a perfect success.

Sunday, January 10, 1864.

Have been at home all day except when I was out for a walk with Denton. It was cold this morning and the streets are very slippery but I wish now that we had gone [to church]. Mrs. Colt went—they had communion at the Presbyterian church. Four weeks from today we will have communion at home—wonder if I will be there. Mr. Boggs was there when Mary wrote. Would like to see him.

Monday, January 11, 1864.

Went to camp this P.M. with Denton. Mrs. Cage was here again today. I am not very well. don't know what ails me. Denton feels quite alarmed. He felt so badly over it that he scarcely wanted to go out at all today. He was invited out this evening but will not leave me. How good and kind he is: I do hope his fears will not be realized—more because he would suffer so much for me—If it is so strength will be given me to endure it.

Tuesday, January 12, 1864

Am alone. Denton went to camp immediately after breakfast and has not come back. Mrs. Colt has been with me part of the time. Perhaps we will go to housekeeping. Dr. Patterson, Lieut. Commel and Maj. Elliott all be one family. Dont know when I will go home. Denton feels slightly uneasy, and I might feel rather more comfortable but all will be well.

Wednesday, January 13, 1864

We have succeeded. Today we ate dinner of our cooking. We are keeping house. It is 17 months today since we were married. It don't seem so long. I have been with Denton more than a month now. I wonder how long I will stay and how many more weary months must pass before he will be at home. My anxiety is all removed. It was a false alarm, and I am thankful it was so. rec'd a letter from home today.

Thursday, January 14, 1864.

This is the second day of housekeeping. It goes pretty well. have been writing letters today. one to Gus and one to Sarah. I would like to sit down and have a good long talk with them at home. There is so much I want to say and so much I want to hear but still I dont want to go home now.

A Union officer and his wife, who is visiting him in his winter quarters in Virginia, much as Emily Elliott visited Denton in Nashville during the early months of 1864. Library of Congress.

Maybe I can stay as long as the reg't does. It will depend on the success of our new arrangement.

Friday, January 15, 1864.

I wonder if I dont feel a little "blue" this P.M. I was in the kitchen nearly all the forenoon and it seems as though it didn't amount to any thing at last. I'll leave Jim to cook alone after this I guess. But he don't know how to "save" as I would like to have him. But then I'll not let that take away my enjoyment. I'll be in better spirits when Major comes. Hope he will come early. What would I do without him.

Saturday, January 16, 1864.

Evening. I believe I could cry without much trouble. But I mustn't. There must of necessity be some little trials along lifes way. The sun does not always shine. I suppose I have erred but it was through ignorance. The result of which Denton speaks would most probably follow. It was I feel sure only his partiality for me that made him think of it. He can see farther than I can.

Sunday, January 17, 1864.

It is afternoon. Major has gone over to camp. I am alone. I wonder if I made good use of that part of today which is past. Conscience reproaches me for not feeling more in accordance with the holy day. I am not very well and did not really feel like reading so went to bed a while but did not sleep. arose, brushed my hair and read a few chapters in Proverbs. It is still raining—no, it has stopped.

Monday, January 18, 1864.

It has been raining and snowing all day and is real cold this evening. A sad night this will be for the poor. I am comfortable and happy. How could I be otherwise than happy here with my husband. He is studying "Military Law." I will read Dickens' David Copperfield. Wonder what they are doing at home and if I am missed from the circle.

Tuesday, January 19, 1864.

It is afternoon. I am alone now. Have had company since dinner. Dr. Mitchell was here again. He will board with us. Hope I can appear hospitable. I know I feel so. Major says I am "the best little wife ever was." Wonder if every husband says so of his wife. I know my husbands heart reposes in me. it seems as though I am not half good enough for him. Maybe I can grow better.

Wednesday, January 20, 1864.

It is raining. Have been alone with my husband. He was studying Phonography [a system of writing] and I was reading the "Revised Regulations for the Army." The evening passed so pleasantly. We are never lonely when in each others society. Time is flying—tomorrow it will be six weeks since I came here. I cant believe it. "We take no note of time but from its loss." Very true. Life will be spent and then it will be as a "tale that is told."

Thursday, January 21, 1864.

How do I feel. It is afternoon. I am alone for a few minutes. Believe I feel as though I might have spent the day more profitably. Have today played my first game of "Eucher." I like it and begin to know something about it. But it seems as though it may have "the appearance of evil." I will talk more seriously about it with Denton. He can see distant consequences better than I can. . . .

Friday, January 22, 1864.

At home in Nashville. My husband is with me. He is on the other side of the stand—asked permission to read some in my journal. I gave permission and he is now engaged with it. We visited Fort Negley today. I had no idea of what a fort was like or if I had I am sure it was a very erroneous idea. Why must such things be. War is the cause of it all. When will it all be over. Visited the cemetery.

Saturday, January 23, 1864.

Evening. I feel repentant but why do I say I feel so without resolving to change my course. Is it wrong? Has it "the appearance of evil?"

Sunday, January 24, 1864.

In my room alone. Major has gone over to camp for "Dress Parade." We all attended the Episcopal Church today. It was the first time for me. Was well pleased with the services but they hardly equaled my expectations. Major is very partial to their form. It is much too much form for me. The text was "So run that ye may obtain." General Granger was there and so were a great many officers of inferior rank.

Monday, January 25, 1864.

Evening finds me here alone with my husband. He has just gone out of the room. It is very pleasant this evening. Has been so warm for the past three days that I let the fire go down in the grate and sit by the open window at work. Rec'd a letter from Alice today. She says father was thrown out of the sled and was considerably injured. They are not getting along well at school. I am sorry.

Tuesday, January 26, 1864.

Evening. I can hardly take time to write. It is evening, and we hear serenading in the distance and feel not in the mood to have company this evening so will extinguish the light, go to bed and—then let them come we will listen to the music. We usually like to see company but prefer "private life" this evening. I have been writing to sister Mary.

Wednesday, January 27, 1864.

Company has just left. The Adj. and his wife and all our own family were here. The evening passed very pleasantly. I hear a brass band again. It is serenading somewhere near. Now it is playing "The Battle Cry." I never heard it played by a band before. Was over at camp this afternoon. Saw "Dress Parade." Wrote a letter sister Mary and one to—or commenced one to sister Lib. It is time to retire. So Goodnight Diary.

Thursday, January 28, 1864.

How the time does pass. It will be 7 weeks this evening since I came here. I must go away before as many more weeks pass. How can I be contented at home. It has always been the dearest spot on Earth to me but now that I have been with my husband I know I will feel alone. But there are loved ones there. Father, mother, brothers and sisters all are there. Death has not entered our door.

Saturday, February 6, 1864.

We are in a new home. Came here today. Changed rooms with Mrs. Patterson. Think we will like this as well as the others. It is home already. We have been writing to those at home. Rec'd letters from sister Cynthia and from brother Henry today. All are well. Have decided not to go home as long as I can stay as well as not.

Sunday, February 7, 1864.

The sun is set. One more sabbath is past. Denton is here copying from the bible. We attended church today at the 2nd Presbyterian. The text was "It is appointed to all men once to die and after that the Judgment." It was an exhortation to be ready when Death comes. I feel some compunctions of conscience this evening. I live to so little purpose. Have I not opportunities of being useful more than I am? Life passes and I am not always with the tick.

Tuesday, February 9, 1864.

Mr. & Mrs. Connell were here this evening. We played "Cribbage." I like it. I can't see the harm there is in playing it at home. Denton is reading "The arts and tactics of war." I will read "David". . . . Denton & I were photographed today. I have one in my album.

Wednesday, February 10, 1864.

Was over to Dresland. Visited Capt Gody's folks He will start home in the morning. Capt Mott will be here this evening. Denton says he seems like one of our own folks. I can like every one Denton can. Evening. I can't see very well, and I don't feel very well. I am to tenderhearted I guess, for I know Denton didn't mean to be harsh in the [illegible]. He will feel so bad if I tell him how it hurt me.

Thursday, Feburary 11, 1864.

Spent the evening at the Connells. Played cribbage. Guess I understand it pretty well. Feel better than I did last night. I did feel real bad. Denton is such a dear husband that I am almost sorry that I let him know that he hurt my feelings, but then I know he had told me that he wanted me to do so, so that he could make amends for it. It was only his impatience.

Friday, February 12, 1864.

Evening. Have just come home. Have been out on horse back. Denton said we rode twelve miles. I never rode near so far before. Enjoyed it so much. Denton said I rode well—considering (that is my word tho'). He was so kind to get the horse and saddle for me. Went out far beyond the pickets down to the river past the [illegible]. Climbed the highest point around Nashville.

Sunday, February 14, 1864.

The clock strikes eight. One more day is past. One more sabbath spent. I have one less day to prepare for that great day—the Judgement Day. This day has been one of profit. I hope. My soul has been stirred to its deepest depth. The tears of repentance have flowed. My sins of omissions are like a mountain before me. I believe I have prayed for strength to be a living christian. May my faith be shown by my works.

Monday, February 15, 1864.

Rec'd three letters today—one from Sarah and from May and from Lib. Rather an unusual feat for me. They are all pretty well. Sarah says they want me to come back and take the school next summer. Maybe I will. Suppose

Henry is home before now. Don't know when I will go. Am pretty near ready to go out riding again.

Tuesday, Feburary 16, 1864.

Have been at house all the time. studied phonography. Hope I will soon be able to write it. Wrote home today that I would take the school for next summer. I made Denton so glad today that he hopped up and down. I was glad too. I began to feel slightly serious about it.

Friday, February 19, 1864.

I am happy this evening and have been all day—suppose Denton says my digestive organs are in good condition. Maybe that is it.

Saturday, February 20, 1864.

Evening. Another week is nearly gone. My visit is so much nearer its close. Wonder when I will go home.

Sunday, February 21, 1864.

Denton has just come from camp. He took over the tracts [i.e., religious tracts] that Cyrus sent by me to the reg't. We attended the Episcopal church today and there was preaching in the camp this afternoon but I didn't know of it till Denton came home and it was all over. I would like to have been there.

Monday, February 22, 1864.

Am well and happy. . . . Denton wants to know my heart and he is so perfectly unselfish that his happiness consists solely in promoting mine. May we ever live thus happily. Heaven guard us from all evils.

Wednesday, February 24, 1864.

I am alone. Major has gone over to camp to get the paper. I would be so lonely without him. He is always with [me] in the evening.

Saturday, March 5, 1864.

Afternoon. Have just written to Cyrus telling him that I will start home next week. I want to see them all, but it seems as though I can't leave D. But I'll be brave and strong. I know the distance between us will not seem so great now that I have been here once. I can come again if he can't get home.

Sunday, March 6, 1864.

Must go tomorrow.

Monday, March 7, 1864.

Morning. I'm ready to go. Denton is not well—is lying on the lounge. The trunks are packed waiting for the carriage.

Evening. Supper at Louisville. Capt Scott will see me across the ferry and on the train. I'm tired but want to get home. Denton is lonely I know.

Thursday, March 10, 1864.

I am at home. Came last evening. How differently I feel from what I did on the 10th of Dec. Then I had just arrived in Nashville, then I had first seen my husband after an absence of 16 months. Three months I have been with him and now must be alone. But will try to be happy and to make others so. Sarah's health is very poor, she has had hemorrhage of the lungs. All the rest are well. I was welcomed home.

Wednesday, March 16, 1864.

I rec'd a letter from Denton today. I couldn't help crying over it. He is lonesome. I knew he would be but for him to say so it seems to real. But time always heals. We could not be together all summer. I will try to write cheerful letters. That will do much to cheer him. He says, "It is because I know how sad and lonely you are feeling." I'll try to be brave and worthy of so much love.

Saturday, March 19, 1864.

It is Saturday evening. The second one I have spent at home. Am much happier than a week ago. I was so lonely then. Come from Mother Elliotts today. That was my first ride on the new railroad. There was a letter here for me from Denton. He was in good spirits. Proposed my making another visit. If he stays there till fall I think I will go. How anxious I will be to start, and he to meet me.

Sunday, March 20, 1864.

I attended church today. The sermon was good as Mr. B.'s always are but my heart was so full of worldly things. I fear my next visit to Nashville was there.

Monday, March 21, 1864.

Here I am again all alone. Wonder if Dent is alone. Hope he does not feel lonely. But he says he will look for me again in the fall if they stay there. Guess I wont be slow about going.

We washed today. Tomorrow I will get all my clothes put away in order. Maybe I'll get another letter. If I can only hear from Denton often I'll be in good spirits.

Thursday, March 24, 1864.

Mr. B. says Denton will be promoted. I hope it will be for the best interest of the reg't and for our country.

Friday, March 25, 1864.

I feel now just as though nothing can satisfy me but to sit down by Denton and let him talk away my despondency. I'll cheer up.

Sunday, March 27, 1864.

Three weeks ago I was with Denton. that was the last evening we were together. May we be allowed to spend many happy Sabbaths together in the service of God. Had a [letter] from Denton last night. Hope he has spent the day quietly. there is so much to interfere with the right observance of the day in the army. Heard another of Mr. Barrs good sermons today.

Thursday, March 31, 1864.

A letter from Denton. So why do I feel so. It seems that I am living for no purpose. Am I careless and—I have not that assurance that I am a christian that I once had. I see so many inconsistencies in my life. My bible is too much neglected. My time is too entirely devoted to this world. May my understanding be enlightened. May I be less anxious about the things of Earth. My conversation be in heaven.

Saturday, April 2, 1864.

It is quite late at night. I have been busy with my needle work all day. went up and took tea at Henry's. came home with Cyrus [her brother]. read the news a while. wrote in Mary Hawkins Album and read some in the bible.

There is a letter in the last Republican from our reg't. Maj. Elliott's name is there. Two years ago how little I thought of being the wife of a U.S. Officer.

Sunday, April 3, 1864.

This day has been a profitable one to me. May it long be remembered. May I be enabled to go through this week as will be worthy a true christian. I will praise God by my walk and conversation.

Monday, April 4, 1864.

Did not wash today. the tubs were in the sugar camp [i.e., the grove where maple sugar was being made]. I finished fathers shirt and now have been studying Phonography.

Tuesday, April 5, 1864.

Rec'd a letter from Denton today. He supposes he has been appointed Lt. Col. . . . I have felt so gloomy today. I'm afraid I'm not very well content. I know I have been slightly lonesome. When I think how happy I was with Denton I long to be back and when I think how happy I will be with him.

Thursday, April 7, 1864.

Have been quilting today and this evening I wrote to Denton. Mr. Bowman is here. He read to us a letter from his brother [obviously a Mormon] in Eutah [Utah] who has three wives and eleven children the oldest of which is nine years old. He seems to think that a man can love all his wives alike as much as he can love his children.

Sunday, April 10, 1864.

Was at church today. The sermon was excellent. Today was fathers birth day. He is sixty-seven. How many years will he yet be with us? We dont know. Maybe some of us will be called away first. Will he be here one year from now?

Tuesday, April 12, 1864.

Rec'd such a good letter from Denton today. It was the longest since I came home. His expressions of love were stronger it seems to me than I ever heard before. It seems to me that I am not worthy such love but Denton says he can never deserve the wealth of love I have lavished upon him. May our love ever be pure as now and may we ever stand in the same exalted place in each others affection. Heaven watch over us and preserve us.

Monday, April 18, 1864.

Morning. School begins today. I feel that it will be a responsibility but hope my strength will be equal to my day. The parents of the children seem to expect a great [deal] from me. I guess they think their children can learn if they only just look at me.

Evening, Well the first day of school is past. I guess it went off well enough. They have such a miserable habit of talking loud. It was required last winter.

Tuesday, April 19, 1864.

Well it is evening again. Another day of school is gone. Feel better tonight than I did last night. Had a switch in the desk which I promised to have and I guess that did me some good. I'll get them tamed soon I guess. I get so discouraged sometimes, or worried, maybe that is the right word. I'll try again tomorrow. Was looking for a letter from Denton tonight but got none.

Thursday, April 21, 1864.

Today was pleasant both outdoors and in. School was very pleasant. I did not get so worried as usual. It will be real hard work for me but the scholars all seem to want to learn and I have to help them and to see them improve. Wrote to Denton today. Rec'd a letter from him yesterday.

Friday, April 22, 1864.

This is such a pleasant morning. Just as I wakened I thought I was with Denton and that his arms were around me and drawing me to him and just as our lips met in a loving kiss I had to waken—before it was all over. but then I like to be wakened so sweetly as that. I hope he will be happy all day.

Sunday, May 1, 1864.

It is eight weeks since I spent the last Sabbath with my darling husband. He is alone now. we both feel that nothing can supply the loss of each others society. But we hope in the future. I hope his business has not interfered too much with his devotions this day.

Tuesday, May 3, 1864.

I am weary in body and mind. Everything at school seemed to jar so today. maybe I didn't feel well myself and then it was rainy too. Hope for better things tomorrow.

The letter I got last night says that Denton is promoted again. I am so glad for him, and then he takes me up with him. He is so good. I can't love him as much as he deserves.

Wednesday, May 4, 1864.

This has been a happy day to me. I feel so thankful. School passed off so well and then to crown all, this evening two letters came to me, one from

Denton and one from Em Daley. Denton expected to leave for Tullahoma very soon. He's really Lt. Col. and thinks he will by one more year go up one more step. He is so good. He calls me "love"; there is no other name could be so sweet.

Sunday, May 15, 1864.

It is so quiet. Not a sound do I hear but the singing of a little bird. This has been a happy day. My S[unday] S[chool] class was very interesting. I have been reading the S.S. books. It gives me some new ideas of teaching. I will strive with the blessing of God to be a faithful laborer. May I be permitted to see the fruits of my labor. The sermon to day was good. "Come ye out from among them and be separate from them," were the words of the text.

I think of my dear husband being here soon to spend the sabath with me.

Monday, May 16, 1864.

Was disappointed in getting a letter. Thought I would get one. But I must not think of always having one when I want it. Then Denton said he would write as soon as he had any more news. Wondering is cheap. If it was expensive I could not indulge it so often. What will the next letter bring.

Tuesday, May 16, 1864.

What have we been doing? We've had the greatest frolic for a little while that we have had since I came home. It is well to be merry. I believe I am really looking for Denton. No letter came and I thought there certainly would be one, and now I'm thinking maybe he is coming. Well I'd rather see him than only a letter. Do wonder if he's coming.

Wednesday, May 18, 1864.

The letter came. Denton will have the promotion and so of course will not come home at least at present. . . . I felt a little morsel of disappointment when I found that D had the place. But then he is "Col." now.

Thursday, May 19, 1864.

Not very jubilant tonight. Dont know what is the reason. Maybe it is a slight attack of indigestion. A good nights sleep will bring all right. The news is still so very encouraging. Grant is doing a great work. Maj. Gen. Sedgwick is killed. How many precious lives have been given. Great battles and even great victories are a great expense. But we hope the end of the war is at hand.

Friday, May 27, 1864.

How busy we are nowadays. Too busy to look at my Diary.

Saturday, May 28, 1864.

It is so late I must not write any tonight. May the coming day be well spent. May Thy Spirit Holy Father dwell with us.

Sunday, May 29, 1864.

Have come to my room for the night. Am alone, and feel a little lonely.

Ellens little baby is so sweet. He is just old enough to learn every thing that is pretty in a child. They will go home tomorrow. Went to Oak Grove today. S. S. was not organized. Saw my old scholars. Next Sabbath is our communion. I want to be prepared for it.

Monday, May 30, 1864.

Rec'd a letter from Lt. Col. this evening. How well that looks. I wonder if I am the least bit proud that my husband is a Lt. Col.

Tuesday, June 1, 1864.

I have been writing to Denton. Rec'd a letter from him today. They expect to go to Ala[bama]. He will be at Dodsonville. Their Hd. Qts. will be at Bellefontes. . . . Dentons letter was as good and kind as ever.

Sunday, June 5, 1864.

Evening. This has been a blessed day. We have enjoyed sweet communion with our blessed Savior. Eight have united themselves to us [i.e., joined the church]. Seven upon profession of their faith. May they never lose this first love. May they labor for the advancement of thy kingdom.

Mr. & Mrs. Myers will leave their native land very soon [in order to become missionaries]. they may never see it again. But their love for the immortal souls of the poor heathen is stronger than their love of home.

Friday, June 10, 1864.

A letter this evening. They have marched from Tullahoma to Dodsonville. Denton will send letters every time he can. He is so good. I feel my need of him more and more. When will we be in our sweet home. God preserve the dear one from all harm.

Monday, June 13, 1864.

Twenty two months since I was married. When will we be together.

Wednesday, June 15, 1864.

No letter from my darling and he can get none from me [because engaged in active operations in the field]. But he is busy so maybe he will not feel the need of them so much. They would have to build "block houses" [small defensive structures] as soon as they went there.

I fear—but oh I pray that no evil befall them.

Thursday, June 16, 1864.

Have come up to bed. I'm lonely. How will I live all this long year alone. There are enough here to keep me from being lonely but that one is far away. I do not hear from him. Where is he! It will be one week tomorrow since the last letter came. He is so far from any communication that letters cannot be sent. But others, how must others have suffered and do suffer. I must bear my part.

Friday, June 17, 1864.

Feel better tonight. I must look at my many reasons for thankfulness instead of dwelling on what I would have changed. My lot is unalloyed happiness compared with that of others. My husband is well for what I

know. I have perfect health and every comfort and luxury heart can reasonably ask for. I have no little ones depending upon me for daily food while
many widowed mothers must toil for little dependent ones. No letter yet—
but I will hope.

Saturday, June 18, 1864.

No letter today. How long will this be the rule. Not long, I hope.

Sunday, June 19, 1864.

Sunday is past, and how has it been spent. Sabbath School was more
interesting if possible than ever. The sermon was so good. The text was
"The path of the just is as the shining light that shineth more and more to
the perfect day." I'm almost afraid that I have said some things which had
better not been said. But our religion must not be gloomy. So be cheerful
and [illegible].

Tuesday, June 21, 1864.

Evening. Today one of my little ones [her students] has died. My "little
Willie" is dead. "It is well with the child" I feel constrained to say, but am
I certain that his soul has gone to heaven? Was he of an age to be an
accountable agent? If he is happy it is well that he has gone before his young
soul was blackened by the sins he would be led in to. His father is unfit to
have an infant mind to form.

Wednesday, June 22, 1864.

The long looked for letter has come at last. It was written the very day
they got to Jacksonville, the 12th, but did not reach Nashville till the 18th.
The "Dear" is well and seemed in good spirits. He is so good, he never
forgets the loving wife at home. There will be no school tomorrow. William
will be buried tomorrow. The candle is out.

Sunday, June 26, 1864.

It is so dreadful warm. I don't know how we will sleep. It is so much
warmer than usual this season of the year. Today we had our first S. S.
concert. It was a real success. All seemed so very much interested in it. My
scholars are just the dearest little ones could be. Hope this week has been
well commenced and will be a profitable one to us all.

Monday, June 27, 1864.

O dear how every thing costs. Three dollars for a calico dress, and every
thing else in the same proportion. What a fine thing that I am teaching. I'd
feel as if it was pretty bad for me to be spending so much if I was not
making something.

Wednesday, June 30, 1864.

Martha is ready to go to sleep and I must too or I'll be so sleepy in school
tomorrow. . . . No letter yet. Well I can hope. Maybe tomorrow will bring
it.

Thursday, July 1, 1864.

Rec'd a letter from Denton.

Wednesday, July 6, 1864.

Nothing of importance to record tonight. Have been at work, work, work, all day. Is this then the way to live. Work all the time for the perishable body? "Six days shalt thou labor." well we do it, I guess. All I wish is that I would get a few minutes to look into a book now and then but I must work on. "Better wear out than to rust out."

Sunday, July 10, 1864.

Evening. One more day is numbered with the past. And it has made known to me the expected nearness of death in another place. Cousin Mary, one in the morning of life is fading as a beautiful flower fades and leaves us forever. But the flower seed falls to the ground and come to us in a different form and so will these immortal flowers bloom eternally in heaven.

Sunday, July 17, 1864.

Tis twilight. I have just come from Cousin Mary's room. We have long been looking for death to come and end her suffering. Her breath is growing difficult. She will very soon be at rest?

Tuesday, July 19, 1864.

Mary was laid in her last home today. Mary's body rests till that resurrection when it shall rise to be reunited with the soul.

Wednesday, July 20, 1864.

Have been writing to Denton. He has seemed near me all day. I had such a vivid dream last night. Oh how dear he is. I must leave him only in God. God gave him to me. May I ever be a blessing to him.

Sunday, July 24, 1864.

I believe this day has been spent profitably. I felt troubled this morning. I could not feel my confidence strong in the Lord. I felt that too much depended on ourselves. This afternoon I have felt such peace as only those feel whose minds are stayed on God. Mr. Barrs sermon was so well adapted to those who are afflicted. May that peace which passeth understanding be ours. May my dear one be kept for me.

Monday, July 25, 1864.

This has been the first day of school. It passed very pleasantly. I am more peaceful tonight that sometimes. My dear husband, if I only knew where he is and how he is. He has felt troubled. He tried to conceal it from me— dear one—lest it give me uneasiness. If he could come home—I'm anxious for the next letters.

Tuesday, July 26, 1864.

I'm troubled and can scarcely tell what about. If I could see Denton and know how he feels! Dear good man he tried to conceal from me if he does feel troubled. He says such dear things in his good letters. He could not love me more. That ought to cheer me to know that such a one is my husband and that his whole heart is mine.

Friday, July 29, 1864.

10 P.M. rec'd a letter from Denton. He was in good spirits and I am. How my happiness depends on the arrival of his letters and the spirit they breath.

I will go to Wooster tomorrow. The money goes so fast. But I cant see but it is well spent. Tomorrow I will get books and perhaps a dress. Books are certainly property well invested.

Ellens little Jonas coughs so. What a thing it is to have a baby!

Friday, August 5, 1864.

Have a letter ready to start to Denton. Where is he? How often I ask that question and reply not. I have every reason to believe he is well at least tolerably so, while so many poor wives heart are bleeding at ever pore for their lost loved ones. When will the cause of this end? We will trust all with God. The children picked lint today in school [lint was used in Civil War field hospitals to stop bleeding].

Saturday, August 6, 1864.

Oh what a good kind and loving letter that was today. It could not have been better. Denton says he would feel repaid a thousand fold for writing them if he knew that they keep me from growing old. I can never grow old, old in spirits as long as he is so kind and loving. He says, "You are just the best little wife that any mortal man ever had." I hope I'll be as good in his eyes.

Saturday, August 13, 1864

At twelve oclock I entered upon my 24th year, and at 9 this evening the 3rd of my married life commenced. The second anniversary finds me at home and Denton away in a southern camp—in Ala. The loved and loving one—may he be kept from every danger and may he be spared to enjoy that peace for which he is sacrificing so much. I felt so sad that I could not write to him. God bless the dear one.

Thursday, August 18, 1864.

I like Irving Washington very much. I do want to read to inform myself. I want to be more nearly an equal for Denton. He would—no could—not love me more but our tastes would be so exactly alike Dear one he praises my selection of books so much.

Wednesday, August 24, 1864.

The days don't seem long enough for me. Have now been writing to Denton. Rec'd the best letter from [him] today. He is so good.

Thursday, August 25, 1864.

Prayer meeting was here. More than usual were out. A great number of the scholars. My heart begs to have reason to hope that they are concerned for their salvation. I hope I can be faithful. Began Denton's shirts today. When will he be here so that I can do all for him. He is lonely, dear soul.

Friday, August 26, 1864.

10 o'clock. P.M. A little while ago I was happy. Now I am miserable. Why

does each trifling occurrence disturb me so much. But then the Dr. needn't have said that he thinks "Lincoln is as much a traitor to his country as Jeff Davis is." . . . What will all this talk come too? It makes me sick.

Saturday, August 27, 1864.

Heigho, I wonder what I'm to do. Was out on different business tonight than I ever was before. A muss among the girls at school I'm glad that Mrs. McElvan & Mrs. Bachtell are so plain and honest and come to me so openly. I don't hardly [know] how to overcome this trouble but I must watch and see that there are no impositions.

Monday, August 29, 1864.

Was in school today. Six years since Cousin Mary and I united with the church. We were not cousins then. Now she has passed to the church triumphant.

Sarah came today. Elli's dear child was so overjoyed. He could only say "Aunt Emily, Ma has come" and was off home again. Sarah is so well, or looks so well.

Wednesday, August 31, 1864.

The last day of the month. Only six days more and Denton will be on his last year of service. Oh how I want the time to fly! We will count the months then the weeks and then the days. If I teach this winter the time will seem so short. School was so pleasant today. I rec'd three letters today. Two from Dent and one from Mrs. Patterson. Was so glad to hear from Mrs. Patterson of course Dents [letters] were eagerly devoured.

Sunday, September 4, 1864.

There mother is out in the cow yard. I made Jonas think that they could milk alone and I think they could. I believe mother humors the boys. But then I suppose it is all right. But if I had known mother would go I would have gone myself.

Henry Noys preached today. I never heard him before. The text was "They testify of me." It rained when church was over and Mr. Lewis brought us home in his buggy.

Tuesday, September 6, 1864.

Have been at Sister Sarah's this evening to help her to write to Dr. Wolfe. She has great faith in his treatment. Sister Martha and Lib come here today. Mr. Pool has enlisted and come to Wooster and Martha came with him. Poor woman she says "it is worse than to bury a husband." I hope he will come back to her.

One year only and Denton's time will be out. Yes only one year now. The 6th of Sept 1865 will bring the end of these terrible three years.

Saturday, September 10, 1864.

The week is gone and no letter yet. What is the reason. They must have been called to concentrate at [illegible]. I hope all is well with them. I know in whom I can trust.

Why do I feel so depressed? I am glad that tomorrow is the holy Sabbath. Its rest will be sweet to me. I hope to be strengthened for the duties of another week. I must examine myself to know what I am doing.

Sunday, September 11, 1864.

Sept. is fast going. This is Sabbath evening. I feel a peace of mind to which I am witness & stronger. I believe the sabbath has been one of profit to me. Mr. Myers preached today he thinks probably they will go this fall. Mr. Barr read a circular from the Christian Commission [an organization devoted to ministering to the spiritual and physical needs of the Union soldiers] soliciting contributions. I would like to give myself to the cause of a time. What can I do through all these winter months Am I an efficient teacher in school.

Monday, September 12, 1864.

One more week is begun. When will school be done. I'm tired. But I must not "be weary." I'll feel more cheerful tomorrow.

Tuesday, September 13, 1864.

We pared and cut apples tonight. All felt pretty lively.

Wednesday, September 14, 1864.

No letter. I must not give up to be so disconsolate. There is work for me to do.

Thursday, September 15, 1864.

Prayer meeting was omitted on account of the lecture by Rev. Mr. Ranson. No letter yet. When will it come.

Friday, September 16, 1864.

A dear letter came this evening. . . . I was down cellar setting up milk and crying and then the dear kind letter came to me. How thankful I am that my dear one is spared. So many thousand are dying. That terrible camp at Andersonville Ga. If Denton was there I believe I would almost pray God to end his suffering in death rather than that he should die by slow torture.

Saturday, September 17, 1864.

Have been with sister Sarah. Poor dear thing she was almost [illegible]. I did what little work there was to be done and then we had such a good long talk. I do hope that her present "treatment" will prove beneficial.

Monday, September 19, 1864.

I am tired. This was washday and ironing too, for we want to be off to Wooster early to attend the S.S. convention. . . . Called at Mr. Kings to see Mrs. Barber. She remembered me as a little girl eight years old. It is 15 years since "little Cynthia" died. Her death was my first sorrow.

Tuesday, September 20, 1864.

Have just returned from Wooster, and set up the new books. How well they look: Now when my dear husband gets home so as to enjoy them. I wonder where he is I thought there would be a letter for me. Mrs. McMay rec'd one from Adjt. today. . . . The regt has been on the march.

Wednesday, September 21, 1864.

Charity was here today, and I am real tired. Alice said "go and sit down Emily" she knew I wanted to write to Denton. Have finished my letter. One really good one came from him—two whole sheets full.

Thursday, September 22, 1864.

Did not go to prayer meeting. Staid at home to try to doctor myself. Guess a good rest will bring me around all right. If it doesnt am afraid I'll have neuralgia.

Friday, September 23, 1864.

Feel better today. School passed off well.

Saturday, September 24, 1864.

Hope the coming day will be well spent. But feel that I have not prepared for it. Father forgive me.

Sunday, September 25, 1864.

I feel that a better use might have been made of the holy hours of this day. Sister Cynthia and my self took a walk out through the fields and woods and our thought and conversation wandered too much. God forgive the trespass of this holy day. I would by greater diligence redeem the time thus lost.

Sister Sarah is worse. This morning at 4 oclock she called to Mary and when she came to her bed she found her hands and face all covered with blood. The hemorrhage was much more profuse than ever before. Will she ever be better.

Monday, September 26, 1864.

It is late—11 o'clock. Cynthia is here with me. All the rest are asleep. We waited for Cyrus to come. I wrote part of a letter to Denton. Rec'd one from Lib this evening. She and Morton are doing the farm work [illegible] corn and hauling pumpkins.

Sarah seems some stronger this evening but is not. Dr. Wallace says he thinks she will never be better. Oh God thou knowest. Help us to say "thy will be done."

Tuesday, September 27, 1864.

We feel in a merry mood Cynthia and I. But why should we not, we have had such a fine lot of candy out of the molasses jar and kept it all a secret from Alice because she hid the pumpkin pie from us, and then something so funny happened in the buttery.

Sarah seemed to be some stronger today.

No letters from any of the dear ones.

Monday, October 3, 1864.

Sarah is the same. No letter from Denton yet. Why is it: How can I know.

Tuesday, October 4, 1864.

Willie is here to stay tonight. She is full of her playfulness. She says "I can't go to sleep. I don't feel sleepy." Dear little one she little knows how we fear that she will soon be an orphan. I was at Sarah's this evening—took my [illegible] up for her to use. am afraid it will be of no avail. Dr. Wallace has written a certificate of his care to Dr. Robbeson and says. "Mrs. Keef will probably survive but a short time." Is it so, will Death soon come to us. If so may it be robbed of its sting.

Wednesday, October 5, 1864.

My darling husband was wounded on the 24th Sept. And oh I have not known it till now. Is he living? Oh my God thou knowest.

Monday, October 10, 1864.

My husband I can pray for thee. God's hand is powerful. He can do more than all human strength. Oh that I give thee entirely to Him. But this poor human heart breaks. Oh that one word might be spoken to me. Oh those lips which have often so fondly pressed my own! will they ever give one more token of affection. Heavenly Father relieve his sufferings and if consistent with thy holy will spare him. Can I get to him? Oh help him.

Tuesday, October 11, 1864.

Another day is gone and not one word. Where is Cyrus and what can he do. And my darling husband. Oh could I but go on the wings of the wind! One week more: what will be revealed in that time.

Wednesday, October 12, 1864.

Denton must be getting better or I would have another despatch. Not a word today. Sarah is the same.

Thursday, October 13, 1864.

Why must we wait. I would fly but here I must stay for some repairs to be made. If I could only get to Indianapolis in time. Cyrus will expect me at Jeffersonville [Indiana; opposite Louisville, Kentucky] and what may be the consequence of having to wait. The despatch said Denton was worse [illegible] off. The message came out last night. I think Cyrus has found [out] that I can't get through.

Friday, October 14, 1864.

At Indianapolis. The train was so far behind time that we had to wait. Delay was never so painful before. Cyrus will be to me this P.M. What will he have to tell me then. Awful suspense.

My darling is dead. Oh blessed Lord help me. Thou didst give and hast taken away. Blessed be Thy holy name.

Saturday, October 15, 1864.

When will night come. Oh what a day. Must I stay here in Indianapolis. Oh my darling could I watch by thee could I throw these poor arms about thee and live always by thee. No thy dear spirit is in Heaven. This body must be laid in the grave until that glorious morning when all shall rise to meet Thee, Oh Holy God. May we then rise to sit on Thy right hand.

Sunday, October 16, 1864.

Sweet peace. The Lord is near me and that to comfort me. I feel assured, do I not, that my darling is at home, that he has reached that desired haven. Oh Father give me strength to endure as seeing Him who is invisible. Wilt Thou glorify Thyself in me. Oh I would live for the adornment of Thy kingdom. May strength be given me to bear with Christian meekness. Help me to look above to rejoice that my darling is with Thee. Be with that dear brother [Cyrus] and may he come in safety with the dear form [Denton's body].

Have been in Gallion [Galion, Ohio] all day.

Monday, October 17, 1864.

On the train at Gallion waiting to start. I must meet those dear ones, a widow.

Here I see my darlings picture as I saw him last. He has been cold in death four days. When will dear brother come with the body of my darling. If I can only see that sweet face. Safe at home. A letter says, "Several surgeons see him daily and he has my almost constant attention." Oh how grateful I am for that: He was as comfortable as human help could make him. The last sentence, I feel, is from his own lips. "May God strengthen and support you in your distress." Darling One, thou art gone. Peace to thee.

Tuesday, October 18, 1865.

Another day has been added to those my darling has spent in Heaven. What have they been to him. A thousand years are to God as one day. Do our loved ones count the years and months as they pass? No I think not. For they have done with time. Eternity is all they know now. I have been strengthened today and most of the time could look up but for a little while oh what anguish I suffered. "Denton cannot come to me." I could not endure it. But God raised my thoughts to Him. That dear form is somewhere.

Wednesday, October 19, 1865.

Mrs. Patterson has come. Dear one she can feel as I feel. No she says not as I feel but our feeling are so alike. Her poor Dr. is a prisoner she doesn't know where. But she can hope that he lives. Denton is dead: How calmly I can say it. I know that His grace will sustains me. Why is He so kind to me. I do not deserve His loving kindness, but his goodness surpasses our poor knowledge to fathom. "I will never leave thee nor forsake thee" He says that to me.

Thursday, October 20, 1865.

A telegram came which says. "Can't remove Col. Elliott's body until after the 31st." It is now lying in the ground. I had hoped to see the dear face once more but God softens every disappointment. His grace is sufficient for me. I can still see His hand in all that He is doing. He will make me see the world in its true colors. I'll be weaned from all there is here. It would be sweet now to die. Yet God will call me just when He is done with me here. What has He for me to do.

Monday, October 31, 1864.

This is the last day. Now that dear form can be removed from its southern grave. Oh how dear the dust even the dust of a loved husband is. That will be laid where I can rest beside it. Then will we rise together at that last great day. Beautiful thought. I'll see him in heaven, but Christ will occupy my thoughts there. Denton will come to welcome me to that new home.

Wednesday, November 2, 1864.

Waiting & hoping. How long must it be. So often it all comes to me with such overwhelming force. Only Divine Grace is sufficient for me. In severe trials if Gods arm does not support we must be overcome. "Lord save or I perish."

Thursday, November 3, 1864.

"I cannot bring his body home." Those words how dreadful they were to me. I thought certainly that could come now. This one more trial, but I believe I can bear it with patience If it could come even next winter I will give thanks. The dust can rest in a southern grave as sweetly as here but it would be so sweet to know that I was by it. Our human hearts: how they cling to that.

Friday, November 11, 1864.

Came from Sarah's beside this evening. She is very weak. Today she gave me all directions about her funeral. Can it be that she is so soon to leave us. Our band of brothers and sisters will then no longer be complete. How loudly death is speaking to us. I never saw him so near.

Friday, November 25, 1864.

And is Sarah dead? Yes. So it is. Her spirit is gone to its eternal home. At half past three she died. So peacefully. There is nothing of terror about such a death. Oh Death where is thy sting.

Friday, December 31, 1864.

The year is growing old. Only one more day and we must bid farewell to 1864. Can it be that it is so? The year, part of which was spent with my darling, is so nearly gone. Never to return. Those happy days, Days of bliss, too happy to endure. Oh God help me I'm all alone. Not one heart throbs for me. Not one to respond to this poor hearts tenderness. Why is it so? Life is a dreary wilderness but when it is past, Eternity will satisfy for all my pain.[5]

ANNIE E. POWERS WAITS FOR PA

For other loved ones of Civil War soldiers, the long vigil had a happier ending. Annie Powers, a young Wisconsin girl probably about ten years of age, was the first in the family to see her "pa," William Powers of the Eighteenth Wisconsin Regiment, come marching home. Though his return, as a paroled prisoner of war, was temporary, by the time he would have returned to his unit, danger of death would have been extremely low for troops in that sector. Indeed, it is unlikely that he participated in any further combat.

Annie's letters to her aunt and cousin back in Ohio reveal the interests and concerns of a Civil War–era school girl—the subjects she studied and the types of play she enjoyed. They also reveal childish exuberance as well as imperfections of spelling and grammar. Most interestingly juxtaposed with these endearingly child-like characteristics is a highly accurate and realistic understanding of the military incident that led to her father's capture in Allatoona, Georgia, the previous October.

After Annie's letter is a note added by her mother, Annette Powers. Annette displays some of the same grammatical shortcomings as her daughter but, still worried about the continued threat to her husband's life, takes a more somber tone.

William Powers's capture came about while he and the detachment of troops of which he was part were guarding a key railroad bridge on the supply line of Union General William T. Sherman's army. They had a blockhouse defensive position for use against Rebel marauders, but neither it nor the small numbers of the detachment were any match for the large and determined Southern forces that hit Sherman's supply lines that fall. Though the Confederate move failed to defeat Sherman, it did mean captivity for a number of his men, like Powers. Annette's fear that the Rebels would "starve" him was well founded, as thousands of Union prisoners died in Confederate prison camps during the last two years of the war, particularly the notorious Andersonville camp. That was not, however, to be Powers's lot. The practice of paroling prisoners, since discontinued, involved releasing them to return to their homes on an official promise from them not to take up arms again until officially exchanged. Paroled prisoners thus had little to do besides wait around in camp, and this explains

Annette Powers's wish that her husband would not be exchanged—and thus not have to return to battle.

Annie E. Powers

Jan 7th 1865.
Dear Aunt Adlade,
I now take my pen in hand to write to you. pa will write some by and by. I am well and hope you are the same. we have had some cold weather but it is quite pleasant now. pa is writing to uncle Edwin but he will write to you afterwards. pa got home the 18th of Dec. he was captured at alla-toona with about 80 other men on the 5th of Oct. they fought about 24 hours and the rebels set fire to the bridge and the block house where they was in and it smoked them out so they had to surrender. they was marched around about four days so our cavalry wouldn't get them. then they was marched 12 days before they got on to the cars wich was near the georgia and alabama line from there they took the cars to camp lawton near millan georgia. they was kept there a few weeks and when sherman came near millan the rebels run them off to savannah where pa was paroled from there they took a boat and went by water to Annapolis and where pa got his furlough to come home. if pa had knew that ma had been well enough he would have had ma and me and netty met him at Vermont or massachusetts he would have come and seen you but he thought he had better wait till the war was over. we have had nice times since he came home we was all real glad to see pa. I saw him first. pa starts for camp chase ohio tomorrow morning. I am real sorry pa has got to go back I will now write to cousin lacy.
Dear cousin lacy I now take my pen in hand to write to you I hope you are well have you been to school this winter I have what do you study I study fourth reader intermediate geography practical arithmetic intellectual arithmetic and i am in the first speeling class and grammar and our teacher is learning us to draw her name is Miss Minnie Smith she comes from new york state can you skate I can skate a little I think it is real fun have had fun riding down hill this winter the monday after christmas as mary and joanna miller and i where riding down hill mary and joanna are my playmates as mary got onto the sled and started down the hill joanna and me ran after her mary tombled off of the sled and joanna and I tommbled over her what did you get for christmas pa fitched me home a lot of books for christmas and for new year i got a candy cupid and a candy dove I want you to tell what your brothers and sisters names are i cannot think of any more so good by from your ever affectionate neice and cousin
Annie E. Powers I want you to write to me

Annette Powers

15 Jan 1865
ever dear Sister, I thought I would try to finish this letter William started for camp chais Ohio last Monday morning O I wish this cruel war was over it is hard to part with our loved ones and not know when we will see them again but we must trust in the Lord and he will help us if William had known that I could have come down there to meet him he would have sent for us so that we could have come and made you a visit I have not had a letter from him yet but hope to get one tomorrow I hope he is not exchanged if not we may come and see you befor he has to go back to his rigment his health was good when he at home I hope it will remain so for it frets me to have him sick away from home and not be able to wait on him I wish you could come out here and see me I think we could take lots of comfort together William told me when he left if he had to go back to the rigment that I had better come out there and make a visit this spring he thought it would do me good and pass a way some of the time for my health as been poor ever since he went in the army but I wish you could come and stay with me a month or two I am glad for your sake that your husband as not got to stay more than one year Powers has got two he did not get his discharge right the first time he whent so that is the way that he went back I sufferd much when I knew that he was taken by the rebels for I knew that they would starve him but they did not keep him but 6 weeks he had to live on a half pint of bad peas and half pint of meal a day and that was all they gave them he did not get a chance to write home till he got out well I must close you must excuse this short letter I will write more next time from
your ever loving Sister
Annette Powers
please write soon[6]

ANNE BANNISTER FINDS EMOTIONAL SUPPORT IN A BESIEGED CITY

Anne Bannister was a young girl living in Petersburg, Virginia, during the Civil War. In the last year of the war she experienced loss of family members and the privation of life in a besieged city, but she found emotional support in an unusual quarter.

It was a sad time indeed, for the inmates of old Chelsea House at Petersburg, Virginia, June 9, 1864, for the dear father had been brought home shot through the head while bravely defending the town against [Union general August] Kautz's Raiders. He was an old man and deaf, but there were only a few old men and young boys to defend the town, all the young men being with Lee's Army. The sun had risen that morning over the sleepy old town brightly and except for anxious thoughts of the absent ones, all hearts were happy and bright as the day. When suddenly every bell in the town began to toll and to clang until every household was aroused and alarmed to know what could be the matter. Gentlemen and boys ran from their homes to the court house to ascertain what this could mean. In a short while women and children were clustered together to wait and pray for the loved ones, about fifty in number, who armed with nothing but shot-guns had hastened to the outskirts of the town to try to keep back one thousand raiders. What could these few do? Then Colonel Archer, hero of the Mexican War, with his old body servant, dragged the small cannon from the public square to the water works where they kept up a constant firing. The constancy of this firing from the water works gave the Raiders the impression that it must be a fort. Phil Slaughter, a slave (grandson of that famous body servant of Colonel John Banister of the Revolution, (my great grandfather) who fought with his master) who was a musician, took his little band, rushed to Bragg's Hill, and played as loudly as possible "Dixie," "The Girl I Left Behind" and other bright songs to make the Yankees think reinforcements were coming to the few that met them, thus showing their masters that they loved them more than freedom. After about two hours of fighting the Raiders retreated. Twelve of the fifty men and boys were killed; one boy fifteen years old, my father, William C. Banister, and ten other old men. Three young boys were taken prisoners. I can never forget that day. My mother, my sister and I were standing on our porch calling to each one that passed for news from the fight, when my uncle, Robert Bolling, drove up in a wagon with my father's lifeless body shot through the head, his gray hair dabbled in blood. My precious mother stood like one dazed, but in a few seconds she was kneeling by my father in such grief as I had never seen before. This was only the beginning of the horrors we were to go through. In less than two months Grant with his Army was besieging the town on his way to Richmond. All the citizens who could left, but we were unable to leave due to the fact that my brother, fifteen years of age, was ill unto death, from exposure in camp while fighting in the defense of Petersburg. Chelsea, our home, was opposite the South Carolina Hospital and so we were in exact range of shells from the Yankee's Fort Stedman and Battery No. 5. For safety we were compelled to live in two large rooms in our basement. With hearts crushed already with sorrow we would sit by and nurse my brother—realizing he could be saved, if could we only get proper food and medicine. The shelling was so constant, that there were no stores open in the town. Three times a week a dear old friend, Dr. Thomas Withers, would come in town through shot and shell to bring what help and medicine he could to the sick and to us, and to cheer our heartbroken, but brave and patient, mother.

At last one morning about day break, after my brother had spent a night of most intense agony and had just fallen asleep, it seemed as if the very earth would open and swallow us up. Window panes were shattered and the whole air was filled with rumbling noises which terrified and deafened one. We could not hear each other when we spoke, the din was so great. What was it? Could it be the end of all things? Then through a lull one could hear a battle had begun. My mother seemed as one turned to stone and spoke as though in a horrible dream:

"My husband killed, one boy dying here, and two in the midst of battle, and the rest of us in the midst of shells and balls! Oh, God, what will become of us?"

Aunt Silvy, an old colored servant standing by, said in a confident tone, "The shells IS falling all around us, but, Miss Caroline, you is sech a good woman dat it peers to me dat de Lord jes takes all dese here shells in his hands, and eases 'em right over dis here house, into South Ca'lina Hospital, even if de garden do look like 'tis ploughed up, but he ain't even let one o' 'em shells hit this house, even if de shells has taken off the end o' Mr. Cooper's house cross the street and cut the piano in half."

The trees around our house were cut to pieces yet we were safe. That night, when all was quiet again we found that the Lord had indeed taken care of the brother in battle as well as us, for my brother, Blair, of Mahone's Brigade, came in late and told us of the horrors of that Crater Explosion and fight. His clothes were spattered with blood, he having fought in the crater—that hand to hand fight. As he finished giving the account of it he said he hoped that never again would he be in such a battle and told us that one of his company had become a raving maniac, bayoneting every soul who came up to him (poor fellow he died the next week, still raving).

A few weeks after this my poor sick brother died on his sixteenth birthday. The shelling and fighting was now so constant, that it was impossible to take his body to the Blandford Cemetery, and so his grave was dug in our beautiful garden, under the willows, and there we buried him, no one with us but our faithful servants and our Rector of St. Paul's Church, Dr. Platt. I remember in looking up that I saw in the street outside our fence several officers on horseback, bareheaded, who remained until the service was over. The next day dear old General R. E. Lee came to see my mother, and said his father and my father's grandfather had been most devoted friends, Ligh-thorse Harry Lee and Colonel John Banister. He had tried to locate us, and had come the afternoon before to call, but he had remained, through the service, outside the fence. He had heard of my father's death in defense of the town and of this young son's service, and he wanted to come as often as he could to see and cheer us and do all he could to help us in our great

Blandford Church and cemetery, Petersburg, Virginia. Library of Congress.

sorrow. He spoke of my two brothers in his Army as very gallant fellows. From this time until the evacuation of the town he came every Sunday that there was no fight and dined with us. He was the kindest, dearest friend to my mother and to us all and as loving to me as a father. Our Sunday dinner was like all our other dinners—Irish potatoes, corn bread, coffee made of sweet potato and sweetened with sorghum, dried apricots also sweetened with sorghum, one slice each of bacon.

On Christmas day Mr. Devoss, the French consul, came through the lines from City Point and brought my mother a turkey and it was served with all the ceremony befitting the event. General Lee ate the rest of his dinner but only tasted his generous helping of turkey. My mother was surprised to see he had scarcely touched his turkey and was about to ask him if he liked only dark meat when, with a very grave face, he said:

"Mrs. Bannister, I have taken the liberty of saving this turkey and asking you to let me take it to Colonel Marshall on my staff. He has been very ill, and has had nothing to eat but corn bread and sweet potato coffee. I hope you will allow me to take this to him as I am sure he will be greatly helped by such a delicious meal."

My mother said, "Of course you may, but you shall have a nice portion for the Colonel and you must eat every bit of your own and there is plenty more for you."

He was very happy and ate every bit of his own and my mother insisted on his having a second helping which he enjoyed.

When he left, with a lot of turkey and potatoes all wrapped in a nice linen napkin, he said, "I will take good care of the napkin and bring it back on Sunday."

Colonel Marshall wrote my mother that the turkey had "saved" his life.

The lack of opportunity for me to get a chance to play out of doors in this besieged city lay heavily on General Lee's heart, so he said that when he could he was going to send for me and if I knew any children who were near me in town to bring them with me to headquarters where we could play about freely. After one of the many golden afternoons when we were being driven back in an ambulance behind two Army mules with General Lee on Traveller riding beside us, as he always did until we were safely home, I was sitting in the post of honor beside the driver and was cutting the mules to make them go faster. "Don't do that, my little child," admonished General Lee, riding up close to me. But childlike I forgot and again after a few moments I cut the mules. Then he said,

"Anne, you must not do that again," sternly but very sadly, he said "my conscience is not entirely at ease about using these animals for this extra service, for they are on half feed as are we all." I was ashamed of myself and very quiet the rest of the ride. Yet to my young mind was born a sudden belief that he had lost hope. As soon as I reached home I rushed to my mother telling her the incident, and crying: "Mother, I don't believe General Lee thinks we are going to win the war."

My mother looked down at me and sadly said, "Of course, we cannot win, we are all starving."

When the Fall came the shellings became less frequent and the citizens began to return to town for winter quarters, and so we children got accustomed to the shells and often played out of doors. We really were quite brave and Agnes Dunlop, my near neighbor, and I played in our yard and then in hers. We had been taught how to throw ourselves flat on the ground if we heard a shell coming, and had become expert, by the sound of the shell, in knowing what kind of shell it was. One day we were in our garden playing, when we heard a shell coming and instead of falling flat I ran for our porch and Agnes for the raspberry hedge, but the shell was ahead of her, and when she got to the place, the hedge was gone, only a long deep hole remaining. I shall never forget the amazed look on her face. We both shrieked with laughter and amazement, I on the porch and she in the garden. What little fools we were! After this quite often the old and young would go out at night to watch the mortar shells. They were like arches of fire, and very beautiful. Very few ever fell in the town.

Then in late November the battle of Burgess' Mill was fought and my brother Blair Banister was mortally wounded through the lung and his right arm shattered. My brave mother went to him just outside of the town where he lay in a tent on a mattress on the ground. There were thirty desperately wounded in this long tent lying on mattresses each side of a middle aisle. She went all through the tent and not seeing Blair she said aloud, "Maybe it is a mistake."

Just then a weak voice said, "Mother, don't you know me?"

Then she saw that this ghastly poor fellow was our handsome, gallant Blair. My mother never left him, but my old colored mammy and I went out every day to help her to nurse him. He could seldom speak and after three days he died in the night. My mother said he thought he was in battle again and would try to drag himself up cheering and hurrahing. The young soldier who brought him out of battle on his back said Blair, fearing he would die before he got to the surgeon, said, "Harwell, if I die tell my mother I am not afraid to die." Then several soldiers came to Mother and told how brave and daring a soldier he was. He was brought home to be buried, but at this time it was so quiet along the lines, that the body of Norborne, my youngest brother, was taken up from our garden and the two who had loved each other so much in life were buried in the same grave in old Blandford Cemetery. My brother who was killed had always been a very merry, bright fellow and when my mother would speak to him about the future, for we all knew that the town would have to be given up, as we and our soldiers were nearly starving, he would say, "Mother, when the Yankees come in town you will have to take some officers in the house for protection and you will find many gentlemen among them, but dear old lady, be sure and look out for a commissary and a doctor because one will feed you and, after starving so long, plenty will make you need a doctor."

One morning in April the town was full of great clouds of smoke; acrid, stinging smoke. The tobacco warehouses had all be set on fire, and we knew Richmond was being evacuated. The firing of our warehouses had been agreed upon as the signal, the Confederates not wishing the Yankees to derive any benefit from this great wealth of tobacco. All the morning we watched our troops go quietly by. Not one soldier in five had any shoes. Their clothes were in rags but their heads were held proudly up as they marched by.

General R. E. Lee as they marched had several men carry and leave on the lawn of one of the homes a chair, which had been loaned him for his use in his headquarters and which he had found so comfortable and convenient, with a note of thanks. This chair belonged to Reverend Dr. Theo. Bland Pryor, whose son, Archibald Campbell Pryor, I later married. It was a big sleepy hollow chair, with an extended table on one of the arms for writing and desk drawer, on the other arm you could swing a small table in front of your for reference books. On these arms were penned many of the orders for the Army of Northern Virginia. Years after, in my home here in Washington, a young northerner was calling on one of my daughters. He said he had been told that this was R. E. Lee's chair during the War. He took his seat in it and sat there for some time. At last he rose and stood looking at it ruefully. Then he said: "I never understood before why Lee surrendered. To me its awfully uncomfortable."

"Well," I said, "I reckon it isn't any too comfortable for a Yankee."

To return to the old subject: While Grant's Army had possession of the town what should happen, but two Yankee officers applied to my mother for board. My mother, feeling quite agitated, said "who are you gentlemen?" One said, "I am Captain Sherman, a commissary" and the other said, "I am Dr. Copeland of New York"! They said they had been attracted by our sweet old home and would like her to take them in. So they came the next day and became our real friends for many years after and stayed in our house as long as they were in Petersburg. Mother told them of her dear son's joking and of his telling her to be sure to get a commissary and a doctor, and how, after his remarks, they had so confused her when they came.

A few days before the evacuation of Petersburg, General Lee was at my home and I had previously asked him to give me a picture of himself, for a keepsake. So this morning he handed me a small but splendid photograph of himself, and on the back was written "For Anne to ever remember her best, best friend, R. E. Lee." I would never frame it because I wished to show the back of it as well as the dear face but kept it on my parlor mantel for many years, but here in Washington someone took it and I could never find it again.

Shortly after the war General Rooney Lee was married in Petersburg to my beautiful cousin Mary Tabb Bolling. Dear old General spent the morning of the wedding with us. Knowing my older sister, Mollie Banister, was to be one of the bridesmaids, he said to me, "Of course my young lady friend is to be at the wedding?" "Indeed I will be," I eagerly answered, and began telling him how I was going to wear my first long dress which was also my first party dress. Then he patted me on my hand and said, "Remember, my dear, I am to have the honor of taking you in to supper. Ask your escort to lend you to me. Your aunt, Mrs. Bolling is sick and will not come down so I want to take you in." I was so happy I literally danced all around him in my delight. That night I was the proudest sixteen-year-old girl in the whole Southland, when I went in to supper on the arm of General R. E. Lee, my warmest, dearest friend, and Mr. J. B. Robertson, of Baltimore, my escort, was quite as happy to wait upon and be with us.

In the published letters of General R. E. Lee his son includes one written to Mrs. Rooney Lee (nee Tabb Bolling) in which he says in part, "I hope you will be able to pay some attention to your poor brother Robert. Don't let his elder brother monopolize you altogether. You will have to take care of both till you find someone, like yourself, to take Robert and Romancoke in hand. Do you think Miss Anne Banister will consent?" I had never seen this until Major Giles B. Cook, one of General R. E. Lee's staff, wrote telling me that my name had been immortalized on such and such a page of "Letters of General R. E. Lee," published by his son Robert Lee. At once my oldest daughter got the book and presented it to her father, Mr. A. Campbell Pryor, and very naturally I feel proud, for I always felt that Gen. Lee loved me as a daughter and he was to me all greatness and loving kindness—my idol.[7]

GEORGE WELLS THANKS GOD FOR UNION VICTORY

Religion was extremely important to the people of Civil War America, as indeed it has been to the American people throughout most of their history. Soldiers and civilians of both sides spoke of the war in terms of a contest between good and evil as well as of God's chastening and purifying of his chosen people. There was of course considerable disagreement between North and South as to which side represented those chosen people.

After Robert E. Lee's surrender at Appomattox Court House, Virginia, April 9, 1865, and Joseph E. Johnston's surrender at Durham Station, North Carolina, April 18, the remaining Confederate forces east of the Mississippi, under Lt. Gen. Richard Taylor, surrendered to Union Maj. Gen. Edward R. S. Canby near Mobile, Alabama, on May 4. In celebration of several victories immediately prior to this that led to the fall of Mobile and pointed toward the coming surrender of Confederate forces, Gen. Canby issued to his troops a proclamation of thanksgiving. That proclamation in turn prompted the following sermon by Chaplain George Wells of the Eleventh Wisconsin, setting forth the issues of the war as Northerners saw them.

"Thanks be to God who giveth us the victory."—Paul.

War is a terrible calamity. . . .

For over eighty years unparalleled prosperity attended these United States in their triumphal progress toward the zenith of power and greatness . . . [until] A faction of fanatics made fanatical by their blind devotion to and superstitious reverence for the institution of slavery threatened to dissolve the union of States and establish a "Southern Confederacy." . . . The flag of the free having been insulted, as men, patriots, and Christians it was our duty to sustain the honor of that flag. . . . At Sumpter the Gauntlet was thrown down, and it was our duty to take it up, to accept the battle and leave the results with the God of battles. This is the condition of things on the surface. Underneath lay a far more glorious idea than avenging an insult offered the "Star Spangled Banner." Principals were involved. There was then to begin a grand struggle between truth and error. Right and wrong were to meet face to face, and the great battle between glorious heavenly liberty and hell born, hell bound slavery was to be fought. As to the final results who could doubt but freedom would be triumphant. But it has not always appeared so, for in the struggle we have not been uniformly successful. . . .

The victories of Spanish Fort and Blakeley that resulted in the evacuation of Mobile are certainly among the most brilliant achievements of the war, and General Canby does well to acknowledge deserved gratitude by thanking his victorious army for displaying so much skill and valor. But he desires us to take into consideration the God of all the earth, and render Him thanks for giving us the victory. Now our friends at home have held a day of joy and thanksgiving for all our victories; let us therefore while remembering Spanish Fort and Blakeley take into account the universal success of our national army, and return devout thanks to Almighty God for the great prosperity attending our glorious cause.

Too many people leave the great Author of all events out of the question. . . . Though men in their willfullness ignore His providence in our national affairs, yet His hand controls events, and though silent and unseen, His purposes have been ripening for our good and the nation's welfare.

I would award the mead of praise to President Lincoln for his honest faithfulness, and to the able Generals who have led our armies from conquering to conquer. I give due credit to the brave soldiers who have fought a good fight, and recognize the earnest determination of a patriotic and noble people to sustain so great a war, and yet, with a glowing soul, I endorse the sentiment of our text—Thanks be to God who giveth us the victory.

But why give thanks to God?

1st Because He gave us for a President a good man, devoted Christian wise statesman, and if an honest man is the noblest work of God, Abraham Lincoln was that noble work, and I do not think I disgrace the "Father of his country" by placing him by his side, one the maker and the other the regenerator of his country. "Honest old Abe" was preeminently the man for the times, and he is to be regarded as an unspeakable gift of God.

2nd Because He gave us Generals whose military skill and determined bravery have achieved such great victories. We may with propriety consider our cause honored with the services of the greatest military heroes of the present age.

3rd Because He raised up strong arms and willing hearts to fight our battles. It was a magnificent sight so many thousand leaving the pursuits of civil life to take up arms in defence of their country's honor. History records no scene more sublime, and when the recording Angel shall open the book of time it will be seen that many were inspired by a God given spirit of duty, as well as by motives of interest and patriotism.

4th Because to Him we owe thanks for the vast resources so essential to carry on the conflict. An immence amount of treasure has been expended, and yet we are far from being exhausted, in fact we are just beginning to realize our greatness in this particular. We can without exhausting our means employ millions more to bring about a successful termination of the war.

5th and finally. Thank God because by the proper use of these His gifts we have obtained the victory. We might have used them improperly, and at times, in our ignorance have done so. But we have been taught wisdom by God's varied dealings so that the means so wisely given have answered the desired and designed ends.

But how shall we manifest our thanks? To remain content with a mere expression of thanks is unworthy of us, and yet we too frequently remain satisfied with so doing. But God who searches the heart will accept nothing short of heart felt gratitude, and this alone can repay the debt of love we owe. Of what use is it to say "O Lord I thank thee" when the life is Godless and the soul full of hatred to the things of God. Gratitude is the memory of the heart, and where this feeling is properly exercised towards God it produces remembrance, not only of the blessings received, but of what the donor requires of us. God desires fruits of gratitude. A manifestation of our thanks in prayer and holy living.

1st Prayer. To pray is certainly the will of God concerning us, and gratitude will draw the soul into this delightful exercise. Pray therefore that God would still continue and preserve us a nation. Though the storm of war may cease its ragings, yet there will remain waves of trouble that will require a God to say "Peace be still" before we are blest with a perfect calm. The physical war is fought and won, but the moral conflict continues, and God with us can alone give the victory. Pray for those whose hearts are made sad by war's desolation. The land is full of mourning for loved ones who "sleep their last sleep," and full of sorrow for lost limbs and shattered health. Pray that God would bestow consolation, and give the oil of joy for mourning with the garment of praise for the spirit of heaviness. And whenever the privilege to render assistance and succor to these noble sufferers presents itself show your gratitude by bestowing your favors, and a gracious God will not suffer you to go unrewarded. But in praying do not forget your own need of pardoning mercy, and a regenerated nature. Pray that God would forgive the past and give you

"A heart in every thought renewed.
And full of love divine"

2nd Holy living. To make our prayers effectual we must lead a holy life, for says the Psalmist, "If I regard iniquity in my heart the Lord will not hear me." If we are grateful to a friend we show it by corresponding acts, and if we are in earnest in thanking God for our successes we shall show it not by rebelling against His will but by keeping His commandments, walking in His statutes, and living to love Him. As a nation we have passed through a very fiery ordeal, and it ought to purify us as gold is purified by fire. God has chastened us, not for our destruction, but to correct and make us a holy people that we may serve Him forever. If we will learn that lesson and obey the teachings of our Almighty Friend our future will be great and glorious beyond our most sanguine expectations, but if we will not serve Him we may expect destruction, for the nation that will not serve God shall perish. The laws of our country are so constituted that every man wields an influence. You and I, my friends, have a power, and we can use it to good advantage if we so choose. Then let us show our gratitude and at the same time benefit our country by living a holy life and exerting a Christian influence around.

Let it be said of the 11th Wisconsin that besides expressions of thanks, they yielded themselves servants to God, and thereby manifested sincere and hearty thanks to God for giving us the victory. Amen.[8]

NOTES

1. DeForest Family Letters, U.S. Army Military History Institute, Carlisle Barracks, Pennsylvania.

2. Alfred E. Willard Papers, Southern Historical Collection, University of North Carolina, Chapel Hill.

3. Napoleon B. Bartlett Letters, Chicago Historical Society.

4. George Phifer Erwin Papers, Southern Historical Collection, University of North Carolina, Chapel Hill.

5. Jonas Denton Elliott Papers, U.S. Army Military History Institute, Carlisle Barracks, Pennsylvania.

6. William H. Powers Papers, Civil War Miscellaneous Collection, U.S. Army Military History Institute, Carlisle Barracks, Pennsylvania.

7. "Incidents in the Life of a Civil War Child," Harrison H. Cocke Papers, Southern Historical Collection, University of North Carolina, Chapel Hill.

8. George Wells Sermon, State Historical Society of Wisconsin, Madison.

PART III

REFLECTING

Chapter 7

Ideas for Exploration

The following questions, grouped in broad topics, will suggest just a few of the many possible areas for student exploration in the large, complex, and highly rewarding field of Civil War studies.

- Why did the Southern states choose to secede in 1860 and 1861? What were the immediate causes? What were the underlying reasons for the conflict? Could secession and/or civil war have been avoided? Why did attempts at compromise and peaceful settlement fail?

The correspondence of James Dawson and Elodie Todd in Chapter 4 of this book might help to shed light on such questions.

- In what ways were Northern and Southern culture different? In what ways were they the same? How did their differences and similarities help to cause the Civil War and influence its course?

A number of documents in this volume addresses such questions. In fact, all of them touch on these issues in one way or another. You might particularly compare the writings of John Reed and David Fleming with those of Sarah Beach Clark, in Chapter 3, for the early part of the war. Then you might compare the diaries of Emilie Quiner (Chapter 5) and Emily Elliott (Chapter 6) with the diary of Laura Beecher Comer (Chapter 5) and the reminiscences of Anne Bannister (Chapter 6), for the latter parts of the war.

• What sorts of attitudes did white Southerners have concerning slavery?
What did white Southerners believe about the nature and attitudes of their
black slaves? How did Northern conceptions differ from Southern ones
on these subjects? What role did slavery play in the coming course of the
war?

Captain R. H. Browne's letter to his wife in Chapter 4 is very re-
vealing on the subject of slavery, as is Laura Beecher Comer's diary
in Chapter 5. The Northern attitude toward slavery and the former
slaves might be deduced from careful reading of such sources as John
and William Barney's letters (Chapter 5) and George Wells's sermon
(Chapter 6).

• What were the primary motivations of the soldiers? How did those motivations differ between North and South? What did each side believe was
at stake in the war?

For this question, the letters, diaries, and memoirs of the soldiers
themselves will be most instructive. See John Reed, David Fleming
(Chapter 3), James Dawson, George Phifer Erwin, William Hardy,
R. H. Browne (Chapter 4), and the five assorted Confederate soldiers
of Chapter 5 to get the Confederate soldiers' perspective. For the
view from Union lines, try Michael Cunningham and Jonathan W. W.
Boynton (Chapter 3), Hamlin Chapman and Aurelius Lyman Voorhis
(Chapter 4), John and William Barney and Michael Cunningham
(Chapter 5), and Frank and Napoleon Bartlett (Chapter 6). These
sources also give you the opportunity of judging how soldiers' impressions of what they fought for may have changed between the time
of the war (when the diaries and letters were written) and the later
decades of the nineteenth century (when memoirs were written). You
might wish to compare diarists and letter writers such as George Phifer Erwin and John and William Barney to memoir writers like John
Reed, David Fleming, and Jonathan Boynton.

• What role did religion play in shaping the attitudes of the two sides about
the war? What role did religion play in the two cultures? What was each
side's understanding of the religious significance of the war? Were any
parts of those two understandings compatible with each other?

References to religion are almost as common in these sources as
statements pertaining to culture. That is because religion was a vital

part of mid-nineteenth-century American culture, both North and South. For exploring such questions, you might particularly wish to look at the writings of James Dawson and Elodie Todd, Laura Beecher Comer, Emily Elliott, and George Wells.

• What hardships and suffering did civilians have to endure during the war? In what ways did the civilian experience differ between North and South or between different regions within the North or the South? What segments of society were most intensely affected by the war?

Here once again, almost all of the documents in this volume shed at least some light on these questions. Of particular interest, however, are Emily Elliott's and Anne Bannister's accounts of personal loss on both sides of the lines. Also of use are the writings of Augusta Kidder, Sophia Bissell, and Michael Cunningham (Chapter 5).

• What were the attitudes of the two sides toward such cultural icons as Lincoln and Lee? What were the qualities that the two sides valued and praised in their leaders? To what degree were those qualities different in the South than they were in the North?

On these points an interesting comparison might be made between Anne Bannister's reminiscences and George Wells's sermon, both in Chapter 6.

Suggestions for Further Reading

The literature of the Civil War is enormous. This section will suggest some starting places for those who wish to delve into it a bit further.

Many excellent overviews of the war are available, including James M. McPherson, *Battle Cry of Freedom* (1988); Allen C. Guelzo, *The Crisis of the American Republic* (1995); Brooks D. Simpson, *America's Civil War* (1996); Herman Hattaway, *Shades of Blue and Gray* (1996); and Charles P. Roland, *An American Iliad* (1991).

On the subject of prewar Southern culture see Clement Eaton's classic *The Mind of the Old South* (1964) and, for a more recent study, Steven E. Woodworth's *A Different Society: The American South, 1787 to 1860* (fourthcoming). For a recent reflection by a very senior scholar, see Eugene D. Genovese, *The Southern Tradition: The Achievement and Limitations of an American Conservatism* (1994). A controversial but thought-provoking interpretation of the culture of the Old South is to be found in Grady McWhiney, *Cracker Culture: Celtic Ways in the Old South* (1988). On the experience of the slaves, see John B. Boles, *Black Southerners, 1619–1869* (1984).

On Northern culture during the Civil War, see Philip S. Paludan, *A People's Conflict: The Union and Civil War, 1861–1865* (1989); J. Matthew Gallman, *The North Fights the Civil War: The Home Front* (1994); Earl Hess, *Liberty, Virtue, and Progress: Northerners and Their War for the Union* (1988); and Richard F. Bensel, *Yankee Leviathan: The Origins of Central State Authority in America, 1859–1879* (1990). For a look at the culture of a single Northern city during the war, see J. Matthew Gallman, *Mastering Wartime: A Social History of Philadelphia during the Civil War* (1990).

Southern society and culture during the war can be examined in Drew

Gilpin Faust, *The Creation of Confederate Nationalism* (1988) and in such local studies as Carl Moneyhon's *The Impact of the Civil War and Reconstruction in Arkansas, 1850–1874* (1994) and Arthur W. Bergeron's *Confederate Mobile* (1991). The "Confederate tories" of which George Phifer Erwin complained can be studied in Wayne K. Durrill, *War of Another Kind: A Southern Community in the Great Rebellion* (1990). Broader studies of the issues of dissent within the Confederacy are discussed in Georgia L. Tatum's classic Disloyalty in the Confederacy (1934) and David Williams, *Rich Man's War: Class, Caste, and Confederate Defeat in the Lower Chattahoochee Valley* (1998).

The role of women is addressed in such works as Catherine Clinton and Nina Silber, *Divided Houses: Gender and the Civil War* (1992); George C. Rable, *Civil Wars: Women and the Crisis of Southern Nationalism* (1989); Drew Gilpin Faust, *Mothers of Invention* (1996); and Catherine Clinton's two books *The Other Civil War* (1984) and *Civil War Stories* (1998).

The experience of children in the Civil War is the subject of James Marten, *The Children's Civil War* (1998), and is also dealt with in Clinton's *Civil War Stories* (1998).

The religious aspect of the conflict can be studied in Eugene D. Genovese, *A Consuming Fire: The Fall of the Confederacy in the Mind of the White Christian South* (1998), and my own forthcoming work, *The Religious World of Civil War Soldiers.*

Index

About the Author

STEVEN E. WOODWORTH teaches history at Texas Christian University in Fort Worth, TX. He is the author of several books, including *The American Civil War*, published by Greenwood Press, as well as *Jefferson Davis and His Generals, Davis and Lee at War*, and *Six Armies in Tennessee.*